HAYNES **MAX** POWER **Ford**

fiesta

The definitive guide to **modifying**

by **Bob Jex**

HAYNES **MAX** POWER **Ford**

fiesta

The definitive guide to **modifying**
by **Bob Jex**

Haynes Publishing

ISBN 1 85960 941 4

Printed by **J H Haynes & Co Ltd,**
Sparkford, Yeovil, Somerset BA22 7JJ, England.

Tel: 01963 442030 Fax: 01963 440001
Int. tel: +44 1963 442030 Fax: +44 1963 440001
E-mail: sales@haynes-manuals.co.uk
Web site: www.haynes.co.uk

Haynes North America, Inc
861 Lawrence Drive, Newbury Park, California 91320, USA

Editions Haynes
4, Rue de l'Abreuvoir
92415 COURBEVOIE CEDEX, France

Haynes Publishing Nordiska AB
Box 1504, 751 45 UPPSALA, Sweden

(3941-7AF1)

It wasn't my idea guv'nor!

1 Advice on safety procedures and precautions is contained throughout this manual, and more specifically on page 210. You are strongly recommended to note these comments, and to pay close attention to any instructions that may be given by the parts supplier.

2 J H Haynes recommends that vehicle customisation should only be undertaken by individuals with experience of vehicle mechanics; if you are unsure as to how to go about the customisation, advice should be sought from a competent and experienced individual. Any queries regarding customisation should be addressed to the product manufacturer concerned, and not to J H Haynes, nor the vehicle manufacturer.

3 The instructions in this manual are followed at the risk of the reader who remains fully and solely responsible for the safety, roadworthiness and legality of his/her vehicle. Thus J H Haynes are giving only non-specific advice in this respect.

4 When modifying a car it is important to bear in mind the legal responsibilities placed on the owners, driver and modifiers of cars, including, but not limited to, the Road Traffic Act 1988. IN PARTICULAR, IT IS AN OFFENCE TO DRIVE ON A PUBLIC ROAD A VEHICLE WHICH IS NOT INSURED OR WHICH DOES NOT COMPLY WITH THE CONSTRUCTION AND USE REGULATIONS, OR WHICH IS DANGEROUS AND MAY CAUSE INJURY TO ANY PERSON, OR WHICH DOES NOT HOLD A CURRENT MOT CERTIFICATE OR DISPLAY A VALID TAX DISC.

5 The safety of any alteration and its compliance with construction and use regulations should be checked before a modified vehicle is sold as it may be an offence to sell a vehicle which is not roadworthy.

6 Any advice provided is correct to the best of our knowledge at the time of publication, but the reader should pay particular attention to any changes of specification to the vehicles, or parts, which can occur without notice.

7 Alterations to vehicles should be disclosed to insurers and licensing authorities, and legal advice taken from the police, vehicle testing centres, or appropriate regulatory bodies.

8 The vehicle has been chosen for this project as it is one of those most widely customised by its owners, and readers should not assume that the vehicle manufacturers have given their approval to the modifications.

9 Neither J H Haynes nor the manufacturers give any warranty as to the safety of a vehicle after alterations, such as those contained in this book, have been made. J H Haynes will not accept liability for any economic loss, damage to property or death and personal injury arising from use of this manual other than in respect of injury or death resulting directly from J H Haynes' negligence.

Contents

What's that then?   06
Fiesta - the first-timer's
favourite   08

Haynes
Max Power

What to buy   10
Don't buy a duffer   12
Sealing the deal   16
Model history   17

Buyer's guide

A necessary evil   18
Valuing your car   19
What type of cover   19
Your car? or your Dad's?   19
Limit your premium   20
Insurance friendly mods   21

Insurance

Suspension

Lowering springs   105
Suspension kit   106
Coilovers   107
Front suspension   108
Rear suspension   113
Nasty side-effects   116
Front strut brace   117

Brakes

The middle pedal   118
Groovy discs   119
Brake discs & pads   120
Cool coloured calipers   124
Painting calipers   125
Painting drums   125

Interiors

Removing stuff   127
Window winders   134
Door sill trims   135
Applying film   138
Painting trim   140
Ready-made panels   142
Knobs/gaiters   143
Under neon light...   147
Retrimming   148
Coloured dials   150
Rev counter   154
Racing starts   156
Boring flooring?   158
Footwell trim plates   161
Fitting a Momo wheel   164
Pedalling your Fiesta   168
Seats/harnesses   169

Mirror, mirror	38
Racing filler cap	41
Fitting a sunstrip	42
Smoothly does it	44
Tinting windows	46
Single wiper conversion	48
Painting by numbers	54
De-locking	56
Remote & central locking	59
Bumpers 'n' bodykits	60
Meshing	63
Tailgate smoothing	64
Badboy bonnet / vents	69
Side skirts	72
Roof spoiler	73
Wheelarch mods	74
Respraying	76

Your most important decision	92
Lead us not into temptation	93
How cheap are you?	94
Bound to drive you nuts	95
Other options	95
Size matters	96
We like a challenge	97
Speedo error? Or not?	97
Hold on to your wheels	98
Locking wheel bolts	99
Changing wheels	101
Tyres	102
Marks on your sidewalls	103
Pressure situation	103

Avoiding trouble	22
A word about your stereo	23
Things that go beep...	23
The knowledge	24
Fitting a basic LED	26
Wiring basics	27
Fitting an auxiliary fusebox	28
Alarm fitting	30

Being scene	78
Morette twin headlights	80
Headlight bulbs	85
Front fog/spotlights	86
Rear light clusters	87
Side repeaters	88
LED washer jets	88

Security

Body styling

Lights & bulbs

Wheels & tyres

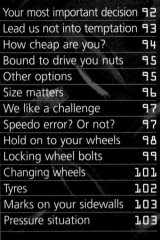

ICE

Head unit	176
Front speakers	178
Rear speakers	182
Amplifier	184
Subs & boxes	186
Wiring	187

Engines

Faster, faster!	190
Replacement filter element	191
Induction kit	192
No quicker but it looks nice	194
Coloured HT leads	195
Adjustable fuel pressure regulator	196
Braided hoses	196
Engine painting	198
Chrome battery cover	199
ECU "chipping"	200
Engine tuning	202
Replacement engine	203

Exhausts

Fitting a back box	206
Four-exit system	208

Reference

Safety and tools	210
Legal modding?	212
Thanks to:	216

Haynes Max Power

What's that then?

Haynes Publishing have, for the last forty years, been helping people keep their cars on the roads in countries all over the world by publishing maintenance manuals. Chances are you've either got one of them yourself or you know somebody who has.

"Lights & bulbs" includes fitting high-power blue headlight bulbs, coloured rear light clusters, etc.

Before

After

Remember what it feels like on your birthday, or at Christmas, when you're faced by a pile of pressies? So do we, that gnawing feeling in your gut, what's in them? What did I get? Take that feeling and multiply it by twelve, that's how we felt when we started this project. When we decided that it was time to try something new, we couldn't wait. Because the same theories apply to modifying your car as servicing it, we reckoned we'd better get on and do it ourselves. We don't pay other people to do it for us, and we get the same dodgy instructions with kit as everybody else.

So if you've ever wondered how to fit a universal door mirror properly, smooth a tailgate or just bolt a seat in, this book is for you.

We've picked up a skip full of tips along the way, and they're all here for you to use. We haven't tried to set any trends, but we've covered every possible process we think you'll need. So where we've tinted a front door window, the same rules apply to a rear one, job done.

If you look in the magazines and want some of that, join us, 'cos so do we, and we'll show you how to get it.

Keeping it real

Modifying a car is not without its problems in the 'real world', as opposed to the seemingly fantasy world of the glossy mags. For instance, it's pretty silly to spend hours fitting illegal window tints or smoked lights if you get pulled the first time you're out

afterwards. Of course, you can get pulled for all sorts of reasons (and just driving a modified car is reason enough sometimes), but keeping the car actually legal is one of the 'hidden' challenges with modifying. Throughout the book, our tips should give all the help you need to at least appear to be on the right side of the law. The annual MOT test is another favourite time for your mods to get panned, and again, we aim to give you all the help necessary to ensure at least that what you've changed doesn't lead to a fail.

Security is another major issue with a tweaked motor, and the perils of insurance cannot be taken lightly, either. We aim to give down-to-earth advice to help you keep the car in the first place, and to help you in not upsetting your insurers too much if the worst happens.

A word about fashion

In producing this book, we're aware that fashions change. What we show being fitted to our car might well be hideously out of date in 6 months time, or might not be your thing in the first place! Also, some of the stuff we've acquired from our various suppliers may no longer be available by the time you read this. We hope that, despite this, our approach of showing you step-by-step how to fit the various parts will mean that, even if the parts change slightly, the procedures we show for fitting will still be valid.

Our main project car was a 1.3 Frascati, 1995 N reg, with some additional work being carried out on other Fiestas.

"Wheels & tyres" takes a detailed look at all the options

"Body styling" shows you how to fit universal mirrors to full body kits

"Interiors" includes seats, painting trim, gear knobs and loads more.

Fiesta - the first-timer's favourite

For the young modifier on a budget, Fords have long been the obvious choice for many, and Fiestas are the pick of the bunch. With Mk 2s just looking a bit too old now (and with rust an increasing problem), the very affordable Mk 3 has come under the modifying spotlight.

If VW "invented" the hot hatch with the Golf GTI, then Ford brought the idea to the masses with the XRs of the 1980s. The old Fiesta XR2 especially was a cracking little car - cheap to buy and run (with very simple Escort mechanicals), brilliant fun to drive with quick steering and excellent grip (in the dry), and it even looked half-decent in standard form. Anyone who couldn't afford a 205 or a Golf was very well served by Ford's alternative.

So where did it all start to go wrong? For reasons best known to themselves, after the demise of the Mk 2 XR2, Ford abandoned the cheap hot hatch market it had created, and moved its game upmarket, beyond the reach of many younger drivers. The new XR2i tried just a bit too hard to be a 205GTi (which it never really had the talent to be), and was just too expensive for what it was - pricing it too high meant that suddenly, all those old XR2 character flaws were exposed. The RS Turbo which followed had the same problems, even though it handled better and went like a scalded cat, it was still a bit too rough n' ready to compete with the very

well-sorted 205 GTi 1.9 and Golf GTI 16-valve. By the time the motoring press had virtually written off the new XR2i, Ford came along and salvaged some pride by dropping in the new 1.8 litre 16-valve Zetec engine, tidying up the looks and the handling at the same time, creating the very talented RS1800 in the process. Trouble is, it was all a bit too late. Rocketing insurance premiums would soon mean that any hot hatch would be fighting for its life - by 1993, the 205 was dead, and the best Golf GTI had died too. Shame.

But hey - ignore the competition when the cars were new. Look at the secondhand market today - XR2is and RS Turbos are a lot more affordable now, and what some motoring journo may have whinged about 10 years ago doesn't matter a stuff. What we've got now are some smart, nippy, cheap-to-run hatches that put a smile on your face. Get real. The only downer to the whole deal is insuring the things - it takes a long while for insurance companies to forget...

Okay, so not everyone can afford the XR and RS - so what does a more basic Mk 3 Fiesta get you? Ford really did start with a blank sheet of paper with the Mk 3, and just as well - the Mk 2 was only a clever update of the Mk 1 Fiesta, which had been around since 1976. Looking at the lines of the Mk 3 (and especially the rear end), it's not hard to tell that Ford's target car when they developed the Mk 3 was the ultra-successful Peugeot 205. As a result, the Mk 3 Fiesta also has a more than sensible ride and handling mix (but not after you've slammed it?), and compared to the Mk 2, the space inside is in a different league (more room for ICE!). The only downside to the base models is that the various HCS pushrod

engines are pretty sad, and there's not much scope for seriously improving these - better to dip into the huge Escort parts bin at your local scrapyard, and sort out a 1.4 or 1.6 CVH conversion, when your insurance/no-claims situation improves. Meanwhile, there's plenty of scope for making even a base Fiesta look the part, with RS Turbo, Si and Cosworth bodykits readily available, as well as an increasing number now of more radical Jap and Euro-look designs. The modifying world seems at last to be waking up to the Fiesta's popularity and potential...

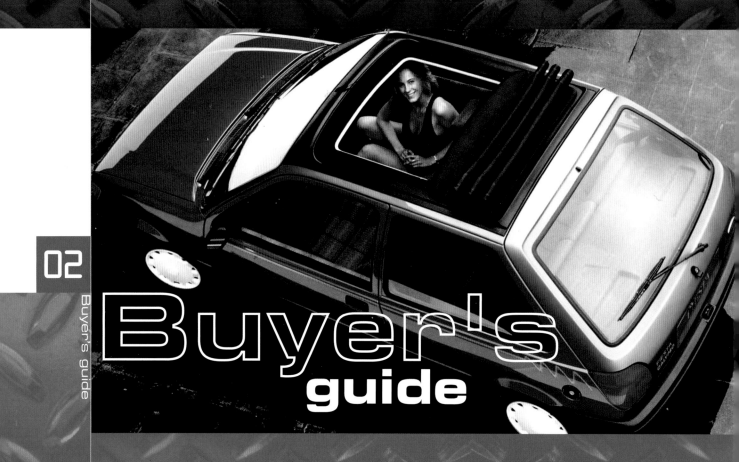

Buyer's guide

What to buy - model guide

'Basic' models

First of all, don't buy a 5-door. The reason? Nobody buys 5-doors for modifying purposes. If it doesn't say in the advert which it is, ask. The 5-door just doesn't lend itself to looking cool - you might have other ideas, but you'll be in a minority! Also, unless you've got a phobia about clutches and gearchanging, avoid the automatics, identified by designations such as 'CTX' 'CVT' and 'LA'.

As with any car, go for the latest model you can afford. Some of the special editions (and there've been plenty of those) had some useful extra kit, like sunroofs, tints and body-colour bumpers, as well as the obligatory ghastly interior re-trim. Many of the lesser Fiestas were bought as second cars, for shopping and for the school run; there's also a fair number in the hands of pensioners. Although some of these will be the less trendy 5-door models, if you can find a 3-door, they can be the best buys of all, provided they've been looked after. Why pay extra for an Si or XR, if you're going to change everything anyway? The base models are, however, fairly sad inside, with a dull dash and virtually no toys - smartening it up with a full interior makeover would be a priority on one of these babies.

A major change was the introduction of catalytic converters, in October 1992 (some models had converters before that). Avoiding a "cat" is a good idea, if you can - if it goes wrong, as in failing the MOT emissions test, it'll be big bucks to sort. And no, you can't just take it off - fit that free-flowing system by all means, but we didn't suggest it - your car will then be illegal on the road. All cat models have fuel injection. Before you get the idea this means more power, think again. Fitting a cat means controlling emissions, which means leaning the engine off - not a recipe for tyre-shredding torque . . . and if the fuel injection starts playing up, it'll be even more dosh.

The 1.0 Popular, Bonus and Fresco models (1989 to 1991) are particularly unimpressive, performance-wise, and there ain't much scope for easy improvement. All you'll be saving is one group on insurance, for a car that struggles to reach the unofficial motorway speed limit. Still, at least a 1.0 litre petrol's lively enough off the motorway, something no-one's going to accuse the 1.8 litre diesels of. Unrefined and not even that economical - just don't do it, okay?

The models you'll see most of will be 1.1 litres (L, LX and so many special editions). With modest performance reflected in Group 5 insurance, these are probably the best bargains in the base models - the 1.3 litre engine is a bit rarer, offers only a little more punch, and insurance is two groups higher. Mind you, when the cats arrived, in October 1992, the 1.1 models lost another 4 bhp (down to a puny 49 horses), while the 1.3s were unaffected, keeping 10 more. Hmmm. Rarer are the 1.4 LX and Ghia - with the grunty CVH engine, these actually have some oomph, but are only in Group 7. Most of these were 5-doors, though, and the LX vanished in 1991.

If you're going to fit fat tyres, get a car with power steering (only available on later special editions, like the Fiesta Mistral, Sapphire or Equipe) - non-assisted steering isn't heavy to start with, but the combination of big rims and a small sporty Momo steering wheel might have you breaking sweat! Base models from February 1994 all had Ford immobilisers fitted, which helps the insurance, but be sure you get the red "master" key handed over with any spares.

'Sporty' models

For a sporty drive that the insurance companies won't sting you for, seek out the Fiesta Si, introduced in February 1994. Intended as a replacement for the by-then deceased XR2i, the Si was offered with the 1.4 CVH engine (re-named the PTE), or the new 1.6 16-valve Zetec. With insurance rated at Group 7E and 8E respectively, and with a sporty styling makeover (rounded bumpers, front fogs, small tailgate spoiler), Ford would have sold these by the shedload if they'd only thought of it sooner. Strangely, the Si was the only sports model fitted with power steering.

Another performance bargain is the early 1.6 S, the spiritual successor to the old Mk 2 XR2, with a carb-fed 1.6 litre CVH motor, and Group 9 insurance. Sadly, it died in 1991.

The main sports model is the XR2i, initially with a 110 bhp 1.6 litre injection CVH engine, offering nippy performance in exchange for Group 14 insurance premiums. Group 14 - gulp - are you sure about this? The standard interior wasn't very sporty, either. Better performance value was the fire-breathing RS Turbo, with 133 bhp and 0-60 times in the seven-second bracket, for only one extra group over the XR - the Recaro interior looks the part, too. A real hairy motor, the rough-diamond RS Turbo won many fans in its 18-month lifespan - just don't mention the naff three-spoke alloys . . .

The sports Fiesta range had a major revamp in early 1992, when the 1.8 litre 16-valve Zetec engine arrived (a thoroughly-modern motor, with excellent torque, and much less top-end thrash than the poor old CVH unit). The new engine came in 105 bhp form for the new XR2i 16v, and in 130 bhp form for the new RS1800 model. The suspension and styling both received worthwhile tweaks at the same time, and at last the motoring press were satisfied.

Don't buy a **duffer**

In general, the Mk 3 Fiesta is a solid used buy, with only a few problems worth noting. Many lesser Fiestas you'll see would've been bought by women and oldies, who generally at least drive sensibly and have their cars dealer-serviced (though there are exceptions!).

Unless you're planning on spending big money on an RS Turbo, it's far better to buy privately, as long as you know what you're doing. Dealers still think they can charge over the odds for small cars, but all you'll get for the extra money is a full valet and some degree of comeback if the car's a dog. Buying privately, you get to meet the owner, and this can tell you plenty about how the car's been treated. Everyone's nervous when buying a car, but don't ignore your "gut feelings" when you first see the car, or meet its owner. Also, don't make the common mistake of deciding to buy the car before you've even seen it - too many people seem to make up their minds before setting out, and blindly ignore all the warning signs. Remember, there are other cars, and you can walk away! Think of a good excuse before you set out.

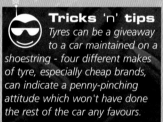

Tricks 'n' tips
Tyres can be a giveaway to a car maintained on a shoestring - four different makes of tyre, especially cheap brands, can indicate a penny-pinching attitude which won't have done the rest of the car any favours.

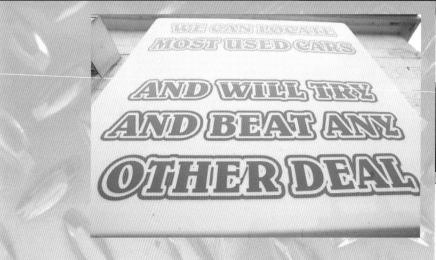

HCS engine number stamped into the block above the gearbox - can you see yours?

Take someone who 'knows a bit about cars' along with you - preferably, try and find someone who's either got a Fiesta, or who's had one in the past.

Never buy a car in the dark, or when it's raining. If you do have to view any car in these conditions, agree not to hand over any money until you've seen it in daylight, and when the paintwork's dry (dull, faded paint, or metallic paint that's lost its lacquer, will appear to be shiny in the rain).

Check that the mileages and dates shown on any receipts and MOTs follow a pattern indicating normal use, with no gaps in the dates, and no sudden drop in the mileage between MOTs (which might suggest the mileage has been 'clocked'). If you are presented with a sheaf of paperwork, it's worth going through it - maybe the car's had a history of problems, or maybe it's just had some nice expensive new parts fitted (like a clutch, starter motor or alternator, for instance).

Check the chassis number (VIN number) and engine number on the registration document and on the car. Any sign of welding near one of these numbers should be treated with suspicion - to disguise the real number, a thief will run a line of weld over the old number, grind it flat, then stamp in a new number. Other scams include cutting the section of bodywork with the numbers on from another car, then cutting and welding this section into place. The VIN number appears on a plate at the front of the engine compartment; if there is any sign that this plate has been tampered with, walk away - the car could be stolen. The chassis number on this plate should match the one stamped into the floor next to the driver's seat (lift the flap for access) - again, if the numbers don't match, or if they're not in a straight line, leave the car well alone - it could be a "ringer" (a stolen car with a fake I.D.). Cars from February 1994 also have the VIN on a small plate on top of the dash, visible through the windscreen.

The engine number is stamped onto a flat machined surface at the front of the engine, at the transmission end (some CVH engines have the number at the cambelt end). This number can be difficult to spot, but keep looking until you find it - if the number's been ground off, or if there's anything suspicious about it, you could be buying trouble.

Check the registration document very carefully - all the details should match the car. If buying privately, make sure that it's definitely the owner's name and address printed on it - if not, be very careful! If buying from a dealer, note the name and address, and try to contact the previous owner to confirm mileage, etc, before handing over more than a deposit. Unless the car's very old, it should

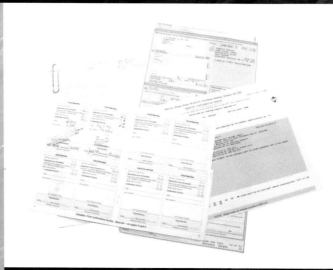

Full service history (fsh)

Is there any service history? If so, this is good, but study the service book carefully:

a *Which garage has done the servcing? Is it a proper dealer, or a backstreet bodger? Do you know the garage, and if so, would you use it?*

b *Do the mileages show a nice even progression, or are there huge gaps? Check the dates too.*

c *Does it look as if the stamps are authentic? Do the oldest ones look old, or could this 'service history' have been created last week, to make the car look good?*

d *When was the last service, and what exactly was carried out? When was the cambelt last changed? Has the owner got receipts for any of this servicing work?*

One sign of a genuine car is a good batch of old MOTs, and as many receipts as possible - even if they're for fairly irrelevant things like tyres.

not have had too many previous owners - if it's into double figures, it may mean that the car is trouble, so checking its owner history is more important.

Problem areas

The dreaded Mk 2 problem of rust isn't much of a factor, but check under the sills for scabs, and around the rear arches (which can start to go quite quickly), front valance and battery tray. Apparently, one unpleasant place they can go is around the fuel filler, which looks pretty hideous, and can come through again even once it's been sorted out. Check too that XR and RS bodykits aren't hiding rust on the arches or sills. Otherwise, major rust anywhere else could be down to badly-repaired crash damage, so walk away.

Brake discs can warp, leading to noticeable judder through the pedal, and suspension wear can lead to the car not tracking straight (and uneven tyre wear) - leaking dampers are not uncommon, either. Of course, you'll be ripping out the standard suspension and fitting some groovy brake discs, so it's not a big deal, but why not use problems like this to haggle the price down? Suspension clonks over bumps means worn balljoints, and they'll still be worn even after some slammage, so get negotiating.

The VIN plate is attached to the bonnet front slam panel . . .

. . . and the VIN is also stamped into the floorpan, in front of the driver's seat.

Any engine will suffer if oil changes have been overlooked, so ask when the oil was last changed, and check the colour (and amount) of oil on the dipstick. The apparently-bulletproof smaller engines (1.0, 1.1 and 1.3 HCS) can suffer camshaft wear, from neglecting oil changes. The HCS engine is rattly anyway, but a severely-worn cam will be very loud - listen to a few examples before deciding.

The CVH engine suffers from top-end oil sludging (take off the oil filler cap, and peer inside for what looks like a coating of thick black tar). Blocked breathers are another result of sludging - after a long time, the sludge in the oil will block oilways, including the pick-up strainer in the sump. Time to administer the last rites, then. Another known killer of CVH engines is neglecting to change the timing belt (or 'cambelt'). A sensible interval here is 2 years or 20 000 miles, and make sure a genuine Ford belt is used (the later Zetec engines are better here, but don't take liberties - for maximum peace of mind, treat these like a CVH too.) All CVH engines have hydraulic tappets, and may rattle slightly when they're first started from cold. Any noise should die down after a few seconds; if not, this might indicate a problem - low oil level, lack of servicing, or the use of poor-quality oil might all be responsible.

High-mileage cars may suffer from hardened/perished valve stem oil seals, giving rise to a trail of blue oil smoke in the exhaust. At start-up from cold, check the exhaust for blue smoke - on the test-drive, try lifting off the throttle for a few seconds (over-run), then accelerate again while watching in the mirror for smoke.

While the trim on a Fiesta is very durable, it should still be obvious whether the car's been abused over a long period, or whether the mileage showing is genuine or not (shiny steering wheels and floppy window winder handles are a good place to start checking if you're suspicious). Okay, so you may be planning to junk most of the interior at some point . . . If a scruffy interior doesn't actually put you off, at least haggle the price down!

Although you may feel a bit stupid doing it, check simple things too, like making sure the windows and sunroof open and shut, and that all the doors and tailgate can be locked. Check all the basic electrical equipment too, as far as possible - lights, front and rear wipers, heated rear window, heater fan; it's amazing how often these things are taken for granted by buyers! If your chosen Fiesta already has alloys fitted, does it have locking wheel bolts? Where's the key?

Is the catalytic converter ("cat") working? These are major bucks to replace - to be sure, only buy a car with a new MOT (the cat is checked during the emissions test).

Many Fiestas will have a driver's airbag fitted - these will have AIRBAG and the initials SRS (supplementary restraint system) on the steering wheel centre pad. The orange airbag warning light should come on and go off when the engine's started - if it stays on, this counts as an MOT fail, and curing the fault could be mega-bucks (it might also indicate that the airbag's gone off, in a crash!). If the light doesn't come on at all, this could still mean there's a fault with the airbag, but your dishonest seller's just taken out the bulb . . . nice try.

Sports models

Has it been thrashed to death? We wouldn't pay top dollar for any sporty Fiesta without evidence of careful maintenance - any car will stand a good ranting much better if it's been properly serviced. A fully-stamped service book only tells half the story, though. Does the owner look bright enough to even know what a dipstick is?

If the car's just too cheap (and even if it's not), never take anything at face value - check everything you can about the car yourself. Getting your hands on a really good sporty Fiesta is not a simple task - dodgy dealers (and owners!) punt out repaired write-offs and stolen cars, and gullible private buyers get ripped every day.

More so than any other model, check for signs of accident damage, especially the front end. Ask if it's ever been shunted - if the seller says no, but there's paint overspray under the bonnet, what's going on? Also check for overspray on window rubbers, light units and bumpers/trim. With the bonnet open, check the headlight shells are the same colour - mis-matched or new-looking ones merit an explanation. Does the front number plate carry details of the supplying garage, like the back one? If not, why has a new plate been fitted?

Check the glass (and even the lights) for etched-in registration numbers - are they all the same, and does it match the car's actual registration? A windscreen could've been replaced innocently enough, but new side glass indicates a break-in at least - is the car a 'stolen/recovered' joyrider special? Find the chassis and engine numbers, as described earlier, and satisfy yourself that they are genuine - check them against the "logbook" (registration document). An HPI check (or similar) is worthwhile, but even this won't tell you everything. If you're at all suspicious, or if the answers to your questions don't ring true, then walk away. Make any excuse you like.

The sporty models get driven hard, and hard driving will take its toll somewhere. The suspension should feel quite stiff and taut - any sogginess is usually caused by worn shock absorbers (not a problem, if you're fitting a full lowering kit, but use it to haggle the price down). Any vibration or juddering through the steering when braking indicates serious brake wear (warped brake discs), or possibly, play in the suspension/steering joints (fitting a lowering kit will not cure this kind of play, which also eats front tyres!). RS Turbos have an appetite for clutches, and evidence of careful servicing is essential if you don't want the bill for replacing a fried turbo.

It's a plus point if an approved (Thatcham Cat 1 or 2) alarm or immobiliser is fitted, and you might find it's an essential fitment, just to get any kind of insurance quote. Make sure that any alarm actually works, that it looks properly installed, with no stray wires hanging out, and that you get the Thatcham certificate or other paperwork to go with it. If the seller fitted it, it's worth finding out exactly how it's been wired in - if it goes wrong later, you could be stranded with no chance of disabling the system to get you home. Models from September 1993 have immobilisers as standard.

Sealing the deal

Everything as expected and the car's just what you want? It's time to start haggling. Never just agree to hand over the full advertised price for the car, but don't be too ambitious, either (it's best to stay friendly at this point - winding-up the owner is the last thing you need). If the ad says "o.n.o.", expect at least 10% off - if not, why bother putting it on the ad? Try a low offer to test the owner's reaction (they can only say no!) then reluctantly increase the offer until you're both happy. Haggling can also include other considerations besides cash - will the owner chuck in the nice stereo and wheels, leave the tax on, or put a new MOT ("ticket") on it?

Bagged a bargain? Sorted! Offer to leave a deposit (this shows you're serious), but before parting with any more cash, it may be worth considering the following.

Ask for time to get in touch with the previous owner shown on the "logbook" (registration document). If you can speak to them, it's a useful exercise in confirming the car's history and mileage.

A wise thing to do is to run a vehicle check on the car with an organisation such as HPI or the AA. It'll cost you (usually around the 30-quid mark) but could save a lot of hassle in future. They'll need the details of all the identification numbers on the vehicle and documents, as well as the mileage etc. For your money, they'll run the details of the car through their computer database. This database contains the records of all vehicles reported stolen, which have been total losses (ie. have been totalled after a serious accident) or have outstanding finance against them. They can then confirm over the phone the vehicle is straight, and in theory you can proceed with the deal, safe in the knowledge you're not about to purchase a ringer. Not only will you receive a nice certificate through the post with your vehicle details on it, but running the check also gives you financial insurance. The information given is guaranteed (usually to the tune of about ten grand) so if Plod turns up on your doorstep a month later, demanding you return your new vehicle to its rightful owner, you should be able to claim your cash back. No worries.

Tricks 'n' tips

If your understanding of the mechanical workings of the modern automobile is a bit vague and you want a second opinion, it may also be worth considering having the vehicle inspected. The AA and RAC offer this service, but there may be other people in your area too - check in the Yellow Pages. This is a bit pricier than the vehicle check, but will give you peace of mind and some comeback should things not be as expected. If you've got a friendly garage, maybe they could be persuaded to check the car over for a small fee.

Model history

Like many small-car ranges in recent years, the number of "special edition" models offered in the Fiesta's history has been enormous. The models listed below are a representative selection - to have listed them all would've taken half the book! Don't pay over the odds for a special edition, unless it's genuinely got some extra kit you're interested in having - most are just the 1.1 or 1.3 base model with a sunroof, stickers and a Ford radio.

April 1989 (F reg) - Fiesta Mk 3 range introduced. 1.0 and 1.1 litre HCS engines, 1.4/1.6 litre CVH, 1.8 diesel. Popular, Pop Plus, L, LX and Ghia trim. Base 1.0 and 1.1 models have 4-speed gearbox. 1.6 S with uprated suspension, "sports" interior, 90 bhp engine. 1.6 XR2i with bodykit, front fogs, optional 13-inch alloys, central locking, electric windows, 110 bhp injection engine.

February 1990 (G reg) - 5-speed gearbox now standard across the range, except on 1.0 litre Popular.

June 1990 (G reg) - RS Turbo introduced. 1.6 CVH turbocharged injection engine, 133 bhp. Bodykit with front fog and driving lights, bonnet vents, Recaro seats, central locking, electric windows, 14-inch 3-spoke alloys.

January 1991 (H reg) - Limited edition 1.1 SX model introduced - sports suspension, wide wheels, tints, sports interior.

July 1991 (H reg) - Production of 1.0 models, 1.4 LX, and 1.6 S, ends. 1.1 litre is new base model, 1.3 litre HCS engine introduced. 1.3 LX and SX available - LX has rev counter, SX has sports suspension, wider wheels, tints, sports interior.

November 1991 (J reg) - 1.3 Calypso limited edition introduced, with catalyst engine. Full-length electric folding sunroof, sports interior.

February 1992 (J reg) - XR2i and RS Turbo replaced by new 1.8 litre 16-valve Zetec-engined XR2i 16v (105 bhp) and RS1800 (130 bhp). 14-inch "starfish" 5-spoke alloys, remote tailgate release, catalytic converter. RS has Recaro seats.

July 1992 (J reg) - SX models discontinued.

September 1992 (K reg) - 1.3 Finesse limited edition introduced. Sports suspension and interior, tints, tailgate spoiler, centre console with leather gear knob and gaiter, electric folding sunroof option, electric pack option.

October 1992 (K reg) - All models now have standard catalytic converter, clear front indicators, "lights-on" warning.

September 1993 (L reg) - 1.1 and 1.8D Finesse limited edition introduced. Sunroof, tints, rev counter. XR2i and RS1800 gain standard immobiliser.

February 1994 (L reg) - All models now have driver's airbag, side impact bars. Safeguard immobiliser and visible VIN plate fitted to all models - 1.1 and 1.3 models now insurance groups 4E and 6E. Si models introduced, with 1.4 PTE (CVH) and 1.6 Zetec 16v engine - rounded front and rear bumpers, front foglights, sports suspension and interior.

May 1994 (L reg) - Mistral, Sapphire and Equipe limited editions introduced, with passenger airbag. 1.1/1.3 Mistral - sunroof, sports suspension and interior, tailgate spoiler. 1.1/1.3 Sapphire - sunroof, electric windows, central locking, alarm, remote tailgate release. 1.3 Equipe - sunroof, power steering, heated windscreen. 1.1 Azura also introduced.

February 1995 (M reg) - 1.3 Frascati limited edition introduced. Passenger airbag, central locking, electric windows, alarm, remote tailgate release, power steering. 1.1 Quartz introduced.

October 1995 (N reg) - New Fiesta Mk 4 range introduced. Mk 3 models continue - 1.1 base model is "Classic", 1.1 LX is "Classic Quartz", 1.3 LX is "Classic Cabaret".

January 1997 (P reg) - Mk 3 models discontinued.

Performance figures

	0-60 (sec)	Top speed (mph)
1.0	17.5	86
1.1	15.5	94
1.3	14.2	92
1.4 LX	13.4	98
1.4 Si	12.8	102
1.6 S	10.0	109
1.6 Si	12.0	109
1.6 XR2i	8.7	114
1.6 RS Turbo	7.9	129
1.8 XR2i 16v	9.3	114
1.8 RS1800	8.7	121
1.8 Diesel	17.6	91

Insurance
A necessary evil

Ah, insurance - an awful lot of money, for a piece of paper you're not really supposed to use! Of course, you must have insurance - you're illegal on the road without it, and you won't be able to get the car taxed, either. If you drive without insurance and are caught, you may have great trouble ever getting an insurance quote again - the insurance companies seem to regard this offence nearly as seriously as drink-driving on your record, so don't do it!

Tricks 'n' tips
When ringing for quotes, watch your language. Arguing with the bloke/girl on the other end will always get you a higher quote, even if it makes you feel better. Also, don't say anything if you get put on hold. Some companies will put you on speaker - if you're trying to pull a fast one and they then catch you giggling or bragging to your mates, it's game over.

With modified cars, insurance becomes even more of a problem. By putting on all the alloys, trick body kits, nice interiors, big ICE, you're making the car much more of a target for thieves (yes, ok, I know you know this). The point is, the insurance companies know this too, and they don't want to be paying out for the car, plus all the money you've spent on it, should it go missing. There is a temptation 'not to tell the insurance' about the mods you've made. Let's deal with this right now. Our experience has been that, while it can be painful, honesty is best. Generally, the insurance company line is: "…thanks for telling us - we won't put the car 'up a group' (ie charge you more), but we also won't cover the extra cost of your alloy wheels/body kit/tasty seats in the event of any claim…". This is fair enough - in other words, if your car goes missing, you get paid out, based on a standard car. If you particularly want all the extras covered, you might have a long hard search - most companies (if they'll offer you cover at all) will only offer "modified for standard" policies. There are specialist insurers who are more friendly towards fully-loaded cars, but even they won't actually cover the cost of replacement goodies.

Valuing your car

When your insurance pays out in the event of a total loss or write-off, they base their offer on the current market value of an identical standard model to yours. The only way you'll get more than the average amount is to prove your Fiesta is in above-average nick (with photos?) or that the mileage was especially low for the year.

With this in mind, don't bother over-valuing your Fiesta in the hope you'll get more in the event of a claim - you won't! The only way to do this is to seek out an "agreed-value" deal, which you can usually only get on classic-car policies (with these, the car's value is agreed in advance between you, not worked out later by the company with you having no say in it). By over-valuing your Fiesta, you could be increasing your premium without gaining any benefit - sound smart to you?

Equally though, don't under-value, in the hope you'll get a reduction in premium. You won't, and if there's a total loss claim, you won't get any more than your under-valued amount, no matter how loudly you complain.

Work on what you paid for the car, backed up with the sort of prices you see for similar cars in the ads (or use a secondhand car price guide). Add no more than 10% for the sake of optimism, and that's it.

What type of cover?

For most of us, cost means there's only one option - TPF&T (third party, fire and theft). Fully-comp insurance is an unattainable dream for most people until they reach the "magic" age of 25, but what's the real story?

Third Party only

The most basic cover you can get. Basically covers you for damage to other people's cars or property, and for personal injury claims. Virtually no cover for your own stuff, beyond what you get if you take the optional "legal protection" cover.

Third Party, Fire and Theft

As above, with cover for fire and theft, of course! Better, but not much better. This is really only cover in the event of a "total loss", if your car goes missing or goes up in smoke. Still no cover for your car if you stack it into a tree, or if someone breaks in and pinches your stereo.

Fully-comprehensive

In theory, covers you for any loss or damage. Will cover the cost of repairing or replacing your car regardless of whether it was your fault or not. With a fully-comp policy, you can "protect" your no-claims bonus for a small fee so you don't automatically lose those hard-earned years' worth of discount if you prang it. All this extra cover costs more, but is often a better bet in the long run.

Your car, or your Dad's?

Don't pretend your Fiesta belongs to your Dad, and get him to insure it, with you as a named driver. Insurance companies are not stupid. They know that your Dad isn't likely to be running around in a modified car, and they treat any "named driver" application with great suspicion in these cases. This dubious practice also does you no favours in future years. All the time you're living the lie, you're not building up any no-claims bonus of your own.

Not telling the insurance the whole truth gets a little tricky when you have to make a claim. You may think your insurance company is there for your benefit, but they're a business like any other, and their main aim in life is to make money. If the insurance assessor comes around to check your bent/burnt/stolen-and-recovered "standard" Fiesta, and finds he's looking at a vehicle fitted with alloys/bodykit/modified interior, he's not going to turn a blind eye.

Limit your premium

When you phone for a quote your fate is pretty much sealed, but there are a few things you can do to help lower the premium .

Golden Rule Number One

If in doubt, declare everything. Insurance companies are legally entitled to dispute any claim if the car is found to be non-standard in any way.

Golden Rule Number Two

Before modifying the car, ring your insurance, and ask them how it will affect things.

Fit an approved alarm or immobiliser

In general, any alarm or immobiliser with a Thatcham rating should be recognised by any insurance company, but it pays to check before fitting. In some cases, the discounts offered are not that great any more - but an alarm is still a nice way to get peace of mind.

Avoid speed cameras and The Law

Yes, okay, easier said than done! One SP30 isn't usually too bad, but much more and you'll pay for it, so go easy.

Make yourself the only driver

Pretty self-explanatory. The more people who drive your car, the greater the risk to the company. If you've built up 2 years' worth of no-claims, but your partner hasn't, putting them on your insurance will bump it up, due to their relative inexperience.

Build up your no-claims bonus

You'll only do this by owning and insuring a car in your own name, and then not making any claims. Simple really. Each claim free year you have will aid lowering how much you pay out.

Hang onto your no-claims bonus

Obviously, the less you claim, the less your insurance will cost. If something happens to your car, don't be in too big a hurry to make a claim before you've thought it all through. How much will it cost to fix? How much is your excess? If you can afford not to claim, then don't do it.

Limit your mileage

Most companies offer a discount if you only cover a small annual mileage. To get any meaningful reduction, the mileage has to be less than 10,000 per year. Don't try and pretend you only do 3000 if it's nearer 20,000. Few companies ever ask what the car's current mileage is - so how are they gonna know if you've gone over your self-imposed limit? But if they do find out you could be in trouble.

Get a garage

If you have access to a garage use it, insurers love a car to be locked away safe and sound at night.

Insurance-friendly mods?

So - what do insurance companies like and dislike, as far as mods go? No two companies will have the same outlook, and your own circumstances will play a big part too.

Engine mods

"Mild" mods such as induction kits and exhausts don't often change premiums, but just the merest mention of "chipping" can make many companies load the premium, or even completely refuse to offer cover. With complete engine transplants, you may be required to give an engineer's report on the mods before they'll grant cover.

Interior mods

As with bodykits, unless you go absolutely mental it really shouldn't make a difference, but make sure you tell your insurers all the same.

Body mods

Even a tiny rear spoiler can be classed as a "bodykit" (yes, it's daft, but that's how it is). Anything which alters the exterior appearance should be declared. As long as the mods aren't too radical, the jump in premium should be fairly small. If anything at all.

Lights

As they're safety-related, you'll probably get asked for lots of details, but as long as you've kept it sensible (and legal, as far as possible) you'll be fine.

Security

Make sure you mention all security stuff - alarms, immobilisers (including mechanical devices), and locking wheel nuts. Don't tell them you've got a Cat 1 if your alarm really came from Argos, and don't tell them you garage the car at night if it's stuck out in the road. If they find out, you're on your own.

Suspension

Average suspension drops of 30-40mm are fine, go much lower and they may charge you more.

Wheels

The specialist insurers won't mind you having a nice set of alloys, but just about every other insurer will load the premium sadly. Make sure you fit locking wheel bolts.

Brakes

Uprating standard sized discs, maybe with grooved or drilled discs seldom affects the insurance, but some get a bit twitchy when you start fitting bigger discs and replacement calipers.

Security

It's a sad fact, but making your car attractive to the opposite sex also tends to attract attention of a less-welcome kind, possibly from less-than-human pond life.

Avoiding trouble

Now come on - you're modifying your car to look cool and to be seen in. Not a problem - but be careful where you choose to show your car off, and who to. Be especially discreet, the nearer you get to home - turn your system down before you get near home, for instance, or you'll draw unwelcome attention to where that car with the loud stereo's parked at night.

If you're going out, think about where you're parking - somewhere well-lit and reasonably well-populated is the best bet.

Hands up, who doesn't lock their car when they get petrol? Your insurance company has a term for this, and it's "contributory negligence". In English, this means you won't get a penny if your car goes missing when you haven't locked it.

If you're lucky enough to have a garage, use it and fit extra security to the garage door.

Always use all the security you have, whenever you leave the car, even if it's a bit of a chore fitting a steering lock, just do it.

A word about your stereo

From the moment you bolt on those nice alloys, it's taken as read that you've also got stereo gear that's worth nicking - and the thieves know it. All the discreet installation in the world isn't going to deter them from finding out what's inside that nice motor.

If you have a CD player, don't leave discs or empty CD cases lying around inside the car. 6x9s on the rear shelf are also very inviting to thieves, and very easy to steal. When you're fitting your system, give some thought to the clues you could accidentally leave in plain view. Oxygen-free speaker cable is great stuff, but it's also a bit bright against dark carpets, and is all the clue necessary that you're serious about your speakers.

Most modern sets are face-off or MASK, so if they've got security features like this, use them - take your faceplate off when you leave the car, and take it with you rather than leaving it in the door pocket or glovebox (the first places a thief will look).

Things that go beep in the night

Don't skimp on an alarm, it may never even be put to the test, but if it is, you'll be glad you spent wisely ...

The simplest first step to car security is to fake it. It's obviously risky if the thief calls your bluff, but if you really can't afford an alarm just an LED is cheap to buy and easy to fit, and can be rigged to a discreet switch inside the car (we show you how, later on).

Don't overlook the value of so-called "manual" immobilisers, such as steering wheel locks. These are a worthwhile deterrent - a thief not specifically after your car (and yours alone) may move on to an easier target. Some of the items offered may be "Sold Secure" or Thatcham Cat 3, accolades well worth checking out, as it means they've withstood a full-on brute force attack for a useful length of time.

The only way to combat the more determined thief is to go for a well-specified and intelligently-installed alarm. Immobilisers alone have their place, but a pro-fitted immobiliser alone won't stop someone pinching your wheels, or breaking in for the stereo gear.

Finally, one other scam which you might fall victim to. If you find that your alarm is suddenly going off a lot at night, when previously it had been well-behaved, don't ignore the problem. It's an old trick for a thief to deliberately set off your alarm several times, each time hiding when you come out to investigate, then to wait until the fifth or sixth time when you don't reset, leaving him a clear run. If your alarm does keep false-alarming without outside assistance, find out the cause quickly, or your neighbours will quickly become "deaf" to it.

Thatcham categories and meanings:

1 **Cat 1.** For alarms and electronic immobilisers.
2 **Cat 2.** For electronic immobilisers only.
3 **Cat 2-1.** Electronic immobilisers which can be upgraded to Cat 1 alarms later.
4 **Cat 3.** Mechanical immobilisers, eg snap-off steering wheels, locking wheel bolts, window film, steering wheel locks/covers.
5 **Q-class.** Tracking devices.

Other alarm features

Two-stage anti-shock - means that the alarm shouldn't go off, just because the neighbour's cat jumps on your car roof, or because Little Johnny punts his football into your car. Alarm will only sound after a major shock, or after repeated shocks are detected.

Anti-tilt - detects any attempt to lift or jack up the car, preventing any attempt to pinch alloys. Very unpopular with thieves, as it makes the alarm very sensitive (much more so than anti-shock). Alarm may sound if car is parked outside in windy conditions (but not if your suspension's rock-hard!).

Anti-hijack - immobiliser with built-in delay. If your motor gets hijacked, the neanderthals responsible will only get so far down the road before the engine cuts out.

Rolling code - reduces the chance of your alarm remote control signal from being "grabbed" by special electronic equipment.

Total closure - module which connects to electric windows or sunroof and central locking, which closes all items when alarm is set.

Pager control - yes, really - your alarm can be set to send a message to your pager (why not your mobile?) if your car gets tampered with.

Current-sensing disable - very useful feature on some cars which have a cooling fan which can cut in after the ignition is switched off. Without this feature, your alarm will be triggered every time you leave it parked after a long run - very annoying.

Volumetric-sensing disable - basically allows you to manually disable the interior ultrasonics, leaving the rest of the alarm features active. Useful if you want to leave the sunroof open in hot weather - if a fly gets in the car, the alarm would otherwise be going off constantly.

Talking alarms - no, please, please no. Very annoying, and all that'll happen is you'll attract crowds of kids daring each other to set it off again. Unfortunately, these are becoming more popular, with some offering the facility to record your own message!

The knowledge

What people often fail to realise (at least, until it happens to them) is the level of violence and destruction which thieves will employ to get your stuff - this goes way beyond breaking a window.

It comes as a major shock to most people when they discover the serious kinds of tools (weapons) at many professional thieves' disposal, and how brutally your lovingly-polished car will be attacked. Many people think, for instance, that it's their whole car they're after, whereas it's really only the parts they want, and they don't care how they get them (this means that these parts are still attractive, even when fitted to a basic car which has yet to be fully modded). Obviously, taking the whole car then gives the option of hiding it to strip at leisure, but it won't always be the option chosen, and you could wake up one morning to a well-mangled wreck outside.

Attack 1 The first option to any thief is to smash glass - typically, the toughened-glass side windows, which will shatter, unlike the windscreen. Unfortunately for the thief, this makes a loud noise (not good), but is a quick and easy way in. The reason for taking this approach is that a basic car alarm will only go off if the doors are opened (voltage-drop alarm) - provided the doors aren't opened, the alarm won't go off.

  Response 1 A more sophisticated alarm will feature shock sensing (which will be set off by the impact on the glass), and better still, ultrasonic sensing, which will be triggered by the brick coming in through the broken window.

  Response 2 This kind of attack can also be stopped by applying security film to the inside of the glass, which holds it all together and prevents easy entry.

Attack 2 An alternative to smashing the glass is to pry open the door using a crowbar - this attack involves literally folding open the door's window frame by prising from the top corner. The glass will still shatter, but as long as the door stays shut, a voltage-drop alarm won't be triggered.

  Response This method might not be defeated by a shock-sensing alarm, but an ultrasonic unit would pick it up.

Incidentally, another bonus with ultrasonic alarms is that the sensors are visible from outside - and act as a deterrent.

Attack 3 The next line of attack is to disable the alarm. The commonest way to kill the alarm is either to cut the wiring to the alarm itself, or to disconnect the battery after taking a crowbar to your bonnet catch.

  Response 1 If your alarm has extra pin-switches, be sure to fit one to the bonnet, and fit it in the bonnet channel next the battery, so that it'll set off the alarm if the bonnet is prised up. Also make sure that the wire to the pin-switch cannot be cut easily though a partly-open bonnet.

  Response 2 Make sure that the alarm module is well-hidden, and cannot be got at from underneath the car.

  Response 3 Make the alarm power supply connection somewhere less obvious than directly at the battery terminal - any thief who knows his stuff will immediately cut any "spare" red wires at the battery. Try taking power from the fusebox, or if you must source it under the bonnet, trace the large red battery lead to the starter motor connections, and tap into the power there.

  Response 4 Always disguise the new alarm wiring, by using black insulating tape to wrap it to the existing wiring loom. Tidying up in this way also helps to ensure the wires can't get trapped, cut, melted, or accidentally ripped out - any of which could leave you with an alarm siren which won't switch off, or an immobiliser you can't disable.

  Response 5 An alarm which has a "battery back-up" facility is best. Even if he's successfully crow-barred your bonnet and snipped the battery connections, the alarm will still go off, powered by a separate battery of its own. A Cat 1 alarm has to have battery back-up.

Fitting a basic LED

All you need for this is a permanent live feed, an earth, a switch if you want to be able to turn it on/off, and the flashing LED itself (very cheap, from any car accessory shop).

An LED draws very little current, so tap into almost any live feed you fancy. If you've wired in your ICE, take a live feed from the permanent (radio memory supply) wire at the back of your head unit, or go into fusebox with your test light (as featured in the alarm fitting procedure). An earth can easily be tapped again from your head unit, or you can make one almost anywhere on the metal body of the car - drill a small hole, fit a self-tapping screw, then wrap the bared end of wire around and tighten it.

The best place to mount an LED is into one of the blank switches the makers love fitting. The blank switch is pried out, and a hole can then be drilled to take the LED (which comes in a separate little holder). Feed the LED wiring down behind the dashboard to where you've tapped your live and earth, taking care not to trap it anywhere, nor to accidentally wrap it around any moving parts.

Connect your live to the LED red wire, then rig your earth to one side of the switch, and connect the LED black wire to the other switch terminal. You should now have a switchable LED! Tidy up the wiring, and mount the switch somewhere discreet, but where you can still get at it. Switch on when you leave the car, and it looks as if you've got some sort of alarm - better than nothing!

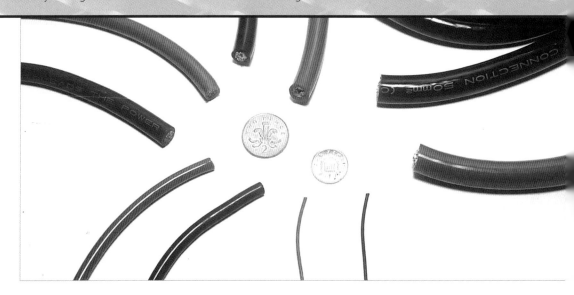

Wiring basics

If you were thinking of taking an alarm live supply direct from the battery - don't. It's better to trace the red lead down to the starter motor, and tap in there.

If a thief manages to get past your bonnet switch, his first thought will be to cut every additional live feed at the battery - of course, if he cuts all the battery leads, you're stuffed (without a battery back-up alarm), but at least you tried…

With your wires identified, how to tap into them?

The best options are:

Soldering - avoids cutting through your chosen wire - strip away a short section of insulation, wrap your new wire around the bared section, then apply solder to secure it. If you're a bit new to soldering, practice on a few offcuts of wire first.

Bullet connectors - cut and strip the end of your chosen wire, wrap your new one to it, push both into one half of the bullet. Connect the other end of your victim wire to the other bullet, and connect together. Always use the "female" half on any live feed - it'll be safer if you disconnect it than a male bullet, which could touch bare metal and send your motor up in smoke.

Block connectors - so easy to use. Just remember that the wires can come adrift if the screws aren't really tight, and don't get too ambitious about how many wires you can stuff in one hole (block connectors, like bullets, are available in several sizes).
Steer clear of connectors like the one below – they're convenient but can give rise to problems.

With any of these options, always insulate around your connection - especially when soldering, or you'll be leaving bare metal exposed. Remember that you'll probably be shoving all the wires up into the dark recesses of the under-dash area - by the time the wires are nice and kinked/squashed together, that tiny bit of protruding wire might just touch that bit of metal bodywork, and cause a fire…

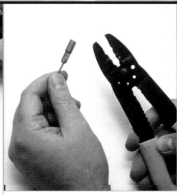

Fitting an auxiliary fusebox

You'll need plenty of fused live feeds from the battery during the modifying process, for stereo gear, neons, starter buttons - and alarms, and it's always a pain working out where to tap into one. If you make up your own little fusebox, mounted somewhere easy to get at, you'll never have this problem again - and it's easy enough to do.

The first job is to disconnect the battery negative lead, then take your main live feed from the battery. Make sure that the main cable is man enough for all the loads you're likely to put on it - starting with four-gauge wire (available from all good ICE suppliers) will mean you're never short of amps. As for where to feed the cable through, see the section on fitting an alarm (next in this section) or the ICE chapter for two good spots for a hole.

Tricks 'n' tips
If a correctly rated fuse keeps on blowing, most likely there's a problem in the circuit. Don't just stick in a higher-rated fuse - you could start a fire.

01 Okay, so you've got your large live wire into the car - where to put the fusebox? It's got to be accessible, and if we can make it look good, so much the better. Our fusebox, by the way, came from our local Lucas store - but you could go for an ICE distribution block. When we had the front kickpanel off to do the alarm, we found the perfect spot for the fusebox, and mounted it on a strip of MDF (the idea being to have it sticking out through a hole in the kickpanel when we're finished).

02 Hold the kickpanel up to your newly-mounted fusebox, and mark it top, bottom and sides. Lower the kickpanel, and mark the whole outline using the clip-on cover, for cutting (a Stanley knife is good enough).

03 The idea is that the fusebox's clip-on cover can be removed once the kickpanel's back in place - check that you've made your hole big enough.

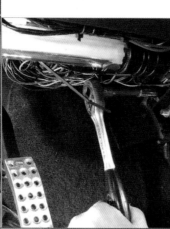

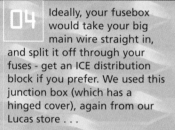

04 Ideally, your fusebox would take your big main wire straight in, and split it off through your fuses - get an ICE distribution block if you prefer. We used this junction box (which has a hinged cover), again from our Lucas store . . .

05 . . . which we fitted just above our new fusebox (plenty of room in here).

06 One piece of 4-gauge, one ring terminal, onto the junction box with this 'ere nut. What could be easier?

07 Now, when you next need a live feed, connect in a short stretch of wire (thick enough to carry the required current, of course) from the junction box to one side of the fusebox . . .

08 . . . connect your component feed to the other side . . .

09 . . . and fit the correct-size fuse. Simple.

10 With the kickpanel back on, it looks like the new fusebox grew there. Make a note of which fuse is for which circuit, and carry the paper around in the glovebox (along with some spare fuses). If a fuse ever blows, you won't end up with your head stuck under the dash, trying to remember where you tapped in, and where the fuse is. You'll just pull the cover off, and replace the fuse. Who would've thought electrical safety could be so cool?

Alarm fitting

The alarm we've chosen to fit is a MicroScan AN213, which, whilst it isn't a Clifford, still offers a decent level of protection, and a useful array of features for a sensible price. When it goes off, it actually sounds like a Clifford, by way of a bonus!

In order to try and make this section as useful as possible, we won't show in detail how this particular alarm is fitted, but instead pick out some of the highlights and tips, in case your chosen alarm is different to ours.

01 Disconnect the battery negative lead, and move the lead away from the battery, or you'll be blowing fuses and your new alarm will go mental the minute it's rigged up. Decide where you're going to mount the alarm/siren. Choose somewhere not easily reached from underneath, firstly, and try the siren in position before deciding. Pick a location away from where you'll be topping up washers, oil or coolant - fluids and alarm modules don't mix. Hold the bracket in place, and mark the first hole . . .

02 . . . drill one hole first, fit the screw tight, then drill the second hole. If you drill all the holes at once, you might get one off-centre - this way, it'll definitely line up.

∧

03 When all the screws are in, hang the alarm module loosely on the bracket. It'll need to be roughly in place, for running all the wiring to it.

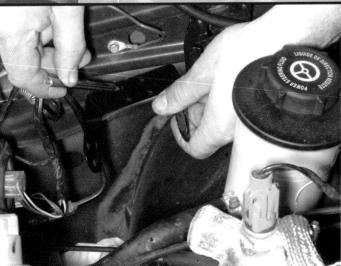

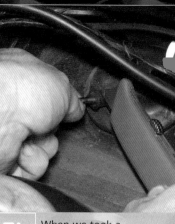

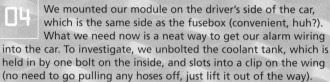

> **04** We mounted our module on the driver's side of the car, which is the same side as the fusebox (convenient, huh?). What we need now is a neat way to get our alarm wiring into the car. To investigate, we unbolted the coolant tank, which is held in by one bolt on the inside, and slots into a clip on the wing (no need to go pulling any hoses off, just lift it out of the way).

05 Behind the tank, we found a huge grommet with a hefty wiring loom already going through it, and this funny little "stump" next to it.

06 When we took a Stanley to the stump, we found it was a capped-off ready-made hole in the huge grommet, ideal for feeding our alarm wiring through - what a bonus!

07 Having consulted our alarm instructions (never a bad idea), we worked out what wires had to go where. Those going inside the car went through our handy new hole we'd found/made. When everything's in (not right now) it's worth sealing any holes you make in the bulkhead (with silicone), to reduce the chance of water getting in, if you're ever a tad over-eager with the hosepipe!

08 Before we did too much wiring inside, what else was there to do under the bonnet? Fitting the bonnet switch, which is essential to the plot. If a thief gets your bonnet open unhindered, he can attack your alarm siren and wiring. Game over. Fit your pin switch close to the battery, to protect the battery connections. To help decide the exact switch position, place a blob of Blu-tac loosely in a likely spot, then close the bonnet onto it. It'll stick to the bonnet, indicating where the switch plunger will hit.

09 Drill yourself a hole for the switch body to pass through . . .

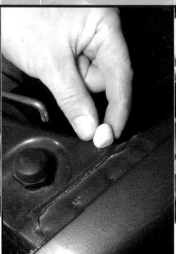

>>

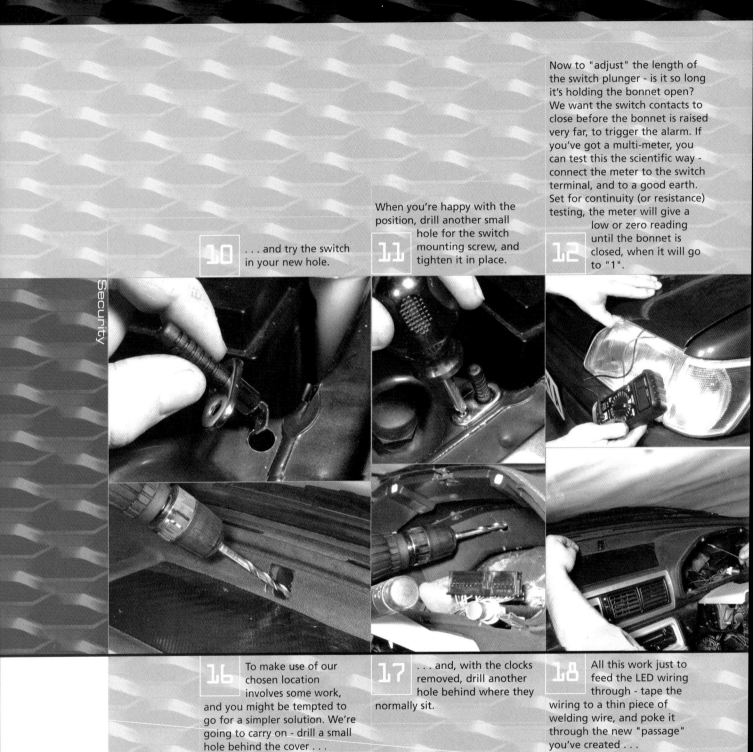

Now to "adjust" the length of the switch plunger - is it so long it's holding the bonnet open? We want the switch contacts to close before the bonnet is raised very far, to trigger the alarm. If you've got a multi-meter, you can test this the scientific way - connect the meter to the switch terminal, and to a good earth. Set for continuity (or resistance) testing, the meter will give a low or zero reading until the bonnet is closed, when it will go to "1".

10 . . . and try the switch in your new hole.

11 When you're happy with the position, drill another small hole for the switch mounting screw, and tighten it in place.

12

16 To make use of our chosen location involves some work, and you might be tempted to go for a simpler solution. We're going to carry on - drill a small hole behind the cover . . .

17 . . . and, with the clocks removed, drill another hole behind where they normally sit.

18 All this work just to feed the LED wiring through - tape the wiring to a thin piece of welding wire, and poke it through the new "passage" you've created . . .

13 Use the meter readings to judge when the switch is opening - by cutting the plunger down, the switch will effectively "go off" sooner. Don't make the switch too sensitive, though, or you might find the alarm gets set off in a strong wind (wind gets under the bonnet, lifts it slightly, alarm sounds).

14 Connect the wire to the switch, and run it neatly round the engine bay to the alarm module. The wire from the bonnet switch has to be joined to the alarm's brown wire, which is what we're doing now, with a soldering iron (don't forget the insulating tape afterwards).

15 Inside the car, it's time to decide where the LED will sit. In the Fiesta, there's a cracking spot at the very top of the dash - prise out this cover (which hides one of the facia mounting screws).

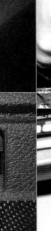
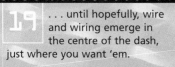
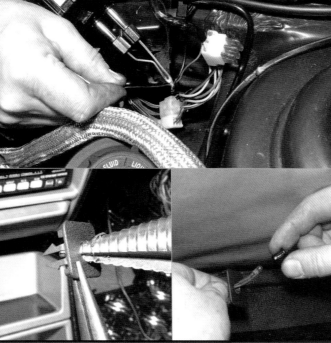
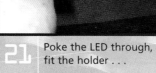

19 . . . until hopefully, wire and wiring emerge in the centre of the dash, just where you want 'em.

20 Now drill a nice hole in the cover you removed earlier, to mount the LED and its holder. Why does this pic remind me of Thunderbirds?

21 Poke the LED through, fit the holder . . .

22 . . . and this is what we end up with. Looks just like it grew there - and in a highly-visible spot. Splendid.

>>

23 No decent alarm is complete without ultrasonics - alarms which are voltage-drop-only rely on the thief considerably opening one of your doors to set it off. What's stopping them crowbarring the door frame, or breaking some glass? Only ultrasonics will help here. Fit the sensors at the top of each A-pillar - first loosen the trim screw at the top . . .

24 . . . and peel back the rubber door seal, so that the sensor wiring can be tucked under the trim panel later.

25 Screw the first sensor into place, making sure it can be angled into the car . . .

29 Now to get the central locking rigged into the alarm (which, if you're de-locking your Fiesta, is the whole point). First, we found a place to mount the central locking interface module - once again, we chose to fit it in the "dead area" behind the instruments.

30 On our car, we have a "positive-pulse" system, meaning the lock and unlock signals are both positive feeds. We know from the Haynes wiring diagram that we're looking for a yellow wire and a white wire, probably in the vicinity of the driver's door. Having found them, we have to join on a blue and a purple wire from our central locking module - strip the insulation, and solder on the new wires.

31 There's several permanent live feeds needed here. The main fusebox is held in by two screws at the top, and two catches either side - using the Haynes manual wiring diagram, you should be able to identify the wires you'll need (check with a test light or meter). Or - make up an auxiliary fusebox, as described earlier in this Chapter.

26 . . . then tuck the wiring round, and feed it down the door pillar. We fed the sensor wiring from both A-pillars down into the instrument pod area.

27 On our alarm, the sensor wiring plugs into a separate unit before going off to the alarm module . . .

28 . . . we chose to mount this unit in behind where the clocks normally sit. Which is nice.

32 Finding a good earth is easier - look for a brown wire attached to the car body (or make up your own).

33 Now we're nearly there. Connect up the wiring plugs to the alarm/siren, and test it according to its instructions. Most require you to "programme in" the remotes before they'll work. Test all the alarm features in turn, remembering to allow enough time for the alarm to arm itself (usually about 30 seconds). Set the anti-shock sensitivity with a thought to where you live and park - will it be set off every night by the neighbour's cat, or by kids playing football?

34 When you test it for the first time, don't forget to either shut the bonnet completely, or do like us, and hold the bonnet pin switch down. Our way, you can pull out the alarm fuses and shut it up, if something goes wrong!

35 Finally, and most important of all - next time you park up, remember to set it!

Body styling

If you're planning a major body job, you've probably already got some good ideas about how you want your Fiesta to look, from "Max Power" or "Redline", or maybe from a friend's car. While it can be good to have a target car to aim for, if you're just starting out on the road towards a fully-loaded car, you probably don't want (or can't quite afford) to go 'all the way' all at once.

If you're new to the world of modifying, it's a good idea to start with smaller jobs, and work up to the full body kit gradually, as your skills increase; spending loads on a body kit is a waste of money if you then make a mess of fitting it! There's plenty of small ways to improve the look of your Fiesta, which don't cost much, and which are simple enough to fit; start with some of these before you go too mad!

One golden rule with any body mods is to plan what you're going to do, and don't rush it. It's better that the car looks a bit stupid for a week (because you couldn't get something finished) than to rush a job and have the car look stupid forever. Do half the job properly rather than all of it half-right. Try and think the jobs through - don't just say to yourself: "Right! Now I'm going to fit those new mirrors!". Read through the instructions (if any), then see what we say, and plan each stage. Have you got all the tools, screws or whatever before you start, or will you have to break off halfway through? If you get stuck, is there someone you can get to help, or have they gone off for the weekend? Above all, if something goes wrong - don't panic - a calm approach will prove to be a huge bonus (that job doesn't have to be done today, does it?).

If a piece of trim won't come off, don't force it. If something feels like it's going to break, it probably will - stop and consider whether to go on and break it, or try another approach. Especially on an older car, things either never come off as easily as you think, or else have already been off so many times that they break or won't fit back on properly. While we'd all like to do a perfect job every time, working on an older car will, sooner or later, teach you the fine art of 'bodging' (finding valid alternative ways of fixing things!). Bodging is fine (if you've no choice) with interior and exterior trim, but make sure there are no safety implications - gluing an exterior mirror on might just about work with the car stood still, but it's going to fall off half a mile down the road, isn't it? Any Tips & Tricks we give in our procedures are things we've tried ourselves, which we know will work. Also, don't assume that you'll have to bodge something back on, every time - if a trim clip breaks when you take something off, it might be easier and cheaper than you think to simply go to your Ford dealer, and buy a new clip (remember, even Ford mechanics break things from time to time, so they will keep these things in stock!).

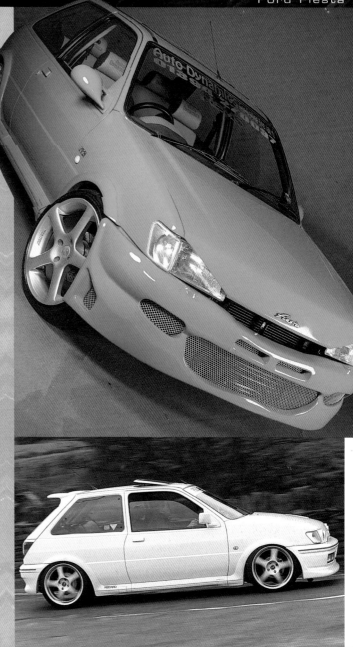

Mirror, mirror

Another simple-to-fit essential accessory, the DTM- or M3-style door mirror is well-established on the modified car circuit, made popular initially either by being fitted to many a car-modifier's dream motor (the BMW M3), or derived from mirrors used in the German Touring Car saloon racing series.

Like the rad grilles and spoilers, most mirrors are supplied in either carbon-look, or (more often) in black for spraying. A cheaper option is to buy carbon-look mirror covers - nowhere near as cool as the real thing, but it might sort you out if funds are tight.

Like so much else, with mirrors, you gets what you pays for. Cheapest option is the "universal-fit"

mirror. Bear in mind that "universal-fit" does not mean "easy-fit", and almost always means a lot of work is involved cutting and shaping to suit. If you can afford it, go for mirrors (or at least mirror bases) which are specifically designed for your Fiesta - they'll be much easier to fit, and chances are, they'll end up looking better too, no matter how long you take fitting the cheapies. Your call.

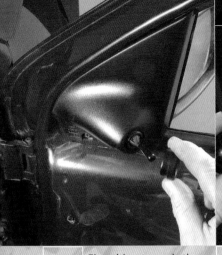

01 First thing to go is the door trim panel, as described in "Interiors" - sorry, but it's necessary, to get to the mirror trim panel screw. On our internally-adjustable mirror, the first job is to unscrew the collar from around the adjuster knob.

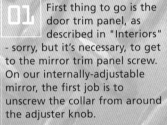

02 Now we'll remove that pesky screw underneath.

03 This next bit's tricky too. Prising off the mirror trim panel carries a high risk of damage to the plastic clips inside. Prise it at the front edge, which releases a locating peg inside, and then unclip the panel at the rear edge (there's two lugs which hook over the door at the back).

04 If you've been successful, this is what you should see next - see how long that front locating peg is?

Fitting **M3 mirrors**

05 There's a single screw at the top, which holds the mirror outer plastic panel to the door . . .

06 . . . then three bolts to undo . . .

07 . . . and finally, the old mirror waves the white flag.

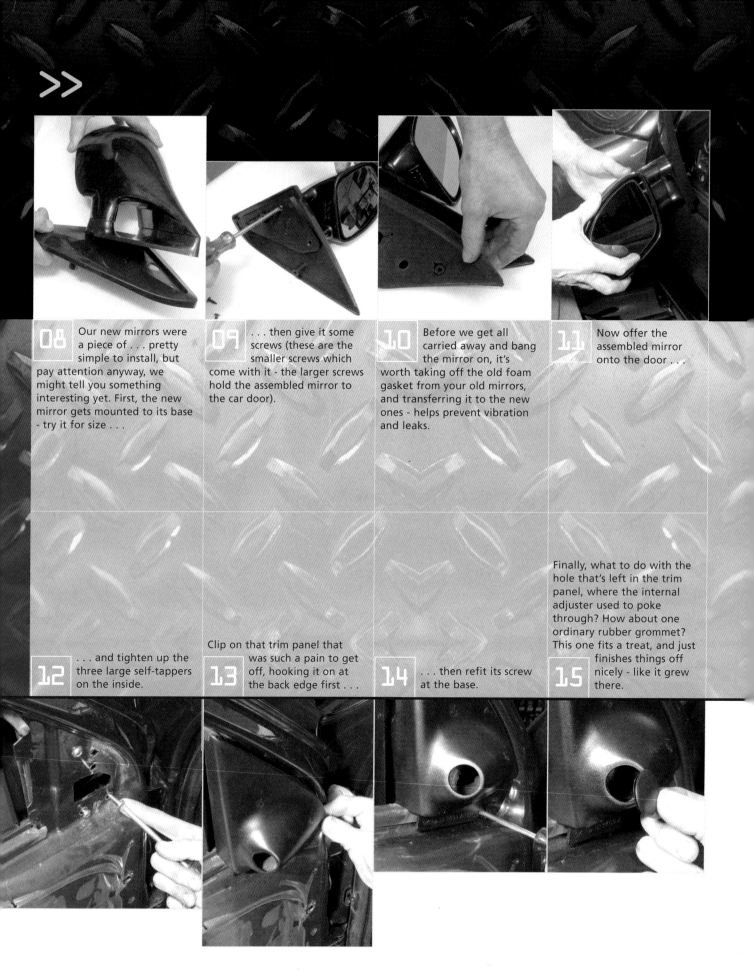

08 Our new mirrors were a piece of . . . pretty simple to install, but pay attention anyway, we might tell you something interesting yet. First, the new mirror gets mounted to its base - try it for size . . .

09 . . . then give it some screws (these are the smaller screws which come with it - the larger screws hold the assembled mirror to the car door).

10 Before we get all carried away and bang the mirror on, it's worth taking off the old foam gasket from your old mirrors, and transferring it to the new ones - helps prevent vibration and leaks.

11 Now offer the assembled mirror onto the door . . .

Finally, what to do with the hole that's left in the trim panel, where the internal adjuster used to poke through? How about one ordinary rubber grommet? This one fits a treat, and just finishes things off nicely - like it grew there.

12 . . . and tighten up the three large self-tappers on the inside.

13 Clip on that trim panel that was such a pain to get off, hooking it on at the back edge first . . .

14 . . . then refit its screw at the base.

15

Racing filler cap

Ah, the humble fuel filler flap. Not much to it, really - just a hinged cover which hides the unsightly filler cap below - what could you possibly do to that?

Well, this really is a matter of taste. With most owners trying to smooth or colour-code everything they can, it's a bit odd to take the already-smooth and colour-coded filler flap, and make it stand out!

At least the Fiesta filler flap is round, unlike a few cars (Golfs, for example), so it's easier to re-create the "racing" look. If you want an easy life, there are stick-on/screw-on fuel cap covers available. Easy to fit, and quite effective. But, for those who really want to impress, it's got to be a complete racing conversion, which does away with the flap and the dull black filler cap below, in favour of a fully-functional alloy item. A pukka working cap will almost certainly need bodyshop assistance to fit successfully.

01 First problem with the Mk 3 Fiesta - there's two sorts of filler cap design. Early cars had the filler cap sticking out of the rear three-quarter, and filler cap covers come in two stick-on parts (very easy to fit). Later cars like ours had a Mk 4-style flap over the filler, so you'll probably need to order a Mk 4 cap cover - okay? The first task with our type is some butchery, so before we went mad with saws and drills, we protected the surrounding paint, with some masking tape.

02 Now it's out with the hacksaw blade, and lop off the finger-pull - the new cover's flat, you see. File the cut edges flat, as you probably won't slice it off flush.

03 Try the new cap in place (mind you don't lose all the screws on the floor, when you first open the pack). Remember that the cap will most often be seen from above, so aim slightly high when centring the new cover.

04 When you're happy with the positioning, get the drill out, and make your first hole, using the cover as a template. Do the top and bottom screws first, as the flap has a slight curve to it, meaning the new cover has to bend to fit.

05 Pin the new cover at the top edge, using the Allen screws and key provided . . .

06 . . . then get the bottom screw in, and re-check the fit. If all's looking good, you can carry on round with the rest of the screws.

07 The screw at the very back edge has nothing to screw into, as you chopped off the finger pull. We tried fitting a nut behind the screw, but then found the flap wouldn't shut. The only thing left was to glue the screw in place, to give the proper look from outside.

 Achtung! *Fuel vapour is explosive. No smoking and no naked lights anywhere near the open fuel filler, please. Even power tools (see step 4) are not strictly allowed - drill slowly to avoid sparks.*

Fitting a
sunstrip

The modern sunstrip - where did it come from? Could it be a descendant of the eye-wateringly naff old shadebands which were popular in the 70s - you know, the ones which had "DAVE AND SHARON" on? If so, things have only got better...

01 This is only stuck to the outside, so only the outside of the screen needs cleaning - excellent! Do a good job of cleaning, though - any dirt stuck under the strip will ruin the effect.

There are two options to make your car look (and maybe even feel) cooler:

a The sunvisor, a screen tint band inside the screen, which is usually a graduated-tint strip. As this fits inside, there's a problem straight away - the interior mirror. The Fiesta mirror is bonded to the screen, and it seriously gets in the way when trying to fit a wet and sticky (nice!) strip of plastic around it. Go for a sunstrip instead.

b The sunstrip, which is opaque vinyl, colour-matched to the car, fits to the outside of the screen. Much more Sir.

A really wide sunstrip imitates the "roof chop" look seen on American hot rods, and colour-coded, they can look very effective from the front - plus, of course, you can use the space to advertise your preferred brand of ICE (no, no, NO! Not a good idea!). As it's fitted to the outside of the screen, the sunstrip has a good chance of seriously interfering with your wipers (or wiper, if you've been converted). If this happens to the point where the wipers can't clean the screen, Mr MOT might have a point if he fails your car . . . The wiper blades may need replacing more often, and the sunstrip itself might start peeling off - still sound like fun?

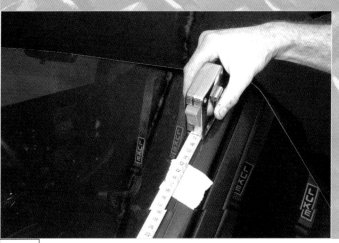

02 With the help of an assistant (if you have one handy), lay the strip onto the car, and decide how far down the screen you're going to go. Legally-speaking, you shouldn't be lower than the wiper swept area - so how much of a "badboy" are you? If you measure and mark the bottom of the strip with masking tape, you'll be sure to get it level, even if it's not legal.

Legal eagle
The rule for tinting or otherwise modifying the windscreen is that there must be no more than a 25% light reduction from standard. In theory, this means you can have a sunstrip which covers up to 25% of the screen area, but some MOT testers may see it differently. A sunstrip's got to come down the screen a fair way, to look any sense (otherwise, why bother?). You could argue that accurately measuring and calculating the windscreen area isn't actually that easy, if you get stopped, and anyway, a sunstrip also cuts out harmful glare! If you go so far down the screen that you can't see out, though - well, that's just stupid.

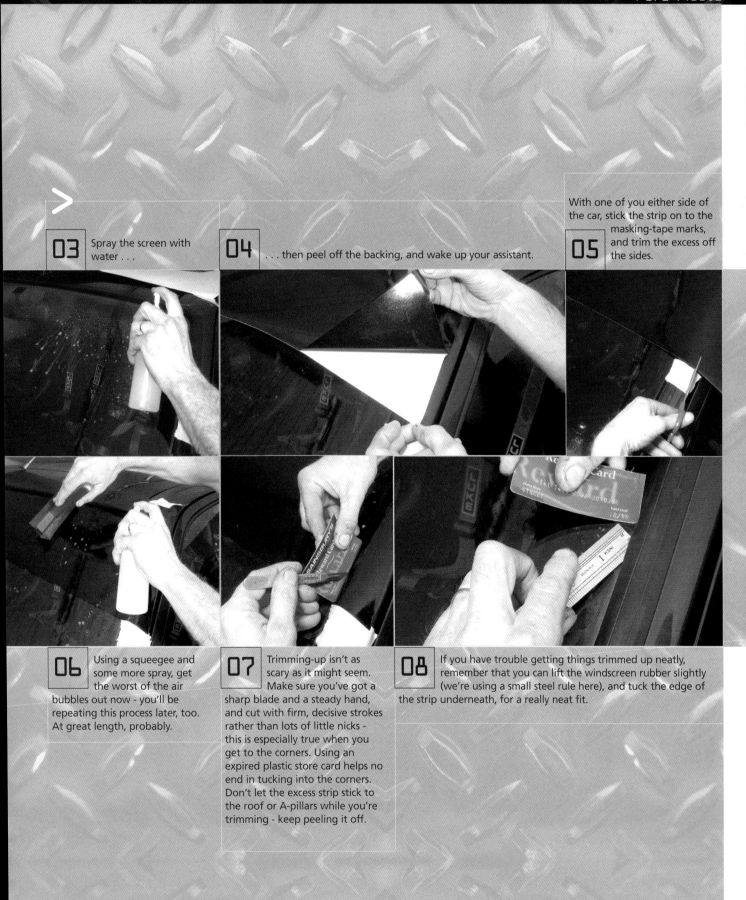

>

03 Spray the screen with water . . .

04 . . . then peel off the backing, and wake up your assistant.

05 With one of you either side of the car, stick the strip on to the masking-tape marks, and trim the excess off the sides.

06 Using a squeegee and some more spray, get the worst of the air bubbles out now - you'll be repeating this process later, too. At great length, probably.

07 Trimming-up isn't as scary as it might seem. Make sure you've got a sharp blade and a steady hand, and cut with firm, decisive strokes rather than lots of little nicks - this is especially true when you get to the corners. Using an expired plastic store card helps no end in tucking into the corners. Don't let the excess strip stick to the roof or A-pillars while you're trimming - keep peeling it off.

08 If you have trouble getting things trimmed up neatly, remember that you can lift the windscreen rubber slightly (we're using a small steel rule here), and tuck the edge of the strip underneath, for a really neat fit.

Smoothly does it

If you've bought a basic Fiesta, it's understandable that you might not want to declare this fact loudly from the rear end of your car. Badges also clutter up the otherwise clean lines, and besides - it's obviously a Fiesta, so who needs a badge? Most Fiestas also come with admittedly-useful but actually quite ugly side rubbing strips of some sort - lose these if you're at all serious about raising your game.

General bodywork smoothing takes an awful lot of time and skill, and is probably best done on a car which is then getting the full bodykit and wicked respray treatment. There's no doubt, however, that it really looks the business to have a fully-smoothed tailgate, or even to have those rather ugly roof gutters smoothed over. Probably best to put the pros at a bodyshop to work on this. De-stripping and de-badging is the next best thing, though, and this can be done at home.

01 Removing the side rubbing strips themselves is easy - heat them up with a hot-air gun, to soften the glue, and peel 'em off.

02 The same technique works for Henry's blue oval . . .

03 . . . and the Fiesta badge on the tailgate.

04 So far, so good. But the problems start when you try removing the industrial-strength double-sided tape underneath the strips and badges. Proper tar remover may do the job, as will solvents like petrol or Gunk. For a neat job with less mess and effort, buy a circular sanding block specifically designed for removing tape and stripes - it's made of rubber, and mounts in a drill. Try a bodyshop or motor factors. Not only does it work on stubborn tape . . .

05 . . . it also makes a neat job of any embarrassing transfer-type logos, disgracing the back end of your motor. Bonus! One tip - keep the "sander" moving, or it can heat-damage the paint. When you're trying to get tape remains off, it also pays to let it cool off for a few seconds every so often, or you end up smearing the gluey-stuff instead of removing it.

06 After applying a little T-Cut (or polish with a light cutting action), your tailgate will never have looked cooler.

Travelling **incognito**

As with so much in modifying, window tinting is a matter of personal taste - it can look right with the right car and colour. There are also a wide variety of films available including coloured films, security films and films which reflect UV rays. The only downside is that it might not be legal to use some tints on the road, which is why many are advertised as "for show cars only".

Kits fall into two main groups - one where you get a roll of film, which you then cut to shape, or a pre-cut kit where the film pieces are supplied to suit your car. In theory, the second (slightly more expensive) option is better, but it leaves little margin for error - if you muck up fitting one of the sections, you'll have to buy another kit. The roll-of-film kit may leave enough over for a few false starts . . . Check when buying how many windows you'll be able to do - some kits are only good for three Fiesta windows - how handy!.

The downside to tinting is that it will severely try your patience. If you're not a patient sort of person, this is one job which may well wind you up - you have been warned. Saying that, if you're calm and careful, and you follow the instructions to the letter, you could surprise yourself.

In brief, the process for tinting is to lay the film on the outside of the glass first, and cut it exactly to size. The protective layer is peeled off to expose the adhesive side, the film is transferred to the inside of the car (tricky) and then squeegeed into place (also tricky). All this must be done with scrupulous cleanliness, as any muck or stray bits of trimmed-off film will ruin the effect (not so easy, if you're working outside). The other problem which won't surprise you is that getting rid of air bubbles and creases can take time. A long time. This is another test of patience, because if, as the instructions say, you've used plenty of spray, it will take a while to dry out and stick . . . just don't panic!

Legal eagle
The law on window tinting currently is that you're allowed up to 25% reduction in light transmission through the windscreen, and up to 30% on all other glass. Many cars come with tinted glass as standard, which has to be taken into account before the tint film is fitted. If in doubt, ask before you buy, and if you can, get a letter from the company to support the legality of the kit, to use in your defence. Some police forces now have portable test equipment they use at the roadside - if your car fails, it's an on-the-spot fine.

Tinting windows

It's worth picking your day, and your working area, pretty carefully - on a windy day, there'll be more dust in the air, and it'll be a nightmare trying to stop the film flapping and folding onto itself while you're working.

Applying window tint is best done on a warm day (or in a warm garage - if there is such a thing), because the adhesive will begin to dry sooner. For fairly obvious reasons, don't try tinting when it's starting to get dark! It's a good idea to have a mate to help out with this job, but you might get fed up hearing "you've missed another bubble" or "you can still see that crease, y'know".

01 If you're doing a front window, the door mirror's got to come off, which means the door trim panel's also got to go. The mirrors are covered elsewhere in this section, with door trim removal in "Interiors". In addition, prise up and remove the rubber strip on the inside of the glass.

02 Get the window being tinted clean - really clean - inside and out. Don't use glass cleaners (or any other product) containing ammonia or vinegar, since both will react with the film or its adhesive, and muck it up. Also clean the area around the window - it's too easy for stray dirt to attach itself to the film - and by the time you've noticed it, it could be too late. On door windows, wind them down slightly, to clean all of the top edge, then close them tight to fit the film.

03 Before you even unroll the film, take note - handle it carefully. If you crease it, you won't get the creases out - ever. First work out which way up the film is, by applying a small bit of really sticky tape to the front and back side - use the tape to pull the films apart, just at one corner.

04 Lay the film onto the glass, with the clear side facing you. Unroll the film, and cut it roughly to the size of the window (on a door window, leave plenty at the bottom edge for now). Some kits have a logo on the film, which seems daft - tinting's difficult enough, without having to get a logo straight! The only benefit of a logo is to establish which layer is the tint. Make life easier - lose the logo.

05 Spray the outside of the window with a weak soapy water solution (Folia Tec supply a small bottle of Joy fluid in their kit, but you could use a few drops of ordinary washing-up liquid). Get one of those plant sprayers you can buy cheap in any DIY store, if your kit doesn't contain a sprayer.

06 Lay the roughly-cut sheet of tint back onto the glass, and spray the outside of the film with soapy water . . .

07 . . . then use a squeegee to get out the air bubbles, sticking the film to the outside of the glass.

On a door window, trim the bottom edge to leave some excess to tuck down inside the door - this stops the film peeling off on the bottom

08 rubber when you roll the window down!

Using a sharp knife (and taking care not to damage your paint or the window rubber), trim round the outside of the window. An unimportant piece of plastic (like an expired video club card) is brilliant for tucking the film into the edges to get the shape right, but don't trim the film right to the absolute edge - leave a small, even gap of just a few mill all round (this helps to get rid of excess water when you

09 squeegee it on the inside - you'll see).

Now go inside, and prepare for receiving the tint. On fixed glass, waterproof the side trim panels in anticipation of the soapy water which will be used, by taping on some plastic sheet (otherwise, you'll have some very soggy panels. And seats. And carpets). Spray the inside of the

10 glass with the soapy solution.

Back outside, it's time to separate the films. Use two pieces of sticky tape to pull the films slightly apart at one corner. As the films come apart, spray more solution onto the tinted piece underneath, to help it separate cleanly. Try not to lift the tint film too much off the glass when

11 separating, as this increases the risk of creasing.

12 Have your willing helper on standby, to assist with transferring the film to the inside (a prime time for messing it all up). Peel the tint film off the glass, keeping it as flat as you can. Without letting it fold onto itself, move it inside the car and place it fairly accurately on the inside of the glass. The surface which was outside should now be on the inside of the glass (now that you've cut it, it will only fit one way!). Carefully slide the film into the corners, keeping it flat.

13 On a door window, use your unimportant plastic to tuck the film into the door - try to stick it to the glass by wedging-in a wad of paper cloth too.

14 Spray the film with the soapy water . . .

15 . . . then carefully start to squeegee it into place, working from top to bottom. We found that, to get into the corners, it was easier to unscrew the blade from the squeegee, and use that on its own for some of it.

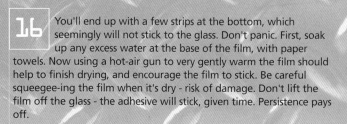

16 You'll end up with a few strips at the bottom, which seemingly will not stick to the glass. Don't panic. First, soak up any excess water at the base of the film, with paper towels. Now using a hot-air gun to very gently warm the film should help to finish drying, and encourage the film to stick. Be careful squeegee-ing the film when it's dry - risk of damage. Don't lift the film off the glass - the adhesive will stick, given time. Persistence pays off.

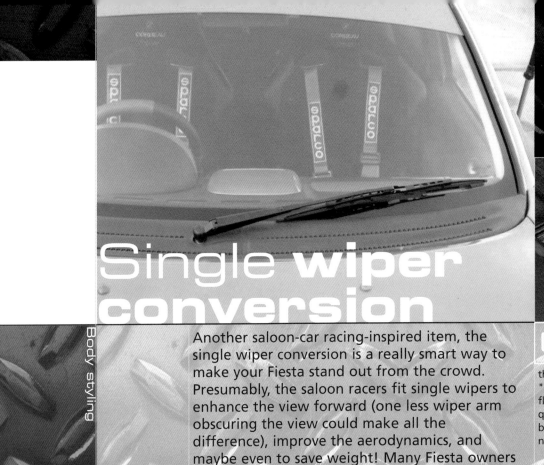

Single wiper conversion

Another saloon-car racing-inspired item, the single wiper conversion is a really smart way to make your Fiesta stand out from the crowd. Presumably, the saloon racers fit single wipers to enhance the view forward (one less wiper arm obscuring the view could make all the difference), improve the aerodynamics, and maybe even to save weight! Many Fiesta owners want the single wiper because it helps to remove clutter - put two Fiestas side by side, and the one with one less wiper looks so much better. It's a fairly "neutral" mod, too - unlike some, it works well no matter what look you're aiming for.

01 Unsurprisingly, the first job is to remove your old wiper arms. Make sure that the wipers are in their "parked" position, if necessary by flicking the wipers on, then quickly off. Flip up the cap at the base of each arm, unscrew the nut . . .

Open the bonnet, and peel off the rubber strip from the top of the bulkhead panel. Removing the air cleaner's a good move on HCS engines, to give you more room (ours had already been replaced by our smaller induction kit - look there for air cleaner removal details).

Now we're looking at removing the bulkhead panel completely. Depending on which model Fiesta you've got, there may be a centre panel section fitted, with several wired-in components fitted - this panel's secured by four screws . . .

02 . . . and pull the arms off their splined fittings.

03

04

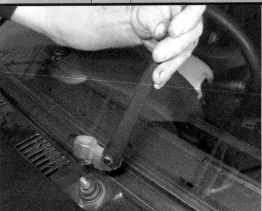

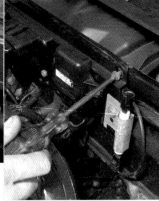

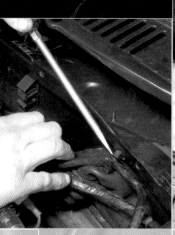

05 . . . and just lifts out (restrained by the wiring, which you can leave connected - just unclip what you can, and move the panel away).

06 Unclip the wiring harness from the remaining sections of bulkhead panel.

07 The panel is now in two sections, secured by a total of eight screws . . .

08 . . . and a 10 mm nut at either end.

Bum notes

As well as having a linkage which needed to be bent before we even got the thing near the car, and having to do major surgery on the heater cover, our Monostyle single wiper kit came with a wiper blade which was 2 inches too long. We had to fit a shorter (20-inch) blade before the kit would sweep the glass without clouting the windscreen rubber (badly) each side. What a bummer.

09 With just a little wiggling and fiddling, the two halves of the panel come free, giving us access to the wiper motor and linkage.

10 To get the linkage out, first prise off the plastic covers from the wiper spindles . . .

11 . . . then undo the large (rusty) nuts underneath.

12 Undo the two bolts from the wiper motor mounting bracket . . .

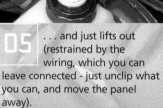

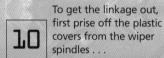

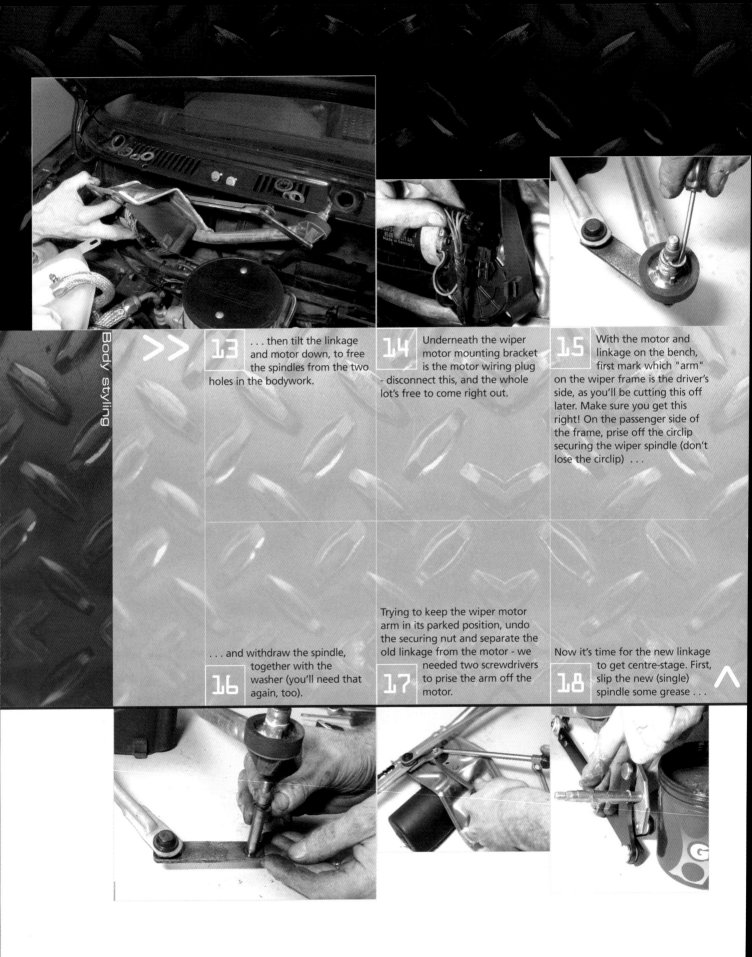

>>

13 . . . then tilt the linkage and motor down, to free the spindles from the two holes in the bodywork.

14 Underneath the wiper motor mounting bracket is the motor wiring plug - disconnect this, and the whole lot's free to come right out.

15 With the motor and linkage on the bench, first mark which "arm" on the wiper frame is the driver's side, as you'll be cutting this off later. Make sure you get this right! On the passenger side of the frame, prise off the circlip securing the wiper spindle (don't lose the circlip) . . .

16 . . . and withdraw the spindle, together with the washer (you'll need that again, too).

17 Trying to keep the wiper motor arm in its parked position, undo the securing nut and separate the old linkage from the motor - we needed two screwdrivers to prise the arm off the motor.

18 Now it's time for the new linkage to get centre-stage. First, slip the new (single) spindle some grease . . .

> **19** . . . and slip on the old washer.

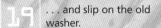

20 Slide the new spindle into the passenger side of the old frame . . .

21 . . . and secure with the old circlip.

22 Now let's get up to the wiper motor arm end of the linkage, and connect it to the motor, using either the old nut, or the new nut and shakeproof washer. Tighten the nut, and - oh dear, we seem to have a problem. What's known in engineering terms as a "touch condition" between the motor arm nut and the linkage rivets. The only answer was to dismantle, and bend the linkage slightly, in two places. Not really good enough, is it?

Before the new linkage can go in for a trial fitting, you'll need to chop off the driver's side of the old frame, together with its section of the old linkage. **23** Unfortunately, that's not the end of the cutting, as we'll soon see.

Offer the new linkage into place, and first off, plug the wiper motor back in. Not much **24** will happen in the wiper department if you don't.

Getting the new linkage into place is, well, rather tricky. Quite **25** problematic. A pain. The main problem we had was getting the short section of linkage below the new spindle to clear the substantial plastic cover fitted over the heater fan motor.

It quickly became apparent that either the cover would have to go, or some cutting would be needed. Losing the cover altogether is not a good idea, or you'll have water coming in the car (that's after the same water has fused out the heater motor). So we decided to mark the required hole, and cut. It's worth turning the motor arm by hand, to see how big a problem you've got (and therefore, how big a hole you'll need).

26

27 Lift out the cover (fortunately, very easy to remove) . . .

28 . . . and give it some with the jigsaw.

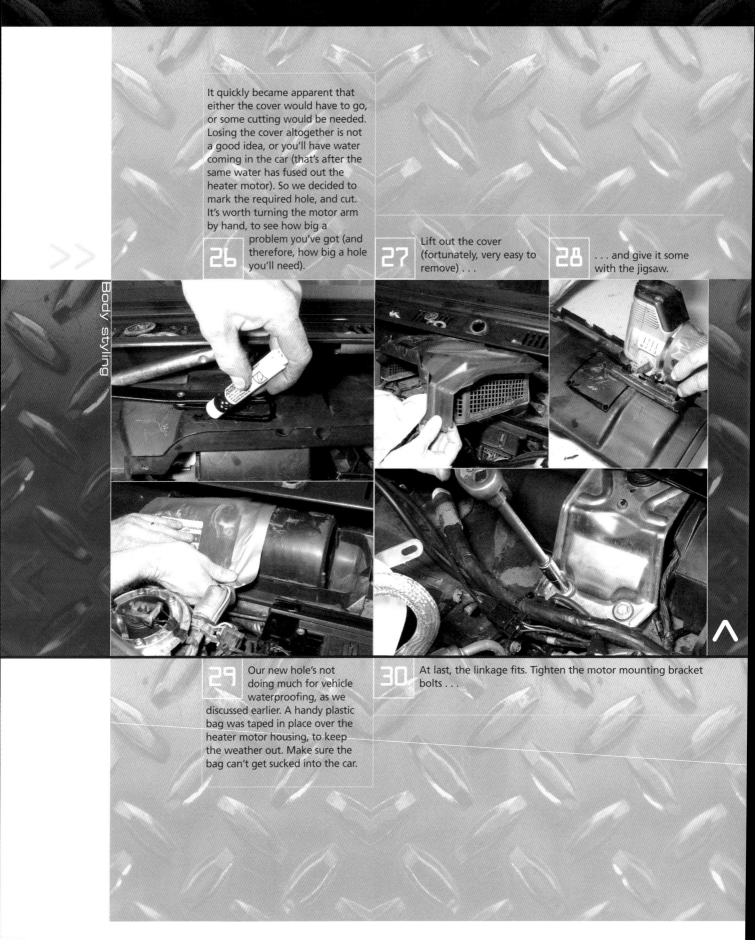

29 Our new hole's not doing much for vehicle waterproofing, as we discussed earlier. A handy plastic bag was taped in place over the heater motor housing, to keep the weather out. Make sure the bag can't get sucked into the car.

30 At last, the linkage fits. Tighten the motor mounting bracket bolts . . .

Do not be tempted to just switch the wiper on at this point - there's plenty still to do. Work the linkage by hand, and see how the wiper moves. What we're trying to do first is to set the wiper blade's sweep - ie we're trying to get it to go equally across both sides of the screen. Re-position the wiper arm on the spindle until it's just right, and tighten the arm nut securely. That part is now done, and the wiper arm is set. Will you need a shorter wiper blade, like we did? See "Bum notes" earlier on.

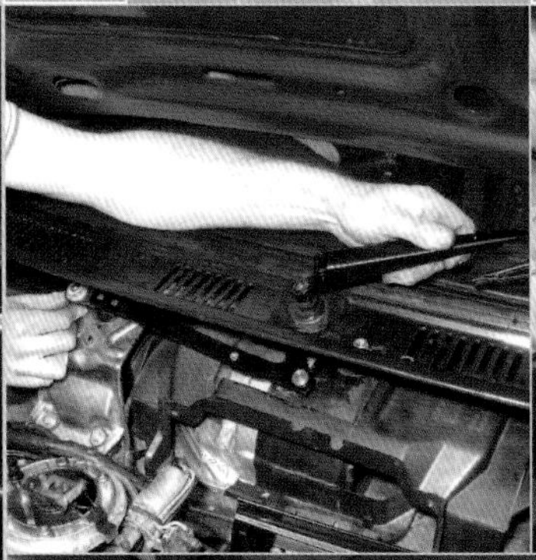

Next, we set the parked position of the motor, by undoing the motor arm nut and re-positioning the arm on its spindle. This can only be done by try-it-and-see - there's no logic to it that we could find! Set the wiper arm in the required position . . .

31 . . . and refit the spindle bush, washer and nut, tightening it firmly and not forgetting its plastic cap.

32 Fit the new wiper arm (as a guess, set it over on the passenger side of the screen until you know better) and tighten the nut enough to just hold it.

33

34

35 . . . undo the nut holding the motor arm on, and remove the arm . . .

36 . . . then re-position the arm on its spindle, and re-tighten the nut. For a true test, you'll have to actually switch the wipers on and off - might be best to start the process with the blade lifted off the screen. We chose to have our blade parked in the middle (possibly not legal, but it looked the best, so we had to. Officer).

37 The final act of consigning your unwanted extra wiper to the bin is to fit the blanking grommet over the driver's side spindle hole. And feel suitably chuffed, obviously.

Painting by numbers

This is not the section where we tell you how to respray your entire Fiesta in a weekend, using only spray cans, okay? Mission Impossible, we ain't. This bit's all about how to spray up your various plasticky bits before final fitting - bits such as door mirrors, light brows, spoilers, splitters - hell, even bumpers if you like. As we've no doubt said before, with anything new, fit your unpainted bits first. Make sure everything fits properly (shape and tidy up all parts as necessary), that all holes have been drilled, and all screws etc are doing their job. Then, and only when you're totally, completely happy with the fit - take them off, and get busy with the spray cans.

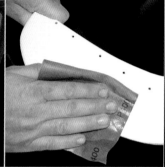

01 The first job is to mask off any areas you don't want painted. Do this right at the start, or you could be sorry; on these door mirrors, we decided to mask off just at the lip before the glass, to leave a black unpainted edge - if we hadn't masked it as the very first job, we would've roughed up all the shiny black plastic next, and wrecked the edge finish.

02 Remove any unwanted "seams" in the plastic, using fine sandpaper or wet-and-dry. Some of these seams look pretty cool, others don't - you decide. Also worth tidying up any other areas you're not happy with, fit-wise, while you're at it.

Especially with shiny plastic, you must rough-up the surface before spray will bite to it, or - it'll flippin' flake off. Just take off the shine, no more. You can use fine wet-and-dry for this (used dry), but we prefer Scotch-Brite. This stuff, which looks much like a scouring pad, is available from motor factors and bodyshops, in several grades - we used ultra-fine, which is grey. One advantage of Scotch-Brite is **03** that it's a bit easier to work into awkward corners than paper.

Once the surface has been nicely roughened, clean up the surface using a suitable degreaser ("suitable" means a type which won't dissolve plastic!). Generally, it's ok to use methylated spirit or cellulose thinners (just don't inhale!), but **04** test it on a not-so-visible bit first, so you don't have a disaster.

Before you start spraying (if it's something smaller than a bumper) it's a good idea to try a work a screw into one of the mounting holes, to use as a **05** handle, so you can turn the item to spray all sides.

Another good trick is to use the screw to hang the item up on a piece of string or wire - then **06** you can spin the item round to get the spray into awkward areas.

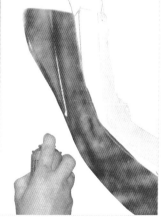

07 If you like a bit of wildlife in your paint, you can't beat the great outdoors. If it's at all windy, you'll end up with a really awful finish and overspray on everything (which can be a real nightmare to get off). Even indoors, if it's damp weather, you'll have real problems trying to get a shine - some kind of heater is essential if it's cold and wet (but not one with a fan - stirring up the dust is the last thing you want).

08 If you're a bit new at spraying, or if you simply don't want to muck it up, practise your technique first (steady!). Working left-right, then right-left, press the nozzle so you start spraying just before you pass the item, and follow through just past it the other side. Keep the nozzle a constant distance from the item - not in a curved arc. Don't blast the paint on too thick, or you'll have a nasty case of the runs - hold the can about 6 inches away - you're not trying to paint the whole thing in one sweep.

09 Once you've got a patchy "mist coat" on (which might not even cover the whole thing) - stop, and let it dry (primer dries pretty quickly). Continue building up thin coats until you've got full coverage, then let it dry for half an hour or more.

10 Using 1000- or 1200- grade wet-and-dry paper (used wet), very lightly sand the whole primered surface, to take out any minor imperfections (blobs, where the nozzle was spitting) in the primer. Try not to go through the primer to the plastic, but this doesn't matter too much in small areas.

13 With a colour like red (notorious for fading easily), blow on a coat of clear lacquer on top - this will also give you your shine, on a very "dry" finish. Apply lacquer before the final top coat is fully hardened. The spraying technique is identical, although pro sprayers say that lacquer should be applied pretty thick - just watch those runs! Lacquer also takes a while to dry - pick up your item too soon, for that unique fingerprint effect!

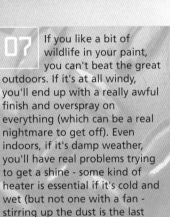

Rinse off thoroughly, then dry the surfaces - let it stand for a while to make sure it's **11** completely dry, before starting on the top coat.

12 Make sure once again that the surfaces are clean, with no bits left behind from the drying operations. As with the primer, work up from an initial thin mist coat, allowing time for each pass to dry. As you spray, you'll soon learn how to build a nice shine without runs - any "dry" (dull) patches are usually due to overspray landing on still-wet shiny paint. Don't worry if you can't eliminate all of these - a light cutting polish will sort it out once the paint's hardened (after several hours).

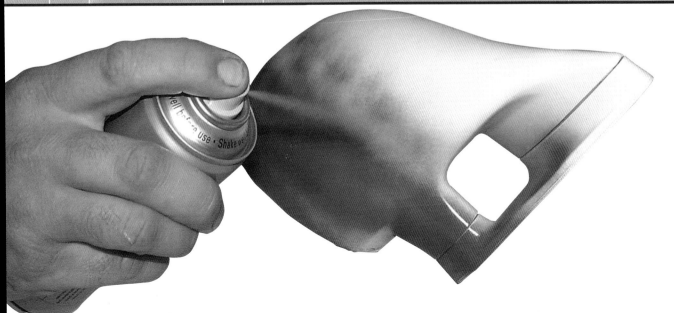

De-locking

Removing door lock barrels

One very popular way to tidy up the Fiesta lines is to do away with the door locks, and even the door handles - but be careful.

Removing the rear door handles (on 5-door models) is okay, legally/MOT-speaking, but removing the front door handles will land you in trouble, come MOT time. There's something in the Construction & Use regs which requires an independent mechanical means of door opening from outside, probably so fire-fighters can get you out, if you stick your Fester on its roof, or in a ditch . . . So - don't spend loads of time (or money, at a bodyshop) having cool and trendy mods done, which you then have to spend more money undoing!

01 First, the door trim panel has to come off - but you knew that already. Look in "Interiors" for door trim panel removal. As with the tailgate lock button we remove later, Ford have helpfully fitted a shield over the door lock barrel too. This is combined with the window rear guide channel, and is removed by taking out this screw from the door rear edge . . .

02 . . . and this screw, from the bottom corner.

With a little wiggling and fiddling, the shield/guide channel comes out **03** through the hole in the door.

It's a bit tricky to show you the next bit, but we done our best. What we're doing here is unclipping the lock barrel operating rod from its grey plastic clip inside the **04** door, with a small screwdriver.

Instead of the easily-removed slide-on clip we found on the tailgate lock button, here we have a circular lock barrel retaining plate, which has to be tapped round anti-clockwise to release it. Shouldn't require more than a **05** screwdriver and the palm of your hand . . .

. . . before the lock barrel and its rod will come out, from outside. Phase 1 of the **06** de-locking process is now complete.

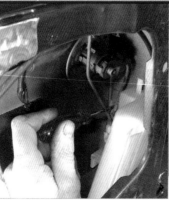
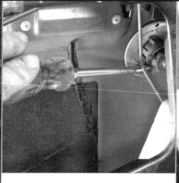

Removing door handles

01 As we've already said, it's not a good idea to remove and flush your handles, unless you've got a very understanding, very unobservant, or very easily-bribed, MOT tester. The only reason we're showing you how to remove your handles is to colour-code them, okay? The first bit's easy - the handles are held on from inside by two screws.

02 To actually release the handles so you can remove them, we're into disconnecting their operating rods, which can be a bit of a pain - try not to bust any of the little plastic securing clips when you prise them with your small screwdriver. Here we see the limitations of trying to photograph inside the door - you can just see the clip at the base of the handle operating rod here . . .

03 . . . the bad news is, you also have to disconnect the handle operating rod at the top end too . . .

Now we're in familiar territory - colour-coding. Roughen and clean the handles with Scotch Brite and panel wipe (these will almost certainly have had silicone on them at some point) . . .

04 . . . before the handle will come out.

05

06 . . . then it's a good coat of primer . . .

07 . . . followed by the top coat and lacquer. Much better.

Removing the evidence

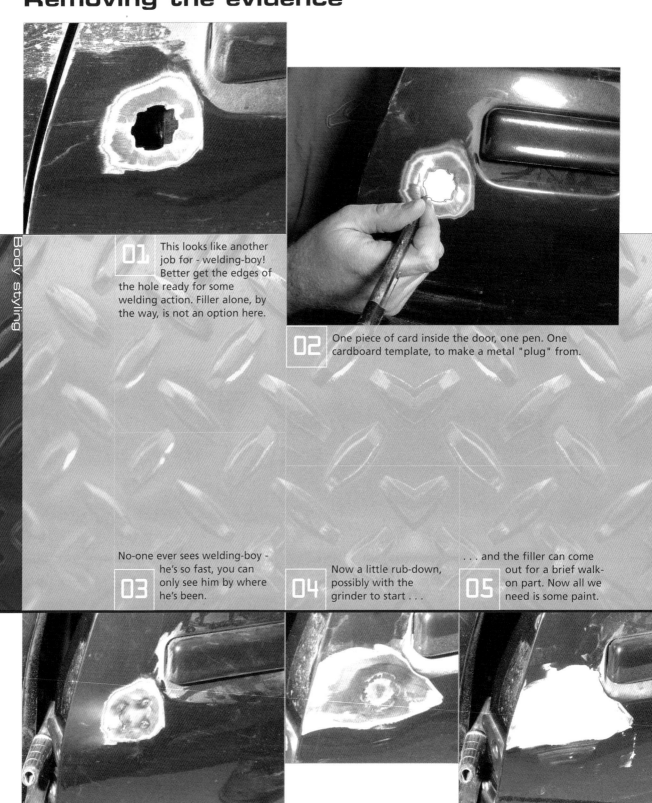

01 This looks like another job for - welding-boy! Better get the edges of the hole ready for some welding action. Filler alone, by the way, is not an option here.

02 One piece of card inside the door, one pen. One cardboard template, to make a metal "plug" from.

03 No-one ever sees welding-boy - he's so fast, you can only see him by where he's been.

04 Now a little rub-down, possibly with the grinder to start . . .

05 . . . and the filler can come out for a brief walk-on part. Now all we need is some paint.

Remote locking

So you can lock and unlock your freshly de-locked doors, you'll need to buy and fit a remote central locking kit, which you can get from several Fiesta parts suppliers (our Microscan kit is really an extension kit for our chosen alarm, but is pretty typical of what you'll get). If your Fiesta already has central locking, you're in luck - buy yourself a cheap car alarm, and a central locking interface.

Tricks 'n' tips
If your battery goes flat, you'll be locked out. We ran two thin wires from the battery terminals (with a 10-amp fuse in the live, and the ends insulated), and tucked them away for access from below in an emergency. By connecting a slave battery to these wires (do not try jump-starting), you'll put enough juice into the system to operate the locks, saving you a red face. Think it over.

To wire up your alarm interface, the best advice is to follow the instructions with the kit - it's impossible to second-guess detailed instructions like this. For what it's worth, though, one piece of advice to bear in mind when tracking down the locking trigger wires is not to disconnect the wiring plugs inside the driver's door, for testing - the locking system won't work at all if you do, and you won't learn anything! On our Fiesta, the lock and unlock trigger wires were yellow (lock) and white (unlock), with a brown earth wire, and a red/yellow live feed - all found inside the driver's door. The yellow and white wires change to yellow/brown and white/brown when we get inside the car.

When you test the operation, make sure at least one window's open, in case you lock yourself out. Also check that the doors are locked when the alarm's armed, and not the other way round!

Central locking kit

If your Fiesta doesn't have central locking as standard, don't despair - there's several kits out there to help you towards your goal.

Our project Fiesta already had central locking, so regrettably there are no Fiesta-specific photos to show you, but hopefully, the details below, together with your kit's instructions, will help you out.

Before you start fitting your new lock solenoids, it makes sense to test them. Connect them all together as described in your kit's instructions - with power connected, pull up on the operating plunger of one, and the rest should pop up too - clever, eh?

Decide where you're going to mount the lock control unit, then identify the various looms, and feed them out to the doors.

The new lock solenoids must be mounted so they work in the same plane as the door lock buttons. It's no good having the lock solenoid plungers moving horizontally, to work a button which operates vertically! Make up the mounting brackets from the metal bits provided in the kit, and fit the solenoids loosely in place.

The kit contains several items which look uncannily like bike spokes - these are your new lock operating rods, which have to be cut to length, then joined onto the old rods using screw clamps. It's best to join the old and new rods at a straight piece of the old rod, so feed the new rod in, and mark it for cutting.

Cut the new rod to the marked length, fit the cut rod to the soenoid, then slip the clamp onto it. Fit the solenoid onto its bracket, and offer the rod into place, to connect to the old rod. Join the new rod and old rod together, and fasten the clamp screws tight. If the clamp screws come loose, you're basically going to be locked out.

Now you can connect up the wires - hopefully, your kit's instructions should be sufficient, but if not, you'll have to resort to the Haynes Service and Repair Manual wiring diagrams.

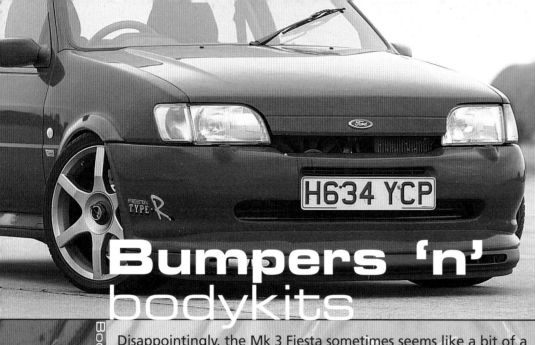

Front bumper

Bumpers 'n'
bodykits

Disappointingly, the Mk 3 Fiesta sometimes seems like a bit of a forgotten vehicle in the modding world - there's certainly not much choice in bodykits at present. The main options are various bumpers 'n' bits which are supposed to make your Fiesta look more like an Escort Cossie, or bolt-on versions of the Si/XR2i bodywork. Not terribly inspiring stuff.

The bodykit we fancied originally is one that actually does make the Fiesta look well-radical, and it's called the Animal. Says it all, really. Combining the best elements of both the Jap and Euro looks, this really makes the Fiesta stand out, especially if you "bad-boy" your bonnet at the same time. What we ended up with (for reasons we won't bore you with - hur-hur) was a "Twelve-Bore" kit, from Fibresports. Nice.

01 The first part of front bumper removal just lulls you into thinking it's going to be simple - undo two screws from each end of the bumper.

02 The bumper's now held on by just two nuts - one either side, roughly below the headlights. But getting at them is, well, a little tricky. First to depart are the front wheelarch liners, which are held on by various screws and clips, and which we probably won't be needing again, if your wheels are anything bigger than 15s.

03 On the driver's side of any Fiesta with a cat, we find the charcoal canister (part of the emissions control gear). This shouldn't be ripped out permanently, so take note of which pipe fits where. Pull the pipes off, remove the screws, and take out the canister.

04 Well, that's one of the two nuts we can get to - now what's in the way, the other side?

05 Oh fine - the washer bottle (can't really do without that, either). It's held on by a bolt you can reach from the engine bay, below the headlight . . .

06 . . . and by another bolt inside the wheelarch.

07 When you lower the bottle out for access to the bumper nut, remember it's hanging by pipes and wires which will serve you better in future if they're not ripped off now - try tying it up out of the way.

08 At last, the old bumper can be slid off its side mounts and removed. Away with the foul grey plastic.

09 Having tried our new bumper on for fit . . .

10 . . . it became obvious that the front arches would need further "adjustment" with the hacksaw . . .

11 . . . and a new end mounting bracket was made up, and spot-welded on.

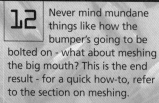

12 Never mind mundane things like how the bumper's going to be bolted on - what about meshing the big mouth? This is the end result - for a quick how-to, refer to the section on meshing.

Rear bumper

01 Removing the rear bumper presents no real challenge to someone who knows. Prise out the number plate light . . .

02 . . . and disconnect the wiring plugs from it.

03 If your Fiesta's as sad as ours was, you might still have rear mudflaps. Remove these now, and never mention that you had them to anyone.

04 There's two screws each side, holding the bumper front edge to the wheelarch . . .

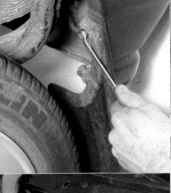

05 . . . and two nuts inside the rear edge of the boot (one each side). Made all the more difficult to get at by our Liquid ICE boot install, which included full carpeting of the boot area. But are we complaining?

06 Unclip the ends, and everything in the bumper department should've gone very floppy, suddenly.

07 It doesn't really matter if you let that grey plastic moulding hit the deck, actually, but you might like to lower it carefully to the floor anyhow.

08 Here's the new rear bumper in place - fortunately, our Fibresports bumper is a quality item, requiring no particular fettling to make fit. However, getting our four-exit exhaust and rear arches to work with it was more of a challenge. For the full story, refer to the relevant sections of this book.

A meshed grille or bumper is just one way to demonstrate who's the daddy of the cruise, and it does a great job of dicing any small insects or rodents foolish enough to wander into the path of your motor. So if you're sick of scrubbing off insect entrails from your paint, and fancy getting even, read on…

Which style of mesh to choose? Well, considering the style of our bodykit, and having already gone for the triangular Focus side repeaters, we thought the classic diamond mesh pattern was best suited. You may disagree. But we don't care.

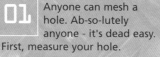

01 Anyone can mesh a hole. Ab-so-lutely anyone - it's dead easy. First, measure your hole.

02 Cut out a roughly-sized piece of mesh, then trim it to size, leaving some over the sides to bend around the edges of your hole.

03 Mesh can be attached using several methods - which one you choose may be dictated by where your hole happens to be. On this fibreglass bumper, using fibreglass made sense, but you could pin the edges using a bead of mastic, or even some weeny self-tappers (as long as they don't come through).

Meshing

Even though you won't see this side of the mesh, it's hardly a cause for embarrassment. **04**

Our bonnet vent was meshed using much the same technique - cut your mesh slightly over-size, and bend it neatly round the edges of the hole. Here, we're using a knockometer as an additional persuading device (don't get too personal - cut edges of mesh could slice your hands quite effectively). **05**

We'd quite like our meshed bonnet vent to look as tidy inside as out, so we're going to do a neat job of sticking it, with a bead of mastic. **06**

Smooth the bead firmly into the mesh to make it neat, and to make sure it's stuck. Total time taken per hole - about 10 minutes. One tip - if you've got to cut another hole in your mesh (such as, for an exhaust or towing eye to poke through), wait until the mastic's dry. Meshing - it's a cinch. **07**

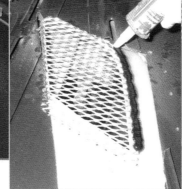

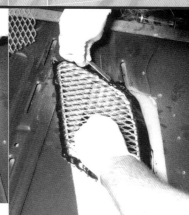

Tailgate smoothing

Achieving the complete "smooth-tailgate" look isn't too involved a procedure, providing you know someone who can weld, and are handy with filler and spray. Completely smoothing the tailgate is a logical extension of de-badging - the first thing to go is the rear wiper. Rear wipers are undoubtedly useful, and were put there for a good reason, but hey - that's just boring. Remove the rear wiper arm and motor (you can leave the washer jet), and the lock button and fill over the holes - easy, eh?

Well, yes, except that most of the holes are too big to just filler over, and will probably need glassfibre matting or welding. The final act of smoothing/flushing is to weld a plate over the rear number plate recess (cutting the recess out would weaken the panel), and finish with filler and spray. The number plate then takes pride of place, nestling in your new bumper, rear diffuser or bodykit - though it will need to be lit at night, remember. The trouble with smoothing is knowing where to stop, and it's best done as part of a full "body job".

If you're going to de-lock the tailgate as well, you'll need to devise a means of opening the darn thing afterwards. Options range from attaching a cable to the lock itself, feeding it through for manual operation, or fitting a solenoid kit and wiring it up to a convenient switch. Some Fiestas (like ours for instance) came with a handy remote release as standard - for those without, you can buy the remote release kit complete from Ford dealers (boxed with fitting instructions) for about thirty quid.

Tailgate button

01 Start work by removing the tailgate trim panel, which we've just done, in removing the rear wiper. Now we find that, presumably in the name of greater security, Ford have fitted a shield over the tailgate lock barrel, which has to go before we can start playing with it. The shield's held on by four rivets, which you have to drill out . . .

02 . . . and then by a further bolt up the side, which you undo . . . .

03 . . . before the shield eventually gives up.

It's all downhill now - there's this clip which holds the barrel in from behind, and this just slides out to the side. Behind it, you can make out the green clip which secures the lock barrel operating rods - but you actually don't need to **04** unclip these, oddly enough.

To remove the lock barrel, all that remains is to pop off this circlip. Being proper mechanic-types, we tried with our proper circlip pliers - and found we had to give up. In the end, the circlip came off using a small screwdriver - which is **05** what you're probably going to use anyway.

06 Now that ugly tailgate button can come out, from outside - so that's two holes we've made in our tailgate today!

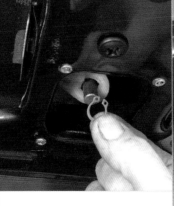

Rear wiper

01 Lift the cover from the tailgate wiper arm, and unscrew the nut underneath.

02 Hopefully your wiper arm will come off without resorting to such drastic means as this little puller, but we thought we'd show you it anyway, just for fun.

03 Going inside, the tailgate trim panel's the next to go. Remove seven screws and prise out one push-in clip (inside the "handle"), then prise the panel off around the edges.

04 If your Fiesta already has a remote boot release, there'll be more than one wiring plug in here. Trace the wiring plug back to the wiper motor before deciding which is which, then disconnect the right one.

05 There's a bolt off to one side with earth wires trapped underneath, so take out the bolt and detach the wires. Again, if you've got a remote tailgate release, the black wire should be put back on, and the bolt re-tightened (otherwise, your remote release won't work again).

06 The wiper motor mounting plate is held on by three bolts. Don't undo the three bolts you can see in the middle, as these just hold the motor itself to the frame - go for the ones around the outside.

07 And at last, the wiper motor comes out. But that's not quite the end of the story - there's a grommet to remove from the outside of the tailgate . . .

08 . . . and this sleeve from the inside, as well. If your Fiesta's not off to the bodyshop immediately, we'd suggest you fit a temporary grommet to the hole you've just created, especially if your boot's got any valuable stereo gear inside!

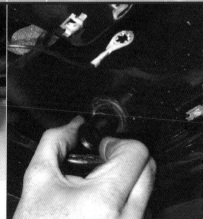

Number plate recess

`02` Transfer the shape to some metal . . .

`03` . . . and cut it out.

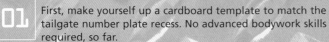

`01` First, make yourself up a cardboard template to match the tailgate number plate recess. No advanced bodywork skills required, so far.

Before digging out the welding gear, check that your new metal is a sound fit. Ours was perfect first time (of course - you believe us, don't you?).

`04`

Strategically remove some of the old tailgate paint where the weld's going to go, then stick the new metal in place using a bead of mastic (useful for sticking, and for keeping the water out - the last thing we need on a Fiesta is another rust trap).

`05`

Time to bring out the welder. A continuous seam isn't needed, nor is it very advisable - you could warp the tailgate if too much heat is applied. Just a few spot welds will do the job nicely.

`06`

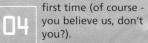
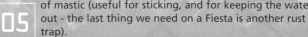

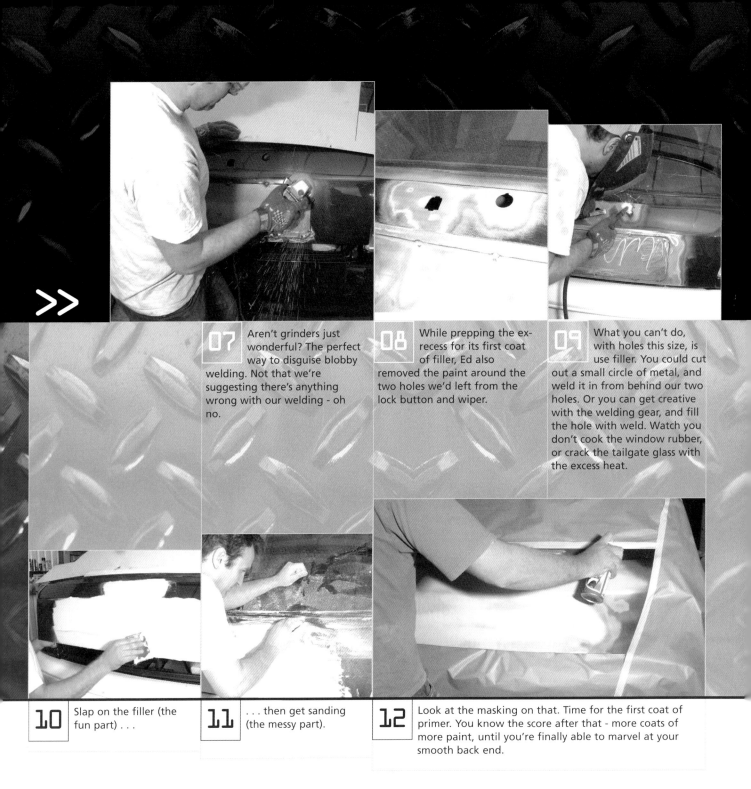

07 Aren't grinders just wonderful? The perfect way to disguise blobby welding. Not that we're suggesting there's anything wrong with our welding - oh no.

08 While prepping the ex-recess for its first coat of filler, Ed also removed the paint around the two holes we'd left from the lock button and wiper.

09 What you can't do, with holes this size, is use filler. You could cut out a small circle of metal, and weld it in from behind our two holes. Or you can get creative with the welding gear, and fill the hole with weld. Watch you don't cook the window rubber, or crack the tailgate glass with the excess heat.

10 Slap on the filler (the fun part) . . .

11 . . . then get sanding (the messy part).

12 Look at the masking on that. Time for the first coat of primer. You know the score after that - more coats of more paint, until you're finally able to marvel at your smooth back end.

An essential fitment for anyone who hasn't gone for Morette lights (which don't always work on Fiestas), it's amazing how adding two small triangular bits of metal can change the front end so much. De-badge the bonnet at the same time, and your Fiesta's own mother wouldn't recognise it.

Badboy bonnet

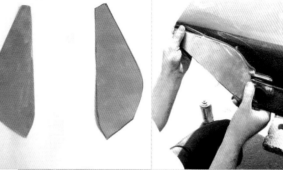

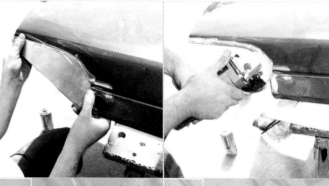

01 Well, this is what we're talking about. Two ready-made metal triangles, which are about to have a majorly appearance-altering effect on our standard Ford bonnet.

02 So - let's try one for fit, first. Looks promising.

03 Show the edge of the bonnet the grinder, and it's ready to be enhanced.

04 Mind your eyes - quality welding in progress from our man Ed.

05 Now we've got both sides done, the welds having been attacked by the grinder, and ready for a skim of filler.

06 Filler also does a nice job of removing that nasty swage line on the front edge of the bonnet. Fiesta goes incognito.

Bonnet vents

Once you've got your bodykit on, it's only natural you'll want a bonnet vent, isn't it? Respect. But this is one scary job to tackle yourself, unless you're really that good, or that brave. Leave it in the hands of the professionals, is our advice. Plenty of options - you can get little louvres stamped in as well, to complement your Evo, Impreza, Integrale or Celica GT4 main vent. There's even been a feature car with a bonnet scoop from a Kia Sedona people carrier! Truly, anything goes. One of the more recent trends is a bonnet vent from a Ferrari F50 - a monster vent which will surely lift our Fiesta above the masses who still think RS Turbo vents are the thing to have.

01 If your chosen vent doesn't have anything handy like a fitting template supplied with it, you'll have some work to do. This means vandalising the paint on your bonnet, before you even get to the hole-cutting stage. Lay the vent onto the bonnet, get it positioned, and mark its shape and where the holes need to be. Take it off, and use a rule to make the marks. Scratch that paint!

02 To any non-professionals, this is the scary bit - making that first cut. After this, there's really no going back.

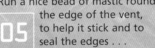

03 Soon, with the aid of his trusty air hacksaw, our man Ed has the first chunk of bonnet almost out.

04 With both holes made, it's time to bring the vent back in, for a trial fitting. Looking good so far. Notice that the major part of the vent sits on top of the old bonnet.

05 Run a nice bead of mastic round the edge of the vent, to help it stick and to seal the edges . . .

06 . . . and slap it back in place.

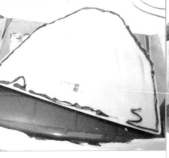

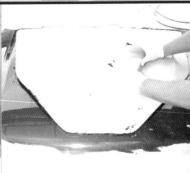

07 Believe it or not, the vent now gets pinned into place with lots of flat-headed self-tappers, straight through into the bonnet below. Drill . . .

08 . . . and screw. But what about the screw heads? They're going to look pretty naff, aren't they?

09 Well, I guess you're not wrong. Kind of an "industrial" look. The vent holes will be cut and meshed later on, but we need a solution for those screws.

10 Ahh... A layer of fibreglass over the top is the answer. The screws can actually be removed once the mastic's set, so the 'glass fills those holes and blends the edges of the vent into the bonnet. You wouldn't really want filler for this - too great a risk of it cracking off as the bonnet flexes.

11 A quick rubdown with a sander, and the next thing it'll need is paint . . .

12 . . . and mesh - we nearly forgot the mesh. With nearly as much bravery as was required to cut the bonnet, we now cut our new vent, to give us some, er, vents. For the lowdown on meshing our new holes, see "Meshing".

13 Sitting pretty (well, it'll look better with paint) in the badboy bonnet, our meshed F50 vent now awaits the coming of the spray booth.

Side skirts

So what's the deal with side skirts, then? Well, they can act as an "artificial" way of visually lowering the car, making it seem lower to the ground than it really is, and they also help to "tie together" the front and rear sections of a full bodykit. This much we know from our magazines. But where did skirts really come from?

As with so much else in modifying, it's a racing-inspired thing. Back in the late 70s, Lotus came up with their famous "ground-effect" F1 cars, which ran very, very low (for the time) and had side skirts made of rubber (or bristles), to give a flexible seal against the track. With the side exits sealed, the car's underbody could be designed to promote fast, clean airflow through from front to rear, which created a low-pressure area underneath, sucking the car onto the track. The Lotus F1 cars blew the opposition away, but were well-dodgy to drive when the side skirts failed to provide a seal. Similar principles for generating under-car downforce survive in modern F1, but without the skirts, which have been banned.

So will fitting skirts to your Fiesta give you race-car levels of downforce, greatly increasing your overtaking opportunities at the next roundabout? You already know the answer, I'm afraid…

01 If the skirts you've got are of decent quality, fitting is a piece of - very easy indeed. With the help of a willing accomplice, offer one on, making sure you've got it the right way round. Does it fit any sense? Now's the time to exercise your right to send it back, if it don't. Otherwise, some minor adjustments with a Stanley knife may be the best solution.

Fitting skirts more-or-less demands that your sills are still in good shape. If your Fiesta's getting a bit crumbly, you won't be best advised to go drilling any more holes - but that's what comes next. Wherever the mounting tabs fall on your new skirts, a hole has to be drilled.

02 Have your assistant assist you by holding the skirt in place while you assist it onto the rear wheelarch with the old drill-and-screw routine. Before we get too carried away, note that it's not a bad idea to run a bead of mastic around the edges of your skirts before fitting - helps keep the damp out of your sills, and you can smooth it off to blend the skirt to the body.

If you find them particularly offensive, those two tiny screwheads could always be de-emphasised with a little filler, or even some of that glassfibre we had left over from the bonnet vent. By the time they're painted, you'll hardly notice anyway. Are we creating a show car here, or what?

03

04 Might not be a bad idea to get some Waxoyl on here.

05 Repeat the drilling and screwing at the front end of the skirt, and we're there.

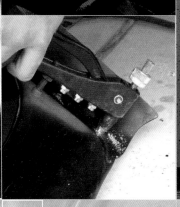

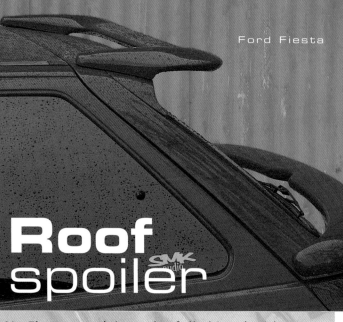

Roof spoiler

No Fiesta can claim to be fully-kitted without a rear spoiler - even if it's just an Si/XR2i standard rear window type, fitted to a basic model. But we don't want to give you that.

The most popular rear wing for the Fiesta at present isn't one from the most obvious source (ie a top modding motor) - it's the good old Mondeo Estate, which, in top-spec form, actually sported rather a tasty roof spoiler. Get hold of one of these, flush your tailgate, and you're well on the way to toning up your rear end. So to speak.

01 Before we could even start fitting our spoiler, we had to "assemble" it - can't beat these "universal-fit" items, can you? Having offered the spoiler up to the car, to establish where the holes in the spoiler would most sensibly need to be, it's out with the drill. Easy so far.

03 This is the finished result - two holes, two sort-of nuts. Ready for fitting, then.

02 To give us a threaded fixing into which to screw our mounting bolts, we need a pop-rivet gun. Our spoiler came with some slightly-odd riveted nuts, which you load up and fit just as you would a normal pop-rivet.

This is one item it'll pay you to take time over fitting - get it off-centre, and you'll never hear the last of it. Ask for a volunteer from the audience to help you hold the spoiler up in place, and establish exactly where your existing bodywork has to be drilled. You need four holes. The big laugh is that you'll need to enlarge your new holes on the inside, to take a socket to tighten the spoiler mounting bolts. Nothing's easy with modifying, but it's worth it.

04

Of course, while you're enlarging the inner holes, you could also do the same to the outer holes, if the drilling stage went slightly to pot. If not, offer the spoiler on, and check that the bolts fit. Do all necessary fettling now, then take the thing off for priming and spraying.

05

And this is the spoiler itself - not as wild as a DTM spoiler, but respect is still due. Now it can come off for a trip to the spray booth and oven - come on, it won't hurt a bit...

06

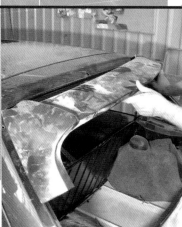

Front arches

Nice chunk of useless metal. Boomerang, anyone?

The law states that not one smidgeon of rubber shall protrude from outside your wheelarches, and the MOT crew will not be impressed if your new rubber's rubbing, either.

This presents something of a problem, if you're fitting wide 17s, especially to a car that's also having a radical drop job (like our Fiesta, on coilovers). If you've exhausted all possibilities with spacers (or wheels with a more friendly offset - see "Wheels 'n' tyres"), those arches are gonna have to be trimmed.

03 Sand that metal edge so you're not slicing up your hands all the time, then get some paint on the bare edge (rust needs no encouragement on a Fiesta).

04 We'll be giving away all his secrets at this rate - this is how you create a new flared edge. That lump of metal Ed's holding is called a dolly - say hello, dolly.

01 The first thing to go is the wheelarch liner - completely, and for good (ours disappeared during the front bumper removal sequence). Removing the liner altogether exposes the engine bay to muck thrown up by the tyres - you might want to trim up a section of the liner, to plug the resulting hole. Meanwhile, it's on with the arch extension, to mark up its profile on the wing.

02 Only those with large *cojones* need apply for this job. With the aid of a large air hacksaw (the rest of us mortals have to make do with something more manual), chop the arches inside the marked line, to leave some metal for our new mounting lip.

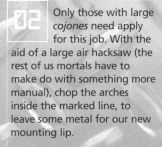

No point in having that nice mounting lip if we're not going to use it. A little drill-and-screw work sees that arch extension on to stay - the screw heads will be wiped out with a little glassfibre or filler, later on.

06 How many tubes of mastic are we up to, now? 1001 uses.

07 (continued above)

05 To locate the bottom edge of our new extensions, we fitted a speed clip to the front of our side skirts, using a tiny right-angled metal bracket, secured with a self-tapper. You could always glassfibre it, but this is a nice touch.

Rear arches

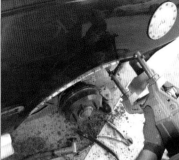

01 Trimming-up the rear arches is essentially the same procedure as for the fronts, with one important difference, which you'll see in a minute. With the arch extensions tried in place and their outline marked on the wing, it's time for the air hacksaw to trim away that return edge of metal.

02 One trimmed arch, ready for further treatment.

03 As before, a lip is created for mounting the new arch extensions by flaring (bending) the metal outwards, with a hammer and suitable dolly.

04 Here's the difference we mentioned earlier - the flared edge of the arch is a double skin, and should really be spot-welded back together, to give us a decent platform to mount the arch extensions on. This contraption on the right is a spot welder - nice if you've got one handy, eh?

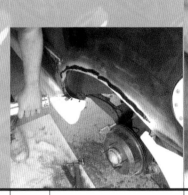

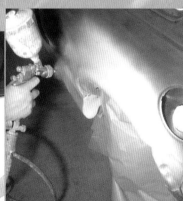

05 A little mastic's always a good idea to help the new glassfibre bits stick . . .

06 . . . but you can't beat a good screw. This one will get fillered-over when we're ready to blend the arches to the wing, so you won't see it.

07 The first job with the glassfibre, though, is to make good the join between the arch extension and the rear bumper. It's all in the details.

08 A quick rubdown and a reference coat of primer, and we're nearly there.

Respraying

Most of the prep work you've already seen, in fitting the various bodykit bits. This, it has to be said, is a major part of the overall effort - most of the cock-ups in any spray job can be traced directly back to poor preparation. For instance, even perfectly sound original paint has to be lightly buffed-up, for the new stuff to "stick".

05

Not happy with your Fiesta's "pensioner blue" paint? Fancy something just a tad more head-turning than stomach-churning? There's really only one answer - and it's time to call in the pros. DIY is what we're all about, but we're not going to pretend this is something we'd undertake lightly ourselves - there's no such thing as a simple respray (not one that'll look good afterwards, at any rate). We just thought you'd like to see some of the stages involved.

06 Oh, and the interior mirror fell off (like they do), so we completely removed the windscreen as well, to stick it back on. You don't have to be mad to want to spray your own car yourself, but it helps.

07 Our bonnet was off anyway, having its new vent fitted. The bonnet should always come off for a respray, or who knows what you'll see when you open it afterwards? To improve our chances still further, the headlights came out too.

Even when you think you've done all the glassfibre or filler work, there's always a little more to do. Rubbing-down the filler shows all the pinholes, which have to be covered somehow - here's how. Filler paste, or stopper, is applied, and then rubbed down - this stuff's "thinner" than ordinary filler, and loves sitting in minute holes.

02

When you're filling close to a swage line, it's vital to re-gain the original bodywork profile, or you'll be the laughing stock of all your mates, despite all your efforts. Here, we're using a sanding block to re-shape the door edge where we de-locked it earlier.

03

For a full respray, it's often better to remove fixed glass completely, rather than spend time masking it all up. Still fancy having a go yourself?

04

Or how about now? Doing a full respray means getting all those door shuts and other areas of painted metal inside. This is the level of masking we're talking about. Unless you're going to completely gut the entire dash and interior afterwards...

05

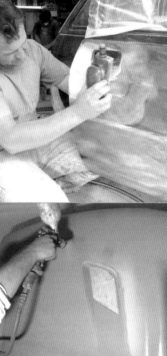

08 Besides all the prep associated with bodykits, now would be a good time to sort all those minor dents and scrapes you've been happily putting up with, all this time. This was a minor ding on our passenger door. We hate to mention it again, but - got any rust damage that wants sorting, while you're there?

09 Anywhere that's had filler will need a reference primer applied now, to see where the high and low spots are. Depending on what we see, it'll either be another quick rubdown, or we could need more filler, or stopper. Or we could be lucky, and need nothing at all.

10 On any panel that's a mixture of glassfibre and metal, it's essential to use an "etch" primer at an early stage, to ensure the new paint will adhere uniformly across the different materials. Looks quite attractive, this stuff. All that's left would be a coat of "high-build" primer (which acts as another sort of filler), more rubbing-down, and the topcoats. And more rubbing-down. And some lacquer.

11 Er... Here's one we didn't do earlier?

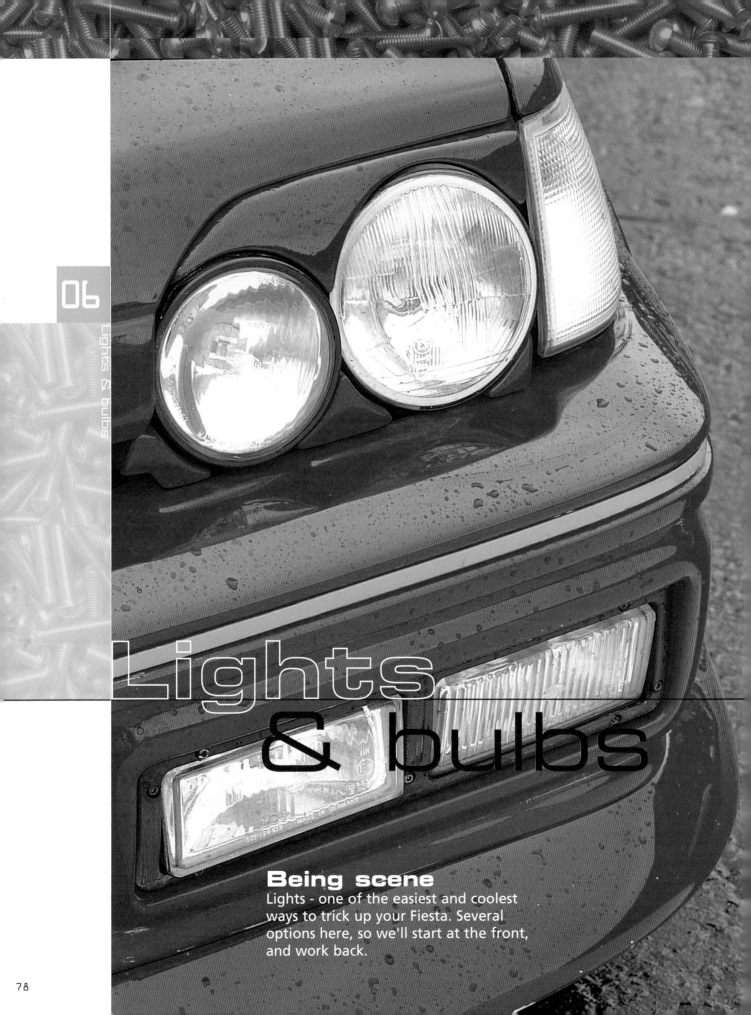

Lights

& bulbs

Being scene

Lights - one of the easiest and coolest
ways to trick up your Fiesta. Several
options here, so we'll start at the front,
and work back.

Headlights

Almost nothing influences the look of your Fiesta more than the front end, so the headlights play a crucial role.

What's available?

For most people, there's essentially five popular routes to modding the Fiesta headlights - three cheap, and two rather less cheap (but more effective).

The popular cheap option is stick-on headlight "brows", which do admittedly give the rather bland Fiesta front end a tougher look. The brows are best sprayed to match the car, before fitting - some have sticky pads, others can be fitted using mastic. Street-cred on the cheap, and (if you want) a cheap alternative to a proper "badboy" bonnet.

Another cheap option is again stick-on - this time, it's stick-on covers which give the twin-headlight look. This is basically a sheet of vinyl (shaped to the headlights, and colour-matched to your car) with two holes cut in it. Dead easy to fit, but dare we say, a bit tacky? Just our opinion. A cheap and simple way to get close to the Morette look.

If you want tinted headlights, you could try spray-tinting them, but go easy on the spray. Turning your headlights from clear glass to non-see-through is plain daft, even if it's done in the name of style. A light tint is quite effective, and gives you the chance to colour-match to your Fiesta. Unlike newer cars, there don't seem to be any companies offering ready-made tinted replacement lights for the Fiesta. At least, not yet. With tinted headlights, you'd be wise to tint those clear front indicators too, of course.

Getting more expensive, we're looking at complete replacement lights - "proper" twin-headlights, available as a kit from the French company Morette. Typically around £300 a set at time of writing, these are for lads who're seriously into their cars - maximum cred, and no-one's gonna accuse you of owning a "boring" Fiesta ever again! The light surrounds have to be sprayed to match your car, and fitting is not without some difficulties, but the finished result is SO worth it.

Another "headlight" option often featured on Fiestas actually belongs in the bodywork section - it's the "badboy" bonnet. By cunningly welding-in a couple of triangular plates to your standard Fiesta bonnet, a bodyshop (or handy DIY-er) can create a really mean look, using just the standard lights. Bonus!

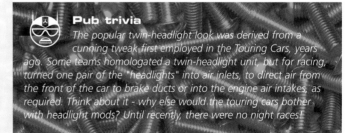

Pub trivia

The popular twin-headlight look was derived from a cunning tweak first employed in the Touring Cars, years ago. Some teams homologated a twin-headlight unit, but for racing, turned one pair of the "headlights" into air inlets, to direct air from the front of the car to brake ducts or into the engine air intakes, as required. Think about it - why else would the touring cars bother with headlight mods? Until recently, there were no night races!

Morette
twin headlights

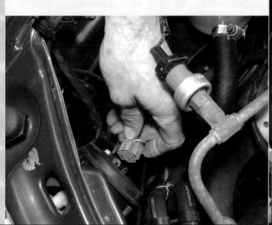

01 Full marks to Ford - removing the old headlights couldn't be much easier. Start with the driver's side headlight, which is where most of the major wiring is done. Pull off the wiring plug from the back of the headlight bulb.

02 Now unplug the sidelight bulbholder from the base of the old headlight - this is a twist-and-pull fitting. When you've got the bulbholder out, pull off the black wiring plug from the back of it - this plug goes onto your new Morette light, and the bulbholder can be chucked.

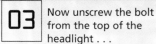

03 Now unscrew the bolt from the top of the headlight . . .

04 . . . then release the spring catch at the top, and pull the light out. Lift it over the bottom lip on the bodywork, and take it away!

05 The first chapter in the Morette story is to remove the headlight shells (held on by four little cross-head screws) and have them colour-matched to the car. Of course, making this your first job runs the risk of knackering the paint finish while you fit the lights (and you only have to loosen off the mountings to get the shells off, once the lights are fitted). Your call. Refit the shells, if removed.

06 Lay the new Morette light into place, and feed in the wiring. Note how the two new bottom mountings will locate over that lip in the bodywork - loosen off the nuts, and the little angle-plates will sit over the lip. Don't actually fit them yet, just eye it up.

07 Full marks to Morette - wiring-up the new lights couldn't be much easier, either. First to go on is the old headlight wiring plug, onto the outer of the twin headlights.

08 Now plug on the black plug you disconnected from the sidelight bulbholder earlier, onto the sidelight (which is below the headlight you just plugged in). If the standard black plug won't fit easily, chop it off and put on some spade connectors instead.

There's a single grey wire with a ring terminal on, which is your earth wire. Connect it to a suitable earth. There's a ready-made earth point on the inner wing, just behind the headlight, which looked pretty suitable to us. Unscrew the little bolt . . .

. . . and add your new grey wire to the existing brown one, then tighten it up.

The inner lights on the Morettes are the main beams, operated through a relay. They're wired up by splicing the relay wire (provided) onto the white wire on the old headlight plug. Here, we have a blue Scotchlok connector - easy to use, but sometimes unreliable in service. At least do the job properly - clip the connector round the white wire and crush the Scotchlok with pliers to make the connection. Close up the plastic clip to seal the connector.

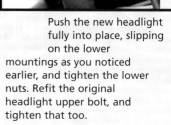

It's the same deal with the short grey wire from the relay, except this must go to an earth. There's a handy brown wire on the sidelight connector plug, which can be Scotchlok-ed onto as before. If you want a more reliable joint on either of these we've just done, strip and solder the wires, remembering to insulate the joint afterwards.

You should now have all the wiring done on the driver's side - woohoo! Feed the remaining two thick wire harnesses across the car, to the passenger side. These wires will have to be clipped up in place (get some cable-ties) when you're done, and not left hanging over hot/moving engine bits. Let's see if we can guess what would happen...

Push the new headlight fully into place, slipping on the lower mountings as you noticed earlier, and tighten the lower nuts. Refit the original headlight upper bolt, and tighten that too.

Now the passenger headlight can be removed and the new unit plonked in, and the headlight/sidelight plugs pushed on.

As with the driver's headlight, you'll be needing a good earth point for the little grey wire with its ring terminal. We fitted the wire onto one of the horn mounting bolts, sitting just below the headlight.

One of the two wire harnesses you just fed across has a flat spade connector, which fits onto the inner light. And - believe it or not - that's the wiring done for the passenger light, too. Sweet.

All that's left is to connect the wire with the fuseholder attached onto the battery positive (+) terminal. We fed the harness up to the terminal, clipping it into the standard Ford cable clip on the way . . .

. . . then on goes the ring terminal, and it's time for a test. Remember the ignition has to be on for the lights to work!

If you're a DIY hero, your Morettes should look something like this. As in - ON, and working. Probably not a bad idea to have the headlight aim checked at a garage, at some point. Don't forget to tighten all the headlight mountings, and tidy up all that wiring, when you're finished.

Headlight bulbs

Currently very popular, the new high-power and "blue" headlight bulbs are an excellent way to boost headlight performance, and to give more of a unique "look". However, like most things, fitting these bulbs is not without its pitfalls. First, some of the bulbs on sale are in fact illegal for use in this country - too powerful - as with all other non-standard lights, the boys in blue will love pulling you over for a word about this, so ask before you buy.

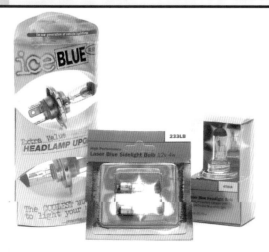

Even if you're not bothered about the legality of over-powerful bulbs (and you might well argue that being more powerful is the whole point of fitting in the first place), there are various problems associated with monster bulbs. It's almost TOO easy to fit mega-powerful bulbs, not realising the dangers.

One thing to realise is that these bulbs give off masses of heat, and plenty of people have melted their headlights before they found this out. If you doubt this, try fitting a 100W headlight bulb, turn it on, and put your hand in front of the light, next to the glass. The excessive heat these bulbs generate will damage the headlights eventually, either by warping the reflector or by burning off the reflective coating. Or both.

The increased current required to work these bulbs has been known to melt wiring (this could lead to a fire) and can also damage the headlight relay. Both the relay and the wiring were designed to cope only with the current drawn by standard-wattage bulbs. If you're going for high power, an auxiliary relay must be fitted (as done with the Morette headlights, page 80).

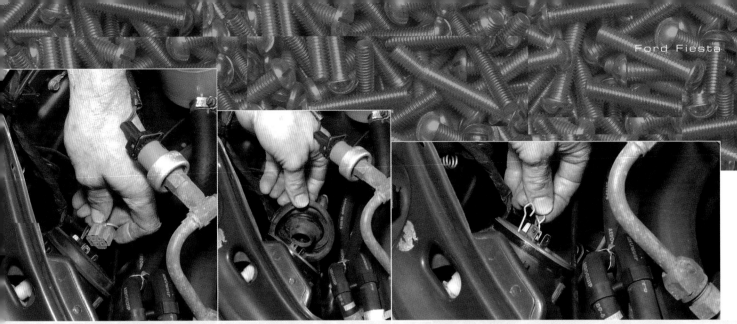

At the back of the headlight, pull off this 'ere plug . . .

. . . then whip off its rubber.

You'll now find a wire clip with two prongs on it, which you squeeze together, and hinge to the side . . .

Blue headlight **bulbs**

. . . and now the bulb falls out - if it hasn't already. If you've any plans to re-use it or sell it, hold it only by the metal bits, not the glass.

Now to fit our blue bulbs (H4 type, of course). Some bulb packaging makes it very easy to pull the bulb out by the glass, which will instantly ruin it - if you touch the bulb glass, wipe it clean with a little meths (methylated spirit - colour purple, not white spirit - colour white). Otherwise, your new bulb will burn out even faster than stated on the packet. Fit the new bulb, secure with the wire clip, fit the rubber boot over the bulb connectors, and plug in. Simple.

Tips 'n' tricks
Put the old bulbs in the glovebox - carrying spare bulbs is a good way to get a let-off from 'Plod', if they stop you for having a bulb gone. Be smart - carry spares.

Front fog/spotlights

Most Fiesta owners seem not to bother much with auxiliary lights, but we'll take you through the theory, should you get the urge to fit some.

If you're fitting fogs, they must be wired in to work on dipped-beam only, so they must go off on main beam. The opposite is true for spotlights. Pop out the main light switch (or pull down the fusebox) and check for a wire which is live ONLY when the dipped beams are on. The Haynes wiring diagrams will help here - on our Fiesta, it was a white wire we needed.

Once you've traced your wire, this is used as the live (+ve) feed for your foglight relay. Did we mention you'll need a relay? You'll need a relay. A four-pin one will do nicely. Splice a new wire onto the feed you've found, and feed it through to the engine (if possible, lift the carpet, and go through one of the bulkhead grommets). Decide where you'll mount the relay (next to the battery seems obvious) and connect the new wire onto terminal 86.

For your other relay connections, you'll need an earth to terminal 85 (plenty of good earth spots around the battery). You also need a fused live supply (buy a single fuseholder, and a 15 or 20 amp fuse should be enough) and take a new feed straight off the battery connection - this goes to terminal 30 on your relay.

Terminal 87 on your relay is the live output to the fogs - split this into two wires, and feed it out to where the lights will go. Each foglight will also need an earth - either pick a point on the body next to each light, or run a pair of wires back to the earth point you used earlier for your relay. Simple, innit?

With the wiring sorted, now you'd best fit the lights. Over to you. Most decent foglights come with some form of mounting brackets. To look their best, hopefully your new lights can slot into pre-cut holes in your new front bumper/bodykit.

To connect the wiring to the lights, you'll probably need to splice on your wires from terminal 87 to the new wiring plugs which came with the lights - not too difficult. Plug it all together, and test - you should now have some rather funky fogs!

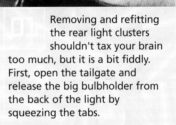

Removing and refitting the rear light clusters shouldn't tax your brain too much, but it is a bit fiddly. First, open the tailgate and release the big bulbholder from the back of the light by squeezing the tabs.

The light cluster itself is held in by four very small nuts. It's a good plan to hold onto the light while the last nut's being loosened, or new clusters will no longer be optional!

Rear light clusters

Available in as many (if not more) colours than the front and side indicators, it's clear rear light clusters that are the most popular among the modded Mk 3 Fiesta fraternity - really freshens up the whole back end. Smoked lights might be okay with the right colour car, but there's no reason not to colour-code, if that's your bag - why not spray-tint your rear lights?

If you want your Fiesta to look really lush, it's got to be the "quad" rear lights, or the "Lexus-style" jewel-effect clusters - any available for a Mk 3 yet? Such style comes at a price, but it's not excessive, considering the finished effect. You decide.

When buying rear light clusters, once again, it's not a good idea to go for the cheapest you can find, because you'll be buying trouble. Cheap rear light clusters don't have rear foglights or rear reflectors, so aren't really legal. Mr. Plod is well-informed on this point, and those sexy rear lights are way too big a come-on for him to ignore. You can buy stick-on reflectors, but these are about as sexy as NHS specs (you'd have to be pretty unlucky to get pulled just for having no rear reflectors, but don't say we didn't warn you). The rear foglight problem could perhaps be solved by spraying the clear bulb itself red, but it won't fool every MOT man. The best solution? Only buy UK-legal lights. Period.

03 At last - the light unit comes out. Peel off the foam gasket fitted on the back - it's there for a reason, or Ford would save money by not fitting it. Want a leaky boot? Thought not - then transfer the foam to your new lights.

04 The new light goes straight back in the hole the old one came from. Just looks way better, that's all. One problem - the rear foglight, fitted on the driver's side. Our lights didn't have a red lens for the foglight, so the bulb showed white through it, which is illegal. A proper solution would be to fit a separate foglight, but we cheated and painted our foglight bulb red, with heat-resistant paint. We're just not sure it's legal...

Side **repeaters**

There's a range of "standard" colours that side reps come in (clear, red, smoked, green and blue). If you're going for the same colour rear clusters, try to buy your lights from the same manufacturer, for greater chance of getting the same shade. Clear lenses can be coloured using special paint, if the particular shade you want isn't one of the "standard" ones, but the paint must be applied evenly to the lens, or this will invite an easily-avoided MOT failure. Bodyshops can colour clear lenses to the exact shade of your car, by mixing a small amount of paint with loads of lacquer - looks quite trick when it's done.

One potential problem here is that side repeaters must still show an orange light, and they must be sufficiently bright (not easy to judge this point, and no two coppers have the same eyesight!). Providing you buy good-quality lenses, and use the recommended bulbs with them, there should be no problem.

Especiallly if you've gone for clear lenses, you'll have to change the bulbs too, to orange ones. Unfortunately, you can then see the orange bulbs through the lenses, leading to what's known as the "fried egg" effect. To get round this, there are special bulbs available which provide the orange light without being as obviously orange from outside. Or get LED side repeaters, like we did.

Besides the various colour effects, side repeater lights are available in different shapes. Any shape goes, really - most popular at the moment are the Focus-style triangular lights.

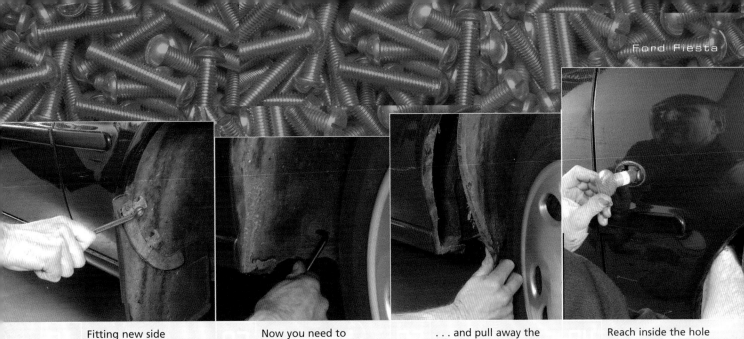

Fitting new side repeaters, in theory, is dead easy - getting the old ones out is a bit of a pain. For once, the easy-to-work-on Ford lets us down. First, unscrew your mudflaps (you haven't still got these, have you? Our only excuse is we'd just bought the car! Take them off, and leave them off).

Now you need to unscrew the little Torx screw that's probably hidden behind a load of… er… muck . . .

. . . and pull away the bottom of the wheel arch liner.

Reach inside the hole you've just made, and push the side repeater out from inside. So why not just prise it out? Well, call us after you've rung the bodyshop for a price on your wing.

Our Focus-style LED lights don't actually have the right wiring plug to connect to the standard wiring - how useful is that? So - it's no going back, and the old wiring plug has to be chopped.

Strip and crimp on some new plugs . . .

. . . and connect up the new lights. We found the Ford black wire was live (goes to the red wire on the new light). We think you can work out where the other wire goes.

Give the wing a good clean, then peel off the backing, and stick 'em on. Straight would be a bonus. Check 'em out!

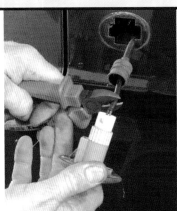

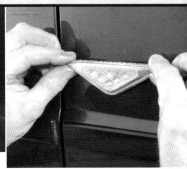

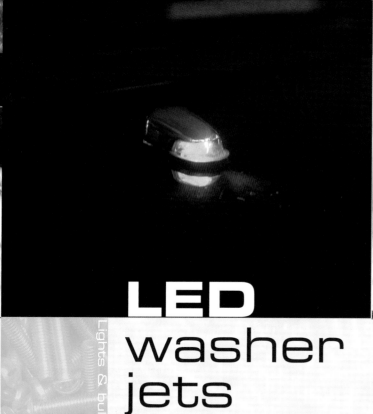

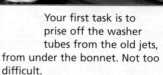

LED washer jets

Now we're talkin'! Very popular at cruises, these are a very easy-to-fit and effective way to make your Fiesta stand out.

Shame they don't seem to be available in many colours yet, but blue works well in any case, and the chrome finish even manages to look good in daylight. Just remember they're not strictly legal - Plod will tell you that you're only meant to be showing white light to the front. But you'd have to say you'd be having a bad night if he pulled you for two little blue lights…

Your first task is to prise off the washer tubes from the old jets, from under the bonnet. Not too difficult.

The tricky part is not losing the washer tubes, once you've disconnected them - you'll be needing them again, remember. This is just one solution - you can poke anything you like up there.

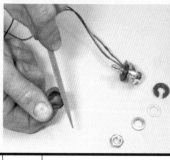

03 Before you can fit your new jets into the bonnet, you need to select the right plastic spacer from the ones provided. The spacer is meant to lock the jet into place, and stop it from being turned. None of our spacers fitted exactly, so here we're filing one down.

04 Pop the jet into the bonnet . . .

05 . . . then fit the spacer in from underneath. We used a blob of grease to hold the spacer in position.

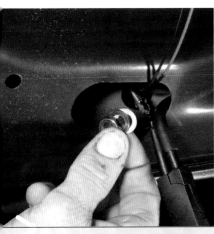
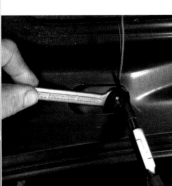

Next, it's on with the washer and nut, which is where things all get a bit fiddly.

Tighten up the nut . . .

. . . then refit the washer tube.

Now we need to start sorting the wiring out. First, the wires have to be fed through the bonnet - this is much easier if you tape the wires to a thicker piece of wire, and poke it through. We chose to feed the wiring for each jet down opposite sides of the car, but you could join them together at this point.

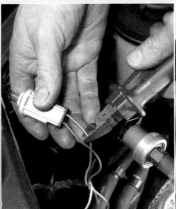
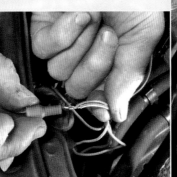
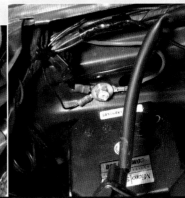

10 Cable-tie the wiring to the bonnet hinge, and make sure it can't get trapped, or stretched, or rubbed through. Okay, we're not talking about huge current here, but if they stop working, it won't make your night, will it?

11 Since the LEDs will only really show up at night, it makes sense to have them come on with the sidelights (which stay on once the headlights are on, by the way). Twist and pull the sidelight bulbholder from the back of the headlight, then cut into the grey/red live wire.

12 Connect the LED red wire to the sidelight live, twisting the two together into one bullet connector.

13 The LED black wire is the earth, and will need a ring terminal on, before it can be connected to a convenient earth point. Here's one we used earlier, just behind the headlight.

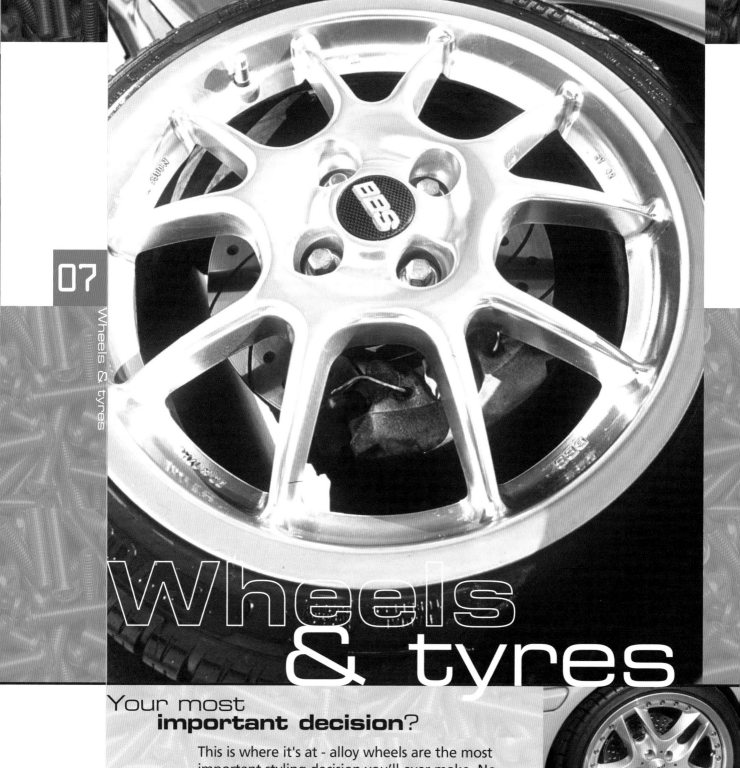

Wheels & tyres

Your most important decision?

This is where it's at - alloy wheels are the most important styling decision you'll ever make. No matter how good the rest of your car is, choose the wrong rims and your car will never look right. Choose a good set and you're already well on the way to creating a sorted motor. Take your time and pick wisely - wheel fashions change like the weather, and you don't want to spend shedloads on a set of uncool alloys.

None of the standard alloys cut it, and should very quickly be dumped. Advice on which particular wheels to buy would be a waste of space, since the choice is so huge, and everyone will have their own favourites - for what it's worth, though, we reckon anything in a five-spoke or multi-spoke design seems to look best on a Fiesta, but go for something a little more original by all means. Beyond those words of dubious wisdom, you're on your own - car colour and your own chosen other mods will dictate what will look right on your car.

Fitting 17s or 18s will be a great deal less stressful if you get wheels with exactly the right offset - otherwise, your arches won't just have to be "trimmed" - they'll be butchered! Fitting wheels with the wrong offset may also do unpleasant things to the handling. The correct offset for all Mk 3 Fiestas is 41.

Lead us not into temptation

Before we go any further into which wheels are right for you, a word about insurance and security. Fitting tasty alloys to your Fiesta is one of the first and best ways to make it look cool. It follows, therefore, that someone of low moral standing might very well want to unbolt them from your car while you're not around, and make their own car look cool instead (or simply sell them, to buy spot cream and drugs).

Since fitting a set of top alloys is one of the easiest bolt-on ways to trick up any car, it's no surprise that the market in stolen alloys is as alive and kicking as it currently is - your wheels will also look very nice on any number of other cars, and the owners of those cars would love to own them at a fraction of the price you paid . . . It's not unknown for a set of wheels to go missing just for the tyres - if you've just splashed out on a set of fat Yokohamas, your wheels look even more tempting, especially if you've got a common-size tyre.

Tell your insurance company what you're fitting. What will probably happen is that they'll ask for the exact details, and possibly a photo of the car with the wheels on. Provided you're happy to then accept that they won't cover the extra cost of the wheels if they get nicked (or if the whole car goes), you may find you're not charged a penny more, especially if you've responsibly fitted some locking wheel nuts. Not all companies are the same, though - some charge an admin fee, and yes, some will start loading your premium. If you want the rims covered, it's best to talk to a company specialising in modified cars, or you could be asked to pay out the wheel cost again in premiums. The worst thing you can do is say nothing, and hope they don't find out - I don't want to go on about this, but there are plenty of documented cases where insurance companies have refused to pay out altogether, purely on the basis of undeclared alloy wheels.

How cheap are you?

Hopefully, you'll be deciding which wheels to go for based on how they look, not how much they cost, but inevitably (for most ordinary people at least), price does become a factor. Some of the smaller manufacturers recognise this, and offer cheaper copies of more expensive designs - this is fine as far as you're concerned, but what's the catch? Surely buying a cheaper wheel must have its pitfalls? Well, yes - and some of them may not be so obvious.

Inevitably, cheaper wheels = lower quality, but how does this manifest itself? Cheap wheels are often made from alloys which are more "porous" (a bit like a sponge, they contain microscopic holes and pockets of air). Being porous has two main disadvantages for a wheel, the main one being that it won't be able to retain air in the tyres. The days of tyres with inner tubes are long gone (and it's illegal to fit tubes to low-profile tyres), so the only thing keeping the air in are the three "walls" of the tyre, with the fourth "wall" being the inside of the wheel itself. If you like keeping fit by pumping up your tyres every morning, go ahead - the rest of us will rightly regard this as a pain, and potentially dangerous (running tyres at low pressure will also scrub them out very effectively - what was that about saving money?).

Porous wheels also have difficulty in retaining their paint or lacquer finish, with flaking a known problem, sometimes after only a few months. This problem is compounded by the fact that porous wheels are much harder to clean (brake dust seems to get ingrained into the wheels more easily) - and the more you scrub, the more the lacquer comes off.

The final nail in the coffin for cheap wheels is that they tend to corrode (or "fizz") more readily than more expensive types. This not only looks terrible if visible from outside, but if you get corrosion between the wheel and the hub, you won't even be able to take the things off! Yes seriously, grown men with all the specialist tools in the world at their disposal will be scratching their heads when faced with wheels which simply will not come off.

Buying wheels from established, popular manufacturers with a large range has another hidden benefit, too. It stands to reason that choosing a popular wheel will mean that more suppliers will stock it, and the manufacturers themselves will make plenty of them. And if you're unlucky enough to have an accident (maybe a slide on a frosty road) which results in non-repairable damage to one wheel, you're going to need a replacement. If you've chosen the rarest wheels on the planet, you could be faced with having to replace a complete set of four, to get them all matching . . . A popular wheel, even if it's a few years old, might be easier to source, even second-hand.

The Sunday morning ritual

It's a small point maybe, but you'll obviously want your wheels to look as smart as possible, as often as possible - so how easy are they going to be to clean?

The multi-spokers and BBS style "wires" are hell to clean - a fiddly toothbrush job - do you really want that much aggro every week? The simpler the design, the easier time you'll have. For those who like nothing better than counting their spokes, though, there are several really good products out there to make your life less of a cleaning nightmare.

Tricks 'n' tips

It's worth applying a bit of car polish to the wheels - provided it's good stuff, and you can be sure of getting the residue out of the corners and edges, a polished wheel will always be easier to clean off than an unpolished one.

Bound to drive you nuts

Don't forget about locking wheel nuts (see "Hold on to your wheels" further on) - bargain these into a wheel/tyre package if you're buying new.

A word of warning about re-using your existing wheel nuts, should you be upgrading from steel wheels. Most steel-wheel nuts are not suitable for use with alloy wheels (and vice-versa, incidentally). Most nuts for use with alloys will have a washer fitted, for two very good reasons - 1) the nut will pull through the wheel hole without it, and 2) to protect the wheel finish.

Another point to watch: by the time you've got your new wheels on, are the wheel studs actually long enough? Is there enough thread showing through the wheel that you can get a nut on, at least by more than a few threads? An engineering works or garage can probably fit new studs to your existing hubs, but this is surely too much grief - little or no thread showing means something's basically wrong with the wheels you're trying to fit, so get the problem sorted.

Tricks 'n' tips

If you're keeping a steel wheel as your spare (or even if you're keeping an original alloy), keep a set of your original wheel nuts in a bag inside the spare wheel.

Other options

If you're on a really tight budget, and perhaps own a real "basic" model Fiesta, don't overlook the possibility of fitting a discarded set of standard alloys, possibly from another Ford entirely - check that the stud pattern's the same, obviously. Getting the right wheel nuts also applies here, not just with aftermarket wheels.

If the Ford range of wheels is too limiting, don't be too quick buying (for instance) alloys suitable for other makes altogether. For instance, Peugeot/Citroën alloys have the same stud pattern (PCD), so they'll go on alright, but the offset is seriously different (like, only 19 or 20, where it should be 41 - have fun). In the case of some alloys (VW for example), the stud pattern may be only fractionally different, but if you put these on, the strain on the studs/nuts is too great, and they can fracture or work themselves loose…

Size **matters**

For us Brits, biggest is best - there are Fiestas out there with 18s and up. And yes, the mags all say you can't have anything less than 17-inchers. In Europe, meanwhile, they're mad for the small-wheel look, still with seriously dropped suspension of course.

On many cars (Fiestas included), 15-inch rims are the biggest you can sensibly fit before you're looking at major work, but they'll still improve the handling (unlike 17s, which often have the exact opposite effect!). We know lots of Fiesta owners who've stopped at 15s, and they're quite happy, thank you. Keep the wheel width to 6.5J as well, if you can - 7J rims may lead to headaches. Don't get too suckered into the whole 17-inch rims thing - if you slam the car down, modern 15s and 16s look nearly as good, and you'll have a much easier life. Tyres will be cheaper, too!

With 17s and up, the problems come front and rear on Fiestas. Wide 17s will rub inside on the front struts, and you won't get full steering lock. Fit hub spacers

Tricks 'n' tips

When you have your new wheels balanced, make sure the fast-fit centre knows to use stick-on weights, inside the wheel (not on the rim edge) - old-type knock-on lead weights look crap on the outer wheel edges, and on the inner edges may foul the suspension. Stick-on weights are, however, notorious for falling off easily, even when applied to pristine new alloys.

to fix this (metal plates which fit between the wheel and hub, and push the wheel outwards). Go too far with spacers, and the wheels will rub on the outside edges. At the rear, 17s will catch on the strut lower spring plate, which is more serious - you can cut away the offending metal, but we wouldn t advise it on safety grounds. The best way to cure this problem is to fit a complete new suspension kit which offers slimmer rear springs, giving more strut-to-wheel clearance (the coilover kit we fitted gave us no problems with our 17s on the back). Explain your concerns to your chosen suspension kit supplier before parting with the folding stuff.

We like a challenge

To be honest, successfully fitting big wheels in combination with lowered suspension is one of the major challenges to the modifier.

At least the Fiesta has reasonably roomy front arches (or they can be made to be easily, by taking out the plastic wheelarch liners). As much as anything, tyre width is what ultimately leads to problems, not so much the increased wheel diameter.

If the tyres are simply too wide (or with wheels the wrong offset), they will first of all rub on the suspension strut (ie on the inside edge of the tyre). Also, the inside edges may rub on the arches on full steering lock - check left and right. Rubbing on the inside edges can be cured by fitting offsets or spacers between the wheel and hub, which effectively pull the wheel outwards, "spacing" it away from its normal position (this also has the effect of widening the car's track, which may improve the on-limit handling - or not). Fitting large offsets must be done using special longer wheel studs, as the standard ones may only engage the nuts by a few threads, which is highly dangerous.

Rubbing on the outside edges is a simple case of wheelarch lip fouling, which must be cured by rolling out the wheelarch return edge, and other mods. If you've gone for really wide tyres, or have already had to fit offsets, the outer edge of the tyre will probably be visible outside the wheelarch, and this is a no-no (it's illegal, and you must cover it up!).

The other trick with fitting big alloys is of course to avoid the "Fiesta 4x4 off-road" look, which you will achieve remarkably easily just by popping on a set of 17s with standard suspension. The massive increase in ground clearance is fine for Farmer Palmer, but won't win much admiration on cruises - guilty of having "fistable" arches, M'lud! Send him down! Overcoming this problem by lowering can be a matter almost of inspired guesswork, as much as anything (see "Suspension").

Speedo error? Or not?

One side-effect of fitting large wheels is that your car will go slower. Yes, really - or at least - it will appear to go slower, due to the effects of the mechanically-driven speedometer.

As the wheel diameter increases, so does its circumference (distance around the outside) - this means that, to travel say one mile, a large wheel will turn less than a smaller wheel. Therefore, for a given actual speed, since the method for measuring speed is the rate of wheel rotation, a car with larger wheels will produce a lower speedo reading than one with smaller wheels - but it's not actually going any slower in reality. So don't worry if you think you've reduced your Fiesta's performance somehow with the monster rims, 'cos you 'aven't.

With the ever-increasing number of those lovely grey/yellow boxes with a nasty surprise inside, spare a thought to what this speedo error could mean in the real world. If (like most people) you tend to drive a wee bit over the posted 30s and 40s, your real speed on 17s or 18s could be a bit more than the bit more you thought you were doing already, and you could get an unexpected flash to ruin your day. What we're saying is, don t drive any faster, to compensate for the lower speedo reading. Actually, the speedo error effect on 17s and 18s really is tiny at around-town speeds, and only becomes a factor over 70. But then, Officer, you couldn't possibly have been going over 70, could you? Officer?

Jargon explained

Rolling radius - the distance from the wheel centre to the outer edge of the tyre, or effectively, half the overall diameter. The rolling radius obviously increases with wheel size, but up to a point, the effects are masked by fitting low-profile tyres, with "shorter" sidewalls. Above 16-inch rims, however, even low-profiles can't compensate, and the rolling radius keeps going up.

PCD - this isn't a banned substance, it's your Pitch Circle Diameter, which relates to the spacing of your wheel holes, or "stud pattern". It is expressed by the diameter of a notional circle which passes through the centre of your wheel studs, and the number of studs/nuts. Unlike the offset, the PCD often isn't stamped onto the wheels, so assessing it is really a matter of eyeing-up and trying them on the studs - the wheel should go on easily, without binding, if the stud pattern is correct. On a Mk 3 Fiesta, the PCD is 108 mm with four studs, which is given as 108/4, or 4 x 108.

Offset - this is determined by the distance from the wheel mounting face in relation to its centre-line. The offset figure is denoted by ET (no, I mustn't), which stands for einpress tiefe in German, or pressed-in depth (now I KNOW you're asleep). The lower the offset, the more the wheels will stick out. Fitting wheels with the wrong offset might bring the wheel into too-close contact with the brake and suspension bits, or with the arches. Very specialised area - seek advice from the wheel manufacturers if you're going for a very radical size (or even if you're not). The correct offset for Fiestas of all sizes is ET 41.

Hold on to your wheels

The minute you bang on your wicked alloys, your car becomes a target. People see the big wheels, and automatically assume you've also got a major stereo, seats and other goodies - all very tempting, but that involves breaking in, and you could have an alarm. Pinching the wheels themselves, now that's a doddle - a few tools, some bricks or a couple of well-built mates to lift the car, and it's easy money.

The trouble with fitting big wheels is that they're only screwed on, and are just as easily screwed off, if you don't make life difficult for 'em. If you're unlucky enough to have to park outside at night (ie no garage), you could wake up one morning to a car that's literally been slammed on the deck! Add to this the fact that your car isn't going anywhere without wheels, plus the damage which will be done to exhaust, fuel and brake pipes from dropping on its belly, and it's suddenly a lot worse than losing a grand's worth of wheels and tyres…

The market and demand for stolen alloys is huge, but most people don't bother having them security-marked in any way, so once a set of wheels disappears, they're almost impossible to trace. Thieves avoid security-marked (or "tattooed") wheels (or at least it's a

pretty good deterrent) - and it needn't look hideous!

When choosing that car alarm, try and get one with an "anti-jacking" feature, because thieves hate it. This is sometimes now called "anti-tilt", to avoid confusion with anti-hijacking. Imagine a metal saucer, with a metal ball sitting on a small magnet in the centre. If the saucer tilts in any direction, the ball rolls off the magnet, and sets off the alarm. Highly sensitive, and death to anyone trying to lift your car up for the purpose of removing the wheels - as I said, the crims are not fond of this feature at all. Simply having an alarm with anti-shock is probably not good enough, because a careful villain will probably be able to work so as not to create a strong enough vibration to trigger it - mind you, it's a whole lot better than nothing, especially if set to maximum sensitivity.

Locking nuts/bolts

Locking wheel nuts will be effective as a deterrent to the inexpert thief (kids, in other words), but will probably only slow down the pro.

What so many people don't realise with their pride and joy is that thieves want to work quickly, and will use large amounts of cunning and violence to deprive you of your stuff. If you fit a cheap set of locking nuts, they'll use a hammer and thin chisel to split the nuts down the sides. Some nuts can easily be defeated by hammering a socket onto them, and undoing as normal, while some of the key-operated nuts are so pathetic they can be beaten using a small screwdriver. So - choose the best nuts you can, but don't assume they'll prevent your wheels from disappearing. Insurance companies seem to like 'em - perhaps it shows a responsible attitude, or something...

There seems to be some debate as to whether it's okay to fit more than one set of locking nuts to a car - some people we know value their wheels so highly that they've fitted four or five sets of nuts - in other words, they've completely replaced all the standard nuts! The feeling against doing this is that the replacement locking nuts may not be made to the same standard as factory originals, and while it's okay to fit one set on security grounds, fitting more than that is dangerous on safety grounds (nut could fail, wheel falls off, car in ditch, owner in hospital . . .).

Obviously, you must carry the special key or tool which came with your nuts with you at all times, in case of a puncture, or if you're having any other work done, such as new brakes or tyres. The best thing to do is rig this onto your keyring, so that it's with you, but not left in the car. The number of people who fit locking nuts and then leave the key to them cunningly "hidden" in the glovebox or the boot . . . incredible stupidity . . . if only the low-lifes out there were as daft! You don't leave a spare set of car keys in your glovebox as well, do you?

How to change a set of wheels

You might think you know all about this, but do you really?

Okay, so you know you need a jack and wheelbrace (or socket and ratchet), but where are the jacking points? If you want to take more than one wheel off at a time, have you got any axle stands, and where do they go? If you've only ever had wheels and tyres fitted by a garage, chances are you're actually a beginner at this. It's surprising just how much damage you can do to your car, and to yourself, if you don't know what you're doing - and the worst thing here is to think you know, when you don't...

What to use

If you don't already have one, invest in a decent hydraulic trolley jack. This is way more use than the standard car jack, which is really only for emergencies, and which isn't really stable enough to rely on. Lifting and lowering the car is so much easier with a trolley jack, and you'll even look professional. Trolley jacks have a valve, usually at the rear, which must be fully tightened (using the end of the jack handle) before raising the jack, and which is carefully loosened to lower the car down - if it's opened fully, the car will not so much sink as plummet!

Axle stands are placed under the car, once it's been lifted using the jack. Stands are an important accessory to a trolley jack, because once they're in place, there's no way the car can come down on you - remember that even a brand new trolley jack could creep down (if you haven't tightened the valve), or could even fail completely under load (if it's a cheap one, or worn, or both).

Under no circumstances use bricks, wooden blocks or anything else which you have to pile up, to support the car - this is just plain stupid. A Fiesta weighs plenty for a "small" car - if you want to find out just how solidly it's built, try crawling under it when it's resting on a few bricks.

Where to use it

Only ever jack the car up on a solid, level surface (ideally, a concrete or tarmac driveway, or quiet car park). If there's even a slight slope, the car's likely to move (maybe even roll away) as the wheels are lifted off the ground. Jacking up on a rough or gravelled surface is not recommended, as the jack could slip at an awkward moment - such as when you've just got underneath…

How to use it - jacking up the front

Before jacking up the front of the car, pull the handbrake on firmly (you can also chock the rear wheels, if you don't trust your handbrake).

If you're taking the wheels off, loosen the wheel nuts before you start jacking up the car. It's easily forgotten, but you'll look pretty silly trying to undo the wheel nuts with the front wheels spinning in mid-air. Our standard alloys had an anti-theft cover fitted over the nuts - well, at least they tried. You'll need the special key (probably in the glovebox) to remove this cover.

We'll assume you've got a trolley jack. The next question is - where to stick it? Ford provide two nice support points at the front, on the square-section "outriggers" just behind the front wishbones. Put a nice flat offcut of wood on your jack head, and get it under there! You can jack on the sill jacking points (which are marked by little notches above the sill edges), but it's better to leave those for your axle stands.

Once you've got the car up, pop an axle stand or two under the front sill jacking points. These points are shown by having a notch cut in the bottom edge of the flange, and this is the only part of the sill it's safe to jack under or rest the car on. On the XRs and RSs, you'll have to unclip a cover for access to the sill jacking points, and even then, access to them might not be all you'd like. With the stands in place, you can lower the jack so the car's weight rests on the stands. Personally, I like to spread the weight between the stands and the jack, so I never lower the jack completely.

I'm sure we don't need to tell you this, but don't jack up the car, or stick stands under the car, anywhere other than kosher jacking and support points. This means - not the floorpan or the sump (you'll cave it in), not the suspension bits (not stable), and not under the brake/fuel pipes.

How to use it - jacking up the rear

When jacking up the rear of the car, place wooden chocks in front of the front wheels to stop it rolling forwards, and engage first gear.

If you're taking the wheels off, you don't have to loosen the wheel nuts before lifting the car, but you'll be relying on your handbrake to hold the wheels while you wrestle with the nuts. Much cooler (and safer) to loosen the rear wheel nuts on the ground too.

Jacking and supporting the rear is a little trickier. You have the choice of jacking under the rear suspension arm (right at the end, under the shock absorber lower mounting), or under the rear axle itself. The axle option's safer, as it won't move as much when you start jacking, and won't load the rear suspension. Of course, if you're fitting your coilovers, jacking under the suspension arm (at least to raise the car up) is not an option! The axle stand can go under the sill jacking point at the rear, again indicated by a notch in the sill edge.

Remember not to put your axle stands under any pipes, the spare wheel well, or the fuel tank, and you should live to see another Christmas.

Achtung!

As far as possible, don't leave the car unattended once it has been lifted, particularly if kids are playing nearby - football goes under your car, they go under to get it, knock the jack, car falls . . . it would almost certainly be your fault.

Changing
wheels

01 No, no, no - this has nothing to do with long-haired interior designers. Changing wheels is a serious business, so pay attention. Before fitting your new wheels, there's stuff to check - first, have you got a nice ally/plastic ring inside the hub? Make sure it's there, as it acts to centre the wheel properly, and may help to stop the wheel rusting on. Ever had a rusted-on wheel? Your local fast-fit centre will have, and they'll tell you it ain't funny...

Pop the wheel onto the studs, then on with the nicely-greased nuts (oo-er), and tighten up as far as possible by hand. You have got some locking nuts, haven't you? Keep your locking wheel nut tool somewhere safe, **05** but not obvious. The glovebox is convenient, but way too obvious!

02 Even with the ring of plastic, the metal bits can still corrode on. Equip yourself with some copper brake grease, and smear some on the wheel boss, inside.

Always tighten the wheel nuts securely (ideally, to the correct torque - 85 Nm). This can only be done properly with the wheel back on the ground. Don't over-tighten the nuts, or you'll never get them undone at the roadside, should you have a flat! D'oh! If your wheels have a centre cap of some kind, fit it. Not only does it look better, but some wheel centre caps cover the wheel nuts - might be all **06** the theft-deterrent you need, to stop an opportunist...

Speaking of corrosion, how rusty are those wheel hubs? Quite to very, we suspect. Take a wire brush, and use it wisely - the less rust and muck there is to start with, the better the wheels will centre-up, too, when you offer **03** 'em on.

This is how us professionals apply copper grease to a hub - mere mortals use their fingers. You'll be doing yourself a favour if some of the same copper grease also finds its way onto the **04** wheel nut threads.

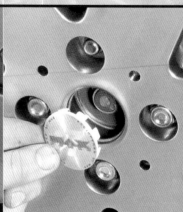

101

Always nice to see a good brand of tyre on a decent alloy. How cool do cheap tyres look?

Tyres

To some people, tyres are round and black, they're nearly all expensive, and don't last long enough. When you're buying a new set of wheels, most centres will quote prices with different tyres - this is convenient, and usually quite good value, too, but look carefully at what you're buying.

Some people try to save money by fitting "remould" or "re-manufactured" tyres. These aren't always the bargain they appear to be - experience says there's no such thing as a good cheap tyre.

Without wanting to sound like an old advert, choosing a known brand of tyre will prove to be one of your better decisions. Tyres are the only thing keeping you on the road, as in steering, braking and helping you round corners - what's the point of trying to improve the handling by sorting the suspension if you're going to throw the gains away by fitting naff tyres? Why beef up the brakes if the tyres won't bite? The combination of stiff suspension and cheap tyres is inherently dangerous - because the front end dives less with reduced suspension travel, the front tyres are far more likely to lock and skid under heavy braking.

Cheap tyres also equals more wheelspin - might be fun to be sat at the lights in a cloud of tyre smoke, but wouldn't you rather be disappearing up the road? Another problem with really wide tyres is aquaplaning - hit a big puddle at speed, and the tyre skates over the water without gripping - this is seriously scary when it first

Tricks 'n' tips
When buying tyres, look out for ones which feature a rubbing strip on the sidewall - these extend over the edge of the wheel rims, and the idea is that they protect the rim edges from damage by "kerbing". Our Toyo Proxes had these strips - discreet and very practical, we reckon.

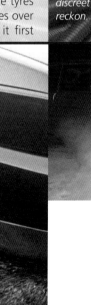

The size markings are obviously the most important, but take note of the directional marks too, if swapping wheels round. Most of the other markings are for anoraks only.

happens. Fitting good tyres won't prevent it, but it might increase your chances of staying in control. The sexiest modern low profile tyres have a V-tread pattern, designed specifically to aid water dispersal, which is exactly what you need to prevent aquaplaning - try some, and feel the difference!

Finally, cheap tyres ruin your Fiesta's appearance - a no-name brand emblazoned in big letters on your tyre sidewalls - how's that going to look? If you're spending big dosh on wheels, you've gotta kit 'em out with some tasty V-tread tyres, or lose major points for style. Listen to friends and fellow modifiers - real-world opinions count for a lot when choosing tyres (how well do they grip, wet or dry? How many miles can you get out of them?) Just make sure, before you splash your cash on decent tyres, that you've cured all your rubbing and scrubbing issues, as nothing will rip your new tyres out faster.

Marks on your sidewalls

Tyre sizes are expressed in a strange mixture of metric and imperial specs - we'll take a typical tyre size as an example:

205/40 R 17 V
for a 7-inch wide 17-inch rim
205 width of tyre in millimetres
40 this is the "aspect ratio" (or "profile") of the tyre, or the sidewall height in relation to tyre width, expressed as a percentage, in this case 40%. So - 40% of 205 mm = 82 mm, or the height of the tyre sidewall from the edge of the locating bead to the top of the tread.
R Radial.
17 Wheel diameter in inches.
V Speed rating (in this case, suitable for use up to 150 mph).

Pressure situation

Don't forget, when you're having your new tyres fitted, to ask what the recommended pressures should be, front and rear - it's unlikely that the Ford specs for this will be relevant to your new low-low profiles, but it's somewhere to start from. If the grease-monkey fitting your tyres is no help on this point, contact the tyre manufacturer - the big ones might even have a half-useful website! Running the tyres at the wrong pressures is particularly stupid (you'll stand to wear them out much faster) and can be very dangerous (too soft - tyre rolls off the rim, too hard - tyre slides, no grip).

Speed ratings

Besides the tyre size, tyres are marked with a maximum speed rating, expressed as a letter code:

T up to 190 km/h (118 mph)

U up to 200 km/h (124 mph)

H up to 210 km/h (130 mph)

V inside tyre size markings (225/50 VR 16) over 210 km/h (130 mph)

V outside tyre size markings (185/55 R 15 V) up to 240 km/h (150 mph)

Z inside tyre size markings (255/40 ZR 17) over 240 km/h (150 mph)

If you've got marks on your sidewalls like this, you're in trouble - this has almost certainly been caused by "kerbing".

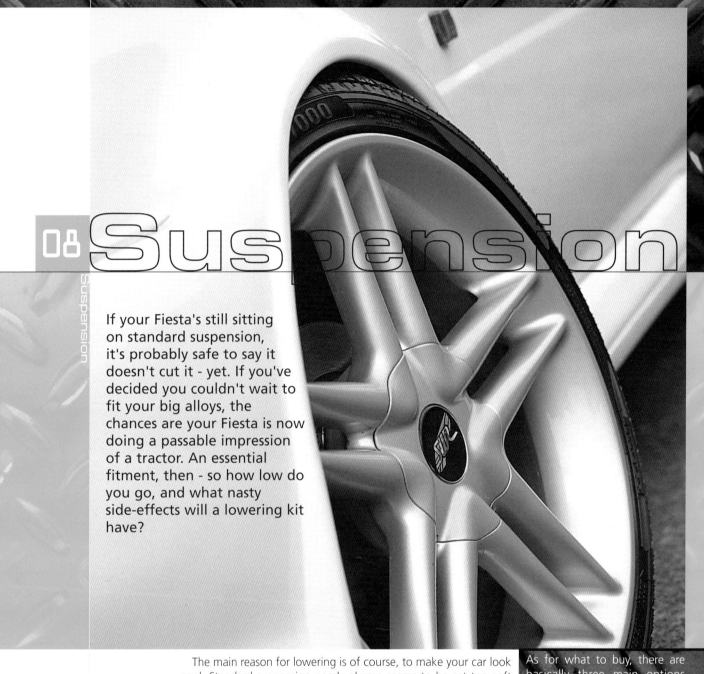

08 Suspension

If your Fiesta's still sitting on standard suspension, it's probably safe to say it doesn't cut it - yet. If you've decided you couldn't wait to fit your big alloys, the chances are your Fiesta is now doing a passable impression of a tractor. An essential fitment, then - so how low do you go, and what nasty side-effects will a lowering kit have?

The main reason for lowering is of course, to make your car look cool. Standard suspension nearly always seems to be set too soft and too high - a nicely lowered motor really stands out instantly. Lowering your car should also improve the handling. Dropping the car on its suspension brings the car's centre of gravity closer to its roll and pitch centres, which helps to pin it to the road in corners and under braking - combined with stiffer springs and shocks, this reduces body roll and increases the tyre contact patch on the road. But - if improving the handling is really important to you, choose your new suspension carefully. If you go the cheap route, or want extreme lowering, then you could end up with a car which doesn't handle at all...

As for what to buy, there are basically three main options when it comes to lowering, arranged in order of ascending cost below:

1 *Set of lowering springs*

2 *Matched set of lowering springs and shock absorbers*

3 *Set of "coilovers"*

Lowering springs

The cheapest option by far, but with the most pitfalls and some unpleasant side-effects.

Lowering springs are, effectively, shorter versions of the standard items fitted to your Fiesta at the factory. However, not only are they shorter (lower), they are also uprated (stiffer) - if lowering springs were simply shorter than standard and the same stiffness (the same "rate"), you'd be hitting the bump-stops over every set of catseyes. With lowering springs, you just fit the new springs and keep the original shock absorbers ("dampers") - even if the originals aren't completely knackered, you're creating a problem caused by mis-matched components. The original dampers were carefully chosen to work in harmony with the original-rate springs - by increasing the spring rate without changing the dampers, you end up with a situation where the dampers will not be in full and effective control of the spring motion. What this usually does before long is wreck the dampers, because they simply can't cope with the new springs, so you really don't save any money in the end.

The mis-matched springs and dampers will have other entertaining side-effects, too. How would you like a Fiesta which rides like a brick, and which falls over itself at the first sign of a corner taken above walking pace? A very choppy ride and strange-feeling steering (much lighter, or much heavier, depending on your luck) are well-documented problems associated with taking the cheap option, and it doesn't even take much less time to fit, compared to a proper solution. Even if you're someone who doesn't object to a hard ride if the car looks cool, think on this - how many corners do you know that are completely flat (ie without any bumps)? On dodgy lowering springs, you hit a mid-corner bump at speed, and it's anyone's guess where you'll end up.

If cost is a major consideration, and lowering springs the only option for now, at least try to buy branded items of decent quality - some cheap sets of springs will eat their way through several sets of dampers before you realise the springs themselves have lost the plot. Needless to say, if riding around on mis-matched springs and shocks is a bit iffy anyway, it's downright dangerous when they've worn out (some inside 18 months!).

Assuming you want to slam your suspension so that your arches just clear the tops of your wicked new rims, there's another small problem with lowered springs - it takes some inspired guesswork (or hours of careful measuring and head-scratching) to assess the required drop accurately, and avoid that nasty rubbing sound and the smell of burning rubber. Springs are generally only available in a very few sizes, expressed by the amount of drop they'll produce - most people go for 60 mm or more, but there's usually 35 to 40 mm springs too if you're less brave (or if you've simply got massive rims). Take as many measurements as possible, and ask around your mates - suppliers and manufacturers may be your best source of help in special cases.

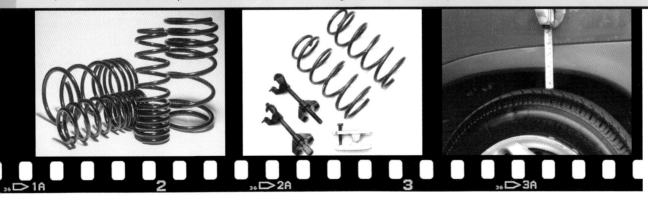

Suspension kit

A far better choice, Sir - a matched set of springs and dampers is a genuine "upgrade", and respect is due. There are several branded kits available, and most of the Ford specialists do their own. With a properly-sorted conversion, your Fiesta will handle even better, and you'll still be able to negotiate a set of roadworks without the risk of dental work afterwards. Actually, you may well be amazed how well the Fiesta will still ride, even though the springs are clearly lower and stiffer - the secret is in the damping.

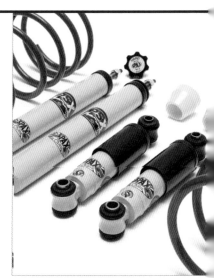

Some of the kits are billed as "adjustable", but this only applies to the damper rates, which can often be set to your own taste by a few minutes' work (don't mistake them for cheap coilovers). This Playstation feature can be quite a good fun thing to play around with, even if it is slightly less relevant to road use than for hillclimbs and sprints - but be careful you don't get carried away and set it too stiff, or you'll end up with an evil-handling car and a CD player that skips over every white line on the road!

Unfortunately, although you will undoubtedly end up with a fine-handling car at the end, there are still problems with suspension kits. They too are guilty of causing changes to steering geometry (have it reset) and once again, you're into guesswork territory when it comes to assessing your required drop for big wheels. Generally, most suspension kits are only available with a fairly modest drop (typically, 35 to 40 mm).

Suspension

Coilovers

If you've chosen coilovers, well done again - you're obviously a person who's serious about their slammage, and not short of the folding stuff, either! This is the most expensive option, and it offers one vital feature that the other two can't - true adjustability of ride height, meaning that you can make the finest of tweaks to hunker down on your new rims. This also gives you more scope to fit those big rims now, lower it down as far as poss, then wait 'til next month before you have the arches rolled, and drop it down to the deck. Coilovers are a variation on the suspension kit theme, in that they are a set of matched variable-rate springs (some have separate "helper" springs too) and shocks, but they achieve their adjustability in a way which might not guarantee as good a ride/handling mix as a normal kit.

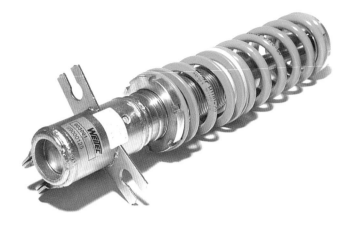

A coilover set replaces each spring and shock with a combined unit where the coil spring fits over the shocker (hence "coil" "over") - nothing too unusual in this, because so far, it's similar to a normal front strut. The difference lies in the adjustable spring lower seat, which can lower the spring to any desired height (within limits). For those bikers among you, have a good look at the rear suspension of a typical modern motorbike to get an idea of the coilover principle - the difference is that on a bike, the adjustable lower seat is used to control the spring "preload", compressing the spring and stiffening the suspension to cope with the weight of a pillion passenger. On a coilover, the spring seat simply sets the ride height.

Unfortunately, you cannae change the laws o' physics, and it has to be understood that coilovers are something of a compromise. Making a car go super-low is not going to be good for the ride OR the handling. Coilover systems necessarily have very short, stiff springs, and this can lead to the similar problems to those found with cheap lowering springs alone. If you go too far with coilovers, you can end up with a choppy ride, heavy steering and generally unpleasant handling (on bikes, incidentally, the rear gets very twitchy at full pre-load, one-up). Combine a coilover-slammed car with big alloys, and while the visual effect may be stunning, the driving experience might well be very disappointing. At least a proper coilover kit will come with shock absorbers (dampers) which are matched to the springs, unlike a "conversion" kit.

Coilover sets are developing all the time, and advances in progressive-rate springs mean that good-quality sets from known makers are well worth the extra over cheaper solutions.

Coilover conversion

Another option gaining ground among the less well-off is the "coilover conversion". If you really must have the lowest, baddest machine out there, and don't care what the ride will be like, these could be the answer. Offering as much potential for lowering as genuine coilovers (and at far less cost), these items could be described as a cross between coilovers and lowering springs, because the standard dampers are retained (this is one reason why the ride suffers). What you get is a new spring assembly, with adjustable top and bottom mounts - the whole thing slips over your standard damper. Two problems with this solution (how important these are is up to you):

1 Your standard dampers will not be able to cope with the uprated springs, so the car will almost certainly ride (and possibly handle) like a pig if you go for a really serious drop - and okay, why else would you be doing it?

2 The standard dampers are effectively being compressed, the lower you go. There is a limit to how far they will compress before being completely solid (and this could be the limit for your lowering activities). Needless to say, even a partly-compressed damper won't be able to do much actual damping - the results of this could be . . . interesting...

Front
Suspension

Suspension

Tricks 'n' tips

Don't start this job without coil spring compressors, or you'll be sorry! A torque wrench is also pretty important.

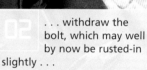

01 Loosen the wheel bolts, jack up the corner of the car you're working on, and take off the wheel. Make sure you've got an axle stand under a solid part of the car in case the jack gives out. Have a look in "Wheels 'n' tyres" for more info on jacking up. First, we've got to split the bottom balljoint, which is held in by a large Torx-headed through-bolt . . .

02 . . . withdraw the bolt, which may well by now be rusted-in slightly . . .

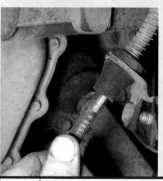

03 . . . then lever down on the lower wishbone to split the balljoint. It's rather vital that the car's well-supported at this point, as some effort will be needed - here, we're using our trolley jack handle (just make sure that nothing slips).

04 Now for some more fun. To remove the strut from the hub, we first need to undo the hub clamp bolt - note which way round the bolt is fitted when you take it out.

05 Next, there's a small bracket holding the brake fluid hose in place - easy enough to unbolt, but on our H&R coilovers, there was no mounting hole provided to refit it. As you can't leave brake hoses hanging (MOT failure), we'll deal with that problem later.

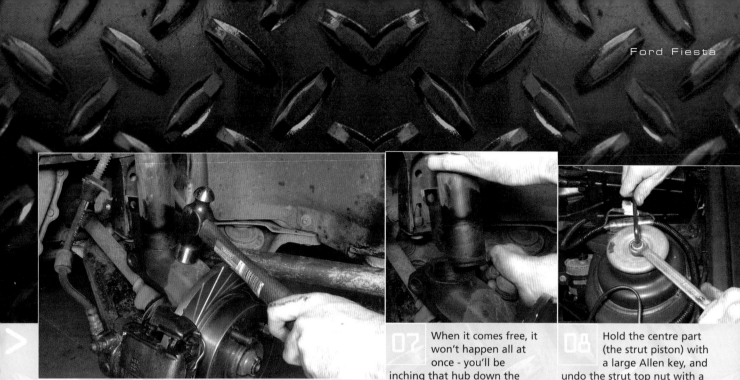

06 For those of you not into physical violence, look away now. These hubs are difficult to separate off the bottoms of the struts, but that's what's got to happen next. We advise lots of WD-40 (try not to get any near your brake discs), and probably, a lot bigger hammer than the one we show here.

07 When it comes free, it won't happen all at once - you'll be inching that hub down the strut, until finally, you'll have something that looks like this. Work the hub around so that the strut is free to drop down from above (once you've undone the top nut, which is the next bit). Support the hub on an axle stand.

08 Hold the centre part (the strut piston) with a large Allen key, and undo the strut top nut with a ring spanner. When the nut gets loose, get ready for the strut to descend rapidly onto the floor . . .

09 . . . or be prepared, and remove it in an orderly fashion from under the wheel arch.

10 Spring compressors are two clamps, each with two hooks, which sit over one of the spring coils. You won't get the hooks over the top and bottom coils, but try the next nearest. Fit the two clamps opposite each other . . .

11 . . . then tighten the big bolt up the middle of each to compress one side of the spring - this must be done evenly, one side after the other, or the un-clamped side might fly off.

Respect

For the next bit, you MUST use coil spring compressors ("spring clamps"). Medical attention will be required if you don't. Do we have to draw you a diagram? The spring's under tension on the strut, even off the car - what do you think's gonna happen if you just undo it? The spring-embedded-in-the-forehead look is really OVER, too.

12 Compress the spring carefully until the tension is off the top mounting. Now undo the inner nut, holding the piston rod with the same Allen key you used earlier . . .

13 . . . then take off the nut and the strut top mounting - you'll be needing both of these again.

14 Though you won't be needing the old spring again, take care when unwinding the spring clamps - that thing's under a lot of tension, so loosen them off in equal amounts until they go slack and can be removed.

15 Though it can be done at any time, we chose to set the lower spring seats on our coilovers roughly now - about halfway up the threaded section seemed as good a place as any, and it's how they were set in the box. Setting them equal on both sides before fitting will make life easier, too, later on - measure the thread above or below the two rings to set it accurately . . .

16 . . . and when you're happy, use the two special C-spanners provided to tighten the two rings against each other.

17 At least we don't need the spring clamps to put it back together. Fit the top mounting and the inner nut we removed from the old strut earlier . . .

18 . . . and tighten the nut using the Allen-key-and-ring-spanner method.

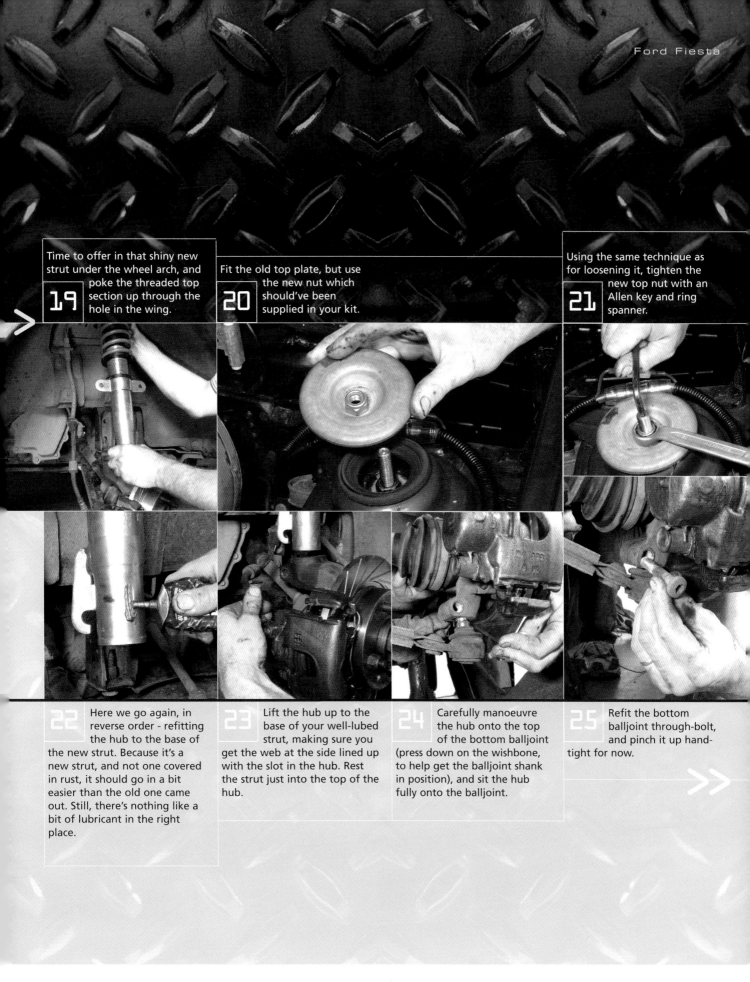

19 Time to offer in that shiny new strut under the wheel arch, and poke the threaded top section up through the hole in the wing.

20 Fit the old top plate, but use the new nut which should've been supplied in your kit.

21 Using the same technique as for loosening it, tighten the new top nut with an Allen key and ring spanner.

22 Here we go again, in reverse order - refitting the hub to the base of the new strut. Because it's a new strut, and not one covered in rust, it should go in a bit easier than the old one came out. Still, there's nothing like a bit of lubricant in the right place.

23 Lift the hub up to the base of your well-lubed strut, making sure you get the web at the side lined up with the slot in the hub. Rest the strut just into the top of the hub.

24 Carefully manoeuvre the hub onto the top of the bottom balljoint (press down on the wishbone, to help get the balljoint shank in position), and sit the hub fully onto the balljoint.

25 Refit the bottom balljoint through-bolt, and pinch it up hand-tight for now.

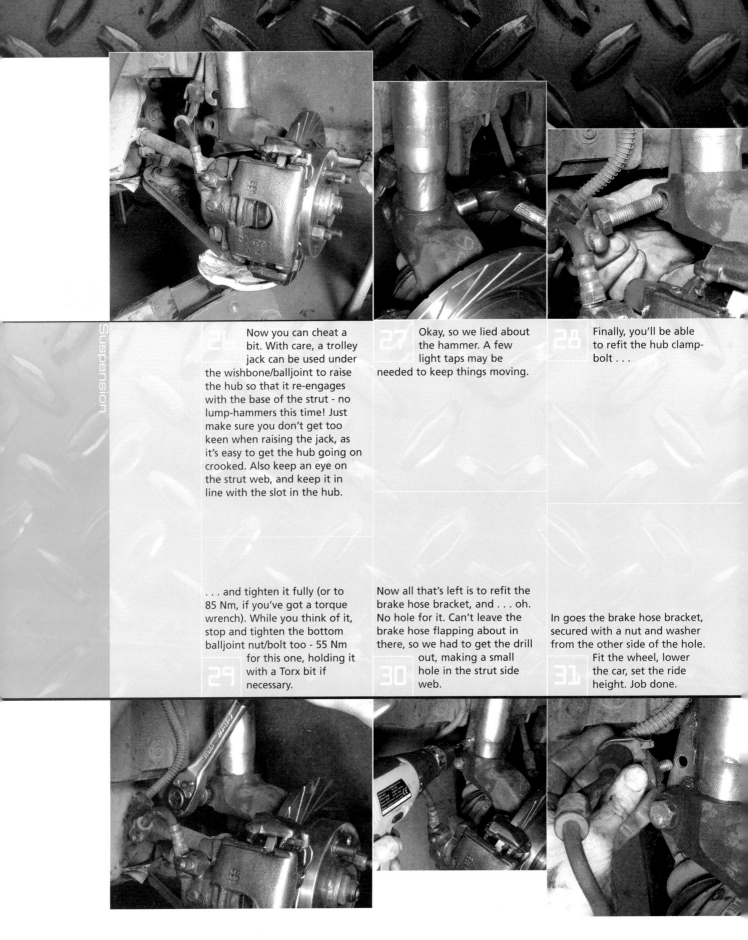

26 Now you can cheat a bit. With care, a trolley jack can be used under the wishbone/balljoint to raise the hub so that it re-engages with the base of the strut - no lump-hammers this time! Just make sure you don't get too keen when raising the jack, as it's easy to get the hub going on crooked. Also keep an eye on the strut web, and keep it in line with the slot in the hub.

27 Okay, so we lied about the hammer. A few light taps may be needed to keep things moving.

28 Finally, you'll be able to refit the hub clamp-bolt . . .

29 . . . and tighten it fully (or to 85 Nm, if you've got a torque wrench). While you think of it, stop and tighten the bottom balljoint nut/bolt too - 55 Nm for this one, holding it with a Torx bit if necessary.

30 Now all that's left is to refit the brake hose bracket, and . . . oh. No hole for it. Can't leave the brake hose flapping about in there, so we had to get the drill out, making a small hole in the strut side web.

31 In goes the brake hose bracket, secured with a nut and washer from the other side of the hole. Fit the wheel, lower the car, set the ride height. Job done.

Rear Suspension

Respect

Coil spring compressors ("spring clamps") are needed on the back suspension too, so don't be taking them back to the hire shop just yet.

01 Loosen the rear wheel bolts, then jack up one rear corner of the car, and support with an axle stand. Have a look in "Wheels 'n' tyres" for more info on jacking up. Remove the rear wheel, then place a trolley jack directly under the suspension arm and raise the rear arms slightly, so it's supported. Phew. Make sure that jack's secure, as the shock lower mounting bolt will be tight.

02 There's a "captive" (welded-in) nut at its other end, so only the bolt comes off. Captive nuts are prone to seizing - got any WD-40 ? Slide out the lower mounting bolt - it might be necessary to adjust the height of the trolley jack if you find that the bolt binds up as it's withdrawn.

03 Lower the jack temporarily, and unhook the bottom end of the shock absorber from the suspension arm. Put the jack back in place afterwards, and take the weight of the arm again.

04 Inside the boot, pull off the plastic cap fitted over the top mounting.

05 First of all, ignore the horizontal centre nut and bolt - if you undo that, things will go off bang (like the strut ejecting itself at high speed from under the wheel arch, straight on your foot). Undoing the two top nuts instead is far less dramatic . . .

06 . . . though you'll still end up with a strut on your foot if you're not careful.

113

07 Here we go with the spring clamps again, as we need that top mounting (and would quite like to live a bit longer). Fit the clamps either side of the spring . . .

08 . . . winding them up evenly until the pressure's relieved from the top mount . . .

09 . . . then undo the top mount nut and bolt. Sliding the bolt out should be easy - if it's at all tight, check that you really have taken the spring pressure off the top mounting before carrying on.

10 Take off that top mounting, and keep hold of the nut and bolt. Apart from the spring and shock, there's very little to throw out with this kit - everything gets recycled. How very green (and how very German? H&R suspension - hand-made in Germany).

15 . . . where you, or a willing accomplice, can do up the two nuts (also new) good 'n' tight, or 35 Nm in torque-wrench speak.

16 Looking good so far. Let's get back underneath, and slot the bottom end of the shock into its home in the suspension arm, ready for that lower mounting bolt. But what's this? It won't fit, and it appears no amount of "persuasion" is going to help.

17 Now we see the problem. The new strut's lower mounting bush is too wide, and not just a bit too wide - try 4 mm too wide (which is a lot to get rid of, as we're about to find out). Did someone say these babies are hand-made in Germany?

18 Filing off 2 mm from each side of the lower bush is a lot like listening to your Dad telling you how he fitted a whiplash aerial and mag wheels to his Capri, back in the 70s - tiresome and boring. But it's got to be done.

11 Fit the old top mount to the new strut . . .

12 . . . then secure it with the old bolt and a new nut (oh well, maybe not so green after all, but it's better the nut doesn't come undone). Do the nut and bolt up nice and tight (50 Nm).

13 As with the front suspension, it's worth setting the rear coilovers to the same ride height before fitting. We also thought a spot of our favourite lube (copper grease - accept no substitute) wouldn't be a bad idea, on the threads.

14 Now feed the strut up into the wheel arch, and poke the top mount through into the boot . . .

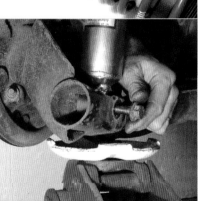

19 Now it fits, and the bolt slides home. Hey - we've got a Fiesta with modified suspension - how cool is that?

20 Tighten that bolt seriously tight - don't be shy, the torque setting's 120 Nm.

21 Now refit the wheel and lower the car. How low did you go? Adjusting the coilovers will probably mean taking the wheel off again, to get decent access, making it a pain-in-the-butt job - but majorly worth it. Use one of the spanners provided to set the spring seat, then use both together to tighten them against each other. We do not want a car which lowers itself as we go along, do we?

22 We know they look nice and shiny now, but one day your new struts might be suffering at the hands of the elements. You could do worse than painting a little Waxoyl onto those coilover threads, so you can still adjust them in six months' time. Just a thought.

Nasty side-effects

Camber angle and tracking

With any lowering "solution", it's likely that your suspension and steering geometry will be severely affected - this will be more of a problem the lower you go. This will manifest itself in steering which either becomes lighter or (more usually) heavier, and in tyres which scrub out their inner or outer edges in very short order - not funny, if you're running expensive low-profiles! Sometimes, even the rear tyres can be affected in this way, but that's usually only after some serious slammage. Whenever you've fitted a set of springs (and this applies to all types), have the geometry checked ASAP afterwards.

If you've dropped the car by 60 mm or more, chances are your camber angle will need adjusting. This is one reason why you might find the edges of your fat low-profiles wearing faster than you'd like (the other is your tracking being out). The camber angle is the angle the tyre makes with the road, seen from directly in front. You'll no doubt have seen race cars with the front wheels tilted in at the top, out at the bottom - this is extreme negative camber, and it helps to give more grip and stability in extreme cornering (but if your car was set this extreme, you'd kill the front tyres very quickly!). Virtually all road cars have a touch of negative camber on the front, and it's important when lowering to keep as near to the factory setting as possible, to preserve the proper tyre contact patch on the road. Trouble is, there's not usually much scope for camber adjustment on standard suspension, which is why (for some cars) you can buy camber-adjustable top plates which fit to the strut tops. Setting the camber accurately is a job for a garage with experience of modified cars - so probably not your local fast-fit centre, then.

Front strut brace

The strut brace (in theory) does exactly what it says on the tin, by providing support between the strut tops, taking the load off the bodyshell. In truth the strut brace has a marginal effect, so one of the reasons to fit one is for show - and why not? Strut braces can be chromed, painted or anodised, and can be fitted with matching chromed/coloured strut top plates - a very tasty way to complement a detailed engine bay.

01 The first thing to do is put the brace in its place. Lay it onto the strut tops, and see how much other stuff it interferes with. If you can, adjust the length of the brace using the centre "screw" until it sits nicely over both struts, then mark the position of the bolt holes. Yes, we know this is a Golf, but our Fiesta brace didn't fit!!! Bummer . . .

02 Now you've got to drill several dirty great holes in the top of the strut towers. As you've probably guessed, the strut towers ain't exactly the flimsiest metal parts to go attacking with your drill. This is one time above all when you must fit the bolts (at least loose) in each hole as you go! You might need a decent round file to adjust your holes slightly, to get them to line up.

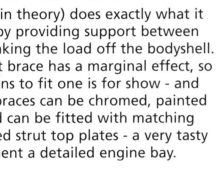

03 Seriously tighten the nuts and bolts on each strut top plate.

04 If you fit an adjustable brace like this one, turn the "screw" adjuster using a stout screwdriver in the hole provided, so that the brace forces outwards. Don't go too mad (the brace is only made of ally). When you're happy, hold the adjuster and tighten the large nuts either side of it.

05 Before you tighten up the bolts at either end of the brace, where it mounts onto the strut plates, check whether you can shut the bonnet without it touching.

09 Brakes

Remember the middle pedal?

It's the one next to the throttle - some people don't use it much. Uprating the brakes is actually a very easy bolt-on upgrade, but there are some points to consider.

Improving the brakes should also improve your chances of avoiding accidents, but insurance companies do not like performance brakes. You should still tell them, but be prepared for bad news. Fitting sporty brakes must automatically make you drive like Colin McRae - the clear implication is that if you need better brakes, you've either also uprated the engine (and not told them?), or you simply drive on the limit everywhere. Shame. We just like to know our cars will stop quickly. That, actually, might be another reason why they don't like better brakes - you stop better, but does the old dodderer behind you? Crunch.

Uprating the brakes will be a complete waste of time if you're a cheapskate on tyres. Cheap, no-name tyres or remoulds won't be able to translate extra braking power into actual vehicle-stopping power - they'll give up their grip on the tarmac and skid everywhere. Something like 90% of braking is done by the front wheels - ie the ones you steer with. If you consider that locked-up wheels also don't tend to steer very well, you'll begin to get an idea why good brakes and poor tyres are a well-dodgy mixture.

Groovy discs

Besides the various brands of performance brake pads that go with them, the main brake upgrade is to fit performance front brake discs and pads. Discs are available in two main types - grooved and cross-drilled (and combinations of both).

Grooved discs (which can be had with varying numbers of grooves) serve a dual purpose - the grooves provide a "channel" to help the heat escape, and they also help to de-glaze the pad surface, cleaning up the pads every time they're used. Some of the discs are made from higher-friction metal than normal discs, too, and the fact that they seriously improve braking performance is well-documented.

Cross-drilled discs offer another route to heat dissipation, but one which can present some problems. Owners report that cross-drilled discs really eat brake pads, more so than the grooved types, but more serious is the fact that some of these discs can crack around the drilled holes, after serious use. The trouble is that the heat "migrates" to the drilled holes (as was intended), but the heat build-up can be extreme, and the constant heating/cooling cycle can stress the metal to the point where it will crack. Discs which have been damaged in this way are extremely dangerous to drive on, as they could break up completely at any time. Only fit discs of this type from established manufacturers offering a useful guarantee of quality, and check the discs regularly.

Performance discs also have a reputation for warping (nasty vibrations felt through the pedal). Now this may be so, but of course, the harder you use your brakes (and ones you've uprated may well get serious abuse), the greater the heat you'll generate. Okay, so these wicked discs are meant to be able to cope with this heat, but you can't expect miracles. Cheap discs, or ones which have had a hard time over mega-thousands of miles, will warp. So buy quality, and don't get over-heroic on the brakes.

Performance pads can be fitted to any brake discs, including the standard ones, but are of course designed to work best with heat-dissipating discs. Unless your Fiesta's got an Escort Cosworth lump under the bonnet, don't be tempted to go much further than "fast road" pads - anything more competition-orientated may take too long to come up to temperature on the road, and might leave you with less braking than before!

Lastly, fitting all the performance brake bits in the world is no use if your calipers have seized up. If, when you strip out your old pads, you find that one pad's worn more than the other, or that both pads have worn more on the left wheel than the right, your caliper pistons are sticking. Sometimes you can free them off by pushing them back into the caliper, but this could be a garage job to fix. If you drive around with sticking calipers, you'll eat pads and discs. Your choice.

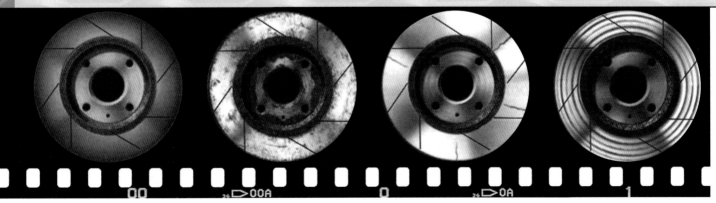

Brake
discs and pads

01 Loosen the wheel bolts, jack up the corner of the car you're working on, and take off the wheel. Make sure you've got an axle stand under a solid part of the car in case the jack gives out. Have a look in "Wheels 'n' tyres" for more info on jacking up. First job is to prise off the pad retaining spring.

02 On the inside of the caliper, prise out the two plugs covering the caliper guide bolt heads. You now need a large Allen key, to undo the two caliper guide bolts.

03 Lift away the caliper, complete with the inner brake pad . . .

Achtung!
Brake dust from old pads may contain asbestos. Wear a mask to avoid inhaling it. Dispose of old brake system components safely at your local waste recycling centre - don't just put them in the bin.

> **04** . . . which is clipped into the caliper piston, and easily un-clipped.

05 To get the new pads to fit, later on, you'll need to push the caliper piston back into the caliper. This will take some effort - here we are, using water-pump pliers (a tool well worth investing in, if you don't have a pair yet).

06 When you push the piston back in, there's a danger that the fluid reservoir will overflow. This can be avoided by connecting a one-man brake bleeding kit to the caliper bleed screw, then undoing the screw. Any fluid will now go into the bleed bottle, not back into the reservoir (this is also a neat way to remove the tired old fluid from the caliper). Tighten the bleed screw afterwards and dispose of the fluid safely.

07 Don't leave the caliper swinging by its hose - that's a good way to end up fitting a new hose (after you've lost your brakes completely, first). Tie it up with a cable-tie.

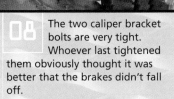

08 The two caliper bracket bolts are very tight. Whoever last tightened them obviously thought it was better that the brakes didn't fall off.

09 Remove both caliper bracket bolts, and lift off the bracket.

10 All that holds the disc in place (apart from the wheel bolts, when the wheel's on) is this clamp washer.

11 Lift off the old disc, and chuck it. It's highly unlikely you'll be removing a pristine brake disc, and worn ones are fit for only one place.

12 Before even thinking about offering on your new discs, take some time cleaning any rust and muck off the hub. If the new discs are prevented from going on completely square, you'll have a run-out condition (as the wheel turns, the disc will "wobble") which will wear out the new pads and the discs. Sound like fun?

13 The new discs must be thoroughly cleaned before you go any further. Most discs are coated with either a sticky or oily substance, to stop them rusting in the box - if this coating isn't removed, your first impressions might not be all that good! Any decent brake-cleaning solvent will do.

14 When you first take out your two shiny new discs, you might think they're identical. Chances are, they're not, and they should only be fitted with the grooves facing a certain way (this is the left front). Check your paperwork - our new multi-grooved discs were supplied with matching pads.

18 Copper brake grease is another must-have item when building brakes. Smear a little around the "corners" of the outer pad (the one without the legs) . . .

19 . . . then clip it into the caliper bracket, and smear some more grease onto the pad backplate.

20 Before clipping the inner pad into the caliper, it's worth smearing a little copper brake grease on the back of the pad, around the spring legs. Helps to prevent brake squeal.

21 Clip the inner pad into the caliper . . .

15 Refit the clamp washer to one of the wheel studs, to hold the new disc in place.

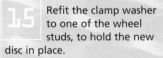

16 It's a good idea not to rely solely on that rather feeble washer when building up your new brakes, so temporarily slip on a couple of wheel nuts (just hand-tight) to do the job properly.

17 Pop the caliper bracket back in place (while it's off, it'd be a good move to clean it up, assuming you're going to paint your calipers later? Just a thought). The old bolts had thread-lock on them, so if you've got some fresh thread-locking fluid available, a drop on the threads is a good idea. A torque wrench is another good idea - set it to 60 Nm (otherwise, just do 'em up really tight).

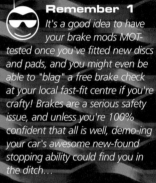

Remember 1
It's a good idea to have your brake mods MOT-tested once you've fitted new discs and pads, and you might even be able to "blag" a free brake check at your local fast-fit centre if you're crafty! Brakes are a serious safety issue, and unless you're 100% confident that all is well, demo-ing your car's awesome new-found stopping ability could find you in the ditch…

22 . . . then untie the caliper, and slip it back over the disc. This is where you find out if you've pushed the caliper piston in far enough.

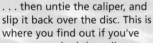

23 Fit the caliper guide bolts, and tighten them to the correct torque, too - this time, it's 25 Nm.

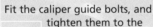

Remember 2
New pads of any sort need careful bedding-in (over 100 miles of normal use) before they'll work properly - when first fitted, the pad surface won't have worn exactly to the contours of the disc, so it won't actually be touching it, over its full area. This will possibly result in very under-whelming brakes for the first few trips, so watch it - misplaced over-confidence in your brakes is a fast track to hospital…

24 The final act is to clip on the pad retaining spring. Easy in theory. The spring ends fit into the holes in the caliper, and the top and bottom lugs spring back round the "ears" on the caliper bracket. Good luck! If you fitted a couple of wheel nuts to hold the disc on, don't forget to remove them before you try refitting the wheels. Don't those calipers look sad, against the posh brakes - how about a lick of paint?

Cool coloured calipers

One downside to fitting massive multi-spoked alloys is that - shock-horror - people will be able to see your brakes! This being so, why not paint some of the brake components so they look the biz, possibly to match with your chosen colour scheme (red is common, but isn't the only choice). Red brake calipers are often seen on touring cars, too, which may well be where the initial inspiration came from. Fiestas don't have rear discs, but painting the brake drums is acceptable under the circumstances - but then, do you paint 'em black, to de-emphasise them, or in your chosen colour for the fronts? It's all tough decisions, in modifying. If you're really sad, you can always buy fake rear discs… For the less-sad among you, Ford performance specialists may be able to sell you a rear disc brake conversion kit, but surely that's going a bit far, just to have red calipers front and rear?

Tricks 'n' tips
If you have trouble reassembling your brakes after painting, you probably got carried away and put on too much paint. We found that, once it was fully dry, the excess paint could be trimmed off with a knife.

Painting the calipers requires that they are clean - really clean. Accessory stores sell aerosol brake cleaner, which (apart from having a distinctive high-octane perfume) is just great for removing brake dust, and lots more besides! Some kits come complete with cleaner spray. Many of the kits advertise themselves on the strength of no dismantling being required, but we don't agree. Also, having successfully brush-painted our calipers, we wouldn't advise using any kind of spray paint.

We know you won't necessarily want to hear this, but the best way to paint the calipers is to do some dismantling first. The kits say you don't have to, but trust us - you'll get a much better result from a few minutes' extra work. We removed the caliper, pads and mounting bracket, then took off the disc, and re-mounted the bracket and caliper on their own. Have a look earlier in this section for more info. Doing it our way means no risk of paint going on the pads or disc.

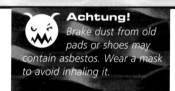

Achtung!
Brake dust from old pads or shoes may contain asbestos. Wear a mask to avoid inhaling it.

Painting **calipers**

01 Attack the rusty old caliper with a wire brush to lose the loose muck. If the caliper's black with brake dust don't breathe it in. Squirt on your brake cleaner, giving the caliper a good dose, and get wiping. Spraying alone will only loosen the muck, and a good scrub is the only answer. If you don't get it spotless, you'll get black streaks in the paint later, which looks really dreadful.

02 Even though we're sure you followed our advice, and removed everything except the caliper (!), there's still a bit of masking-up to do, like round the bleed nipples. How much masking you'll need depends on how big a brush you're using, and how steady your hand is!

03 Our Trillogy paint came in two tins - one paint, one hardener. Pour one into the other, stir, and you then have about four hours max before the paint sets hard in the tin, apparently - so get cracking! If you're painting calipers and drums, it's best to do all the prep work, and be totally ready to start painting at all four corners of the car, before you mix the paint.

04 Stick some card or paper under the brake, 'cos this paint's impossible to get off your driveway. And, er - get painting! Remember that you only have to paint the bits you'll see when the wheels are on. It's best to do more than one coat, we found. Follow the instructions with your kit on how long to leave between coats, but remember the time limit before the paint in the tin's useless. Wait 'til the paint's totally dry (like overnight, or longer) before reassembling.

Painting **drums**

01 At least there's no dismantling with drums - get the rear end jacked up, wheels off (see "Wheels 'n' tyres" if you need jacking info) and just get stuck in with the wire brush, sandpaper (to smooth the surface) . . .

02 . . . then it's spray on the brake cleaner and wipe thoroughly.

03 How much of the rear drums to mask up? Well, you definitely don't want any paint on the wheel studs, so they're a must. You can mask up the section of drum where the wheel bolts on - there's no point painting a bit which is covered by the wheel anyway - and maybe also the edge of the brake backplate (the bit that doesn't turn).

04 Painting the drums is much easier than the rather fiddly calipers. One piece of advice - for the drums, use a thicker, better-quality brush than the one they give you in the kit - you'll get a much smoother paint finish on the drums. Again, two coats of paint seemed like a good idea. Another good idea is to let off the handbrake and turn the drum half a turn every so often until the paint's dry. Nobody likes the runs, after all.

Interiors

The Fiesta dash is best described as functional. It does the job, and that's about it. It might have no style whatsoever, but at least it doesn't feel like it's about to fall apart, or come off in your hands, unlike certain popular French superminis we could mention. Yes, the Fiesta interior (with the exception of some really awfully-nice seat fabrics - not) is dull with a capital D. But you need suffer no longer, because the interior really is one area where most of the goodies are pretty easy to fit, and provided you go for one particular "theme" (rather than a mixture), the end result can certainly help you forget you're in a base model, if indeed you are...

To be fair to the Fester, not many standard interiors are anything to shout about, particularly when you compare them with the sort of look that can easily be achieved with the huge range of product that's out there. As with the exterior styling, though, remember that fashions can change very quickly - so don't be afraid to experiment with a look you really like, because chances are, it'll be the next big thing anyway. Just don't do wood, ok? We've a feeling it's never coming in, never mind coming back...

Removing stuff
Take it easy and break less

Many of the procedures we're going to show involve removing interior trim panels (either for colouring or to fit other stuff), and this can be tricky. It's far too easy to break plastic trim, especially once it's had a chance to go a bit brittle with age. Another "problem" with the Fiesta is that the interior trim is pretty well-attached (and the designers have been very clever at hiding several vital screws), meaning that it can be a pig to get off. They also seem to love using Torx

screws - invest in a set or Torx keys (like Allen keys), otherwise you'll come across one screw that won't come out using any other type of screwdriver. We'll try to avoid the immortal words "simply unclip the panel", and instead show you how properly, but inevitably at some stage, a piece of trim won't "simply" anything.

The important lesson here is not to lose your temper, as this has a highly-destructive effect on plastic components, and may result in a panel which no amount of carbon film or colour spray can put right, or make fit again. Superglue may help, but not every time. So - take it steady, prise carefully, and think logically about how and where a plastic panel would have to be attached, to stay on. You'll encounter all sorts of trim clips (some more fragile than others) in your travels - when these break, as they usually do, know that many of them can be bought in ready packs from accessory shops, and that the rarer ones will be available from a Ford dealer, probably off the shelf. Even fully-trained Ford mechanics aren't immune to breaking a few trim clips!

Door trim panel

You'll find plenty of excuses for removing your door trim panels - fitting speakers, re-trimming the panel, de-locking, even window tinting, so we'd better tell you how ...

Open the window, by whatever means you have. Now, if you've got wind-up windows:

a)   Prise the winder handle to open a gap between it and the circular disc behind. Work the edge of a piece of (clean) cloth/rag into **01** the gap behind the handle, from underneath.

b)   Using a "sawing" action, work the cloth side to side, and also pull the ends of the cloth upwards. It may take some time, but what you're trying to do is snag the ends of the spring clip holding the handle in place - when you do, the sawing action should work the clip up and off, allowing the handle to be pulled from the

splines. With patience, it DOES work - just watch for that spring clip flying off into the blue!

c)   Alternatively, use this special tool (no, don't panic, it's available v. cheap from Draper - tool code WWT) which makes removing the winder handles so much easier, and all professional-looking.

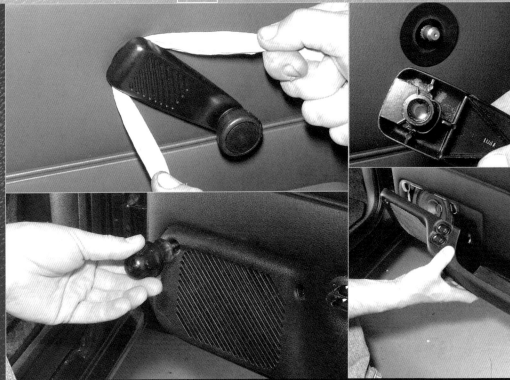

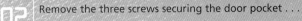

02 Remove the three screws securing the door pocket . . .

03 . . . and lift the pocket to unhook it from the door. Now pick up your shades/lighter/CDs from the floor, and remember to remove them first, next time!

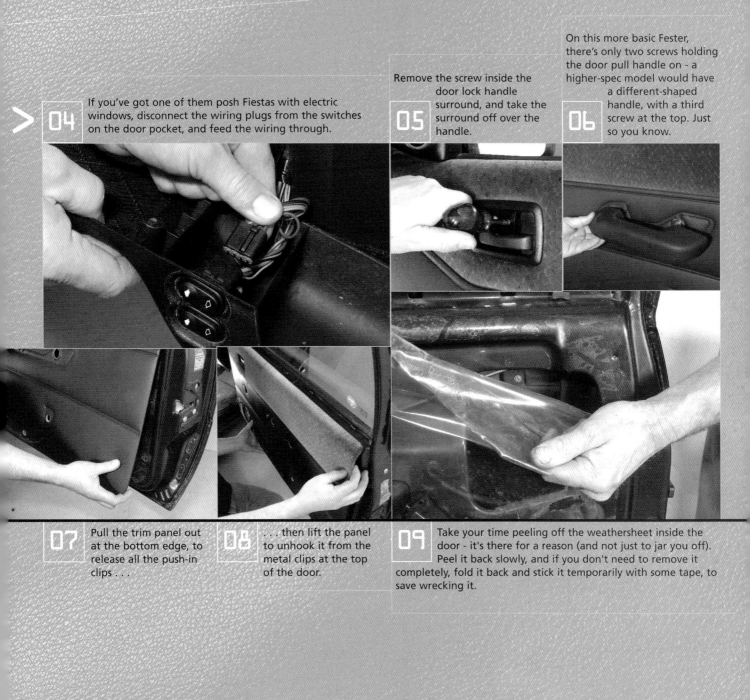

04 If you've got one of them posh Fiestas with electric windows, disconnect the wiring plugs from the switches on the door pocket, and feed the wiring through.

05 Remove the screw inside the door lock handle surround, and take the surround off over the handle.

06 On this more basic Fester, there's only two screws holding the door pull handle on - a higher-spec model would have a different-shaped handle, with a third screw at the top. Just so you know.

07 Pull the trim panel out at the bottom edge, to release all the push-in clips . . .

08 . . . then lift the panel to unhook it from the metal clips at the top of the door.

09 Take your time peeling off the weathersheet inside the door - it's there for a reason (and not just to jar you off). Peel it back slowly, and if you don't need to remove it completely, fold it back and stick it temporarily with some tape, to save wrecking it.

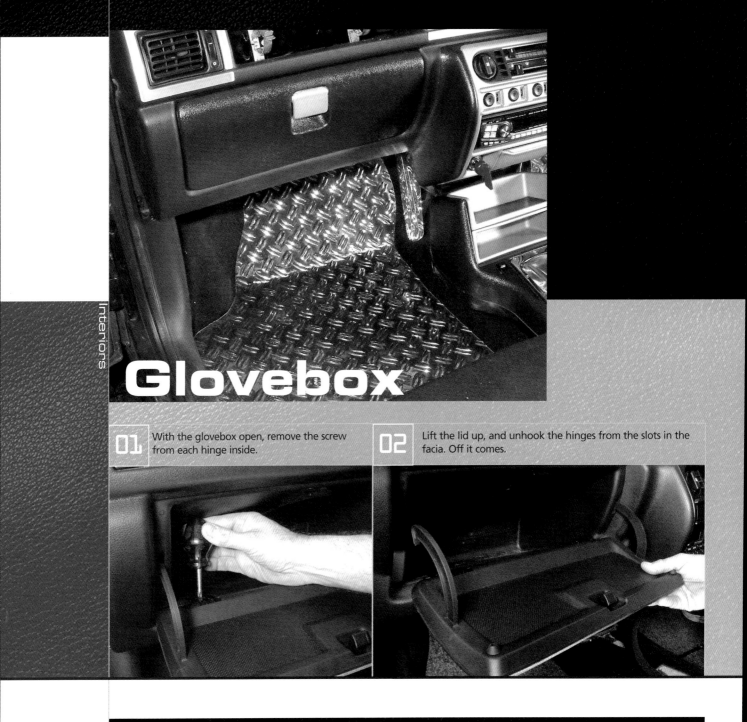

Glovebox

01 With the glovebox open, remove the screw from each hinge inside.

02 Lift the lid up, and unhook the hinges from the slots in the facia. Off it comes.

Dash vents

Good old Uncle Henry - he knows how to make cars easy to dismantle. These fellas just prise out - with some thought to not wrecking the dash, of course.

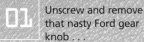

01 Unscrew and remove that nasty Ford gear knob . . .

02 . . . while that equally-unpleasant rubber gaiter unclips, for easy disposal.

03 Undo the two screws behind where the gaiter once sat . . .

04 . . . then remove the screw each side, down in the footwell.

Centre console

05 Now a short interlude, for those of you with a nice internal tailgate release switch. Push it out from underneath . . .

06 . . . and disconnect the wiring plug.

07 Lift the console up over the gear lever, and remove it. We colour-coded ours - the black blob looked much better in purple met.

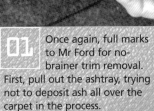

01 Once again, full marks to Mr Ford for no-brainer trim removal. First, pull out the ashtray, trying not to deposit ash all over the carpet in the process.

02 Now the radio's gotta come out. We doubt whether any of you still have a headset this sad, but what can we say? Our new ICE hadn't arrived at this point.

Centre control/
heater panel

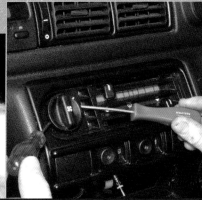

03 Rip out the wiring plugs, and that crummy old Ford set can go down to the car boot. Got its radio code?

04 There's now three screws to undo - one each side at the bottom, and one up inside where the ashtray came out.

05 Now pull off them heater knobs - first the fan switch, noting the two-screwdriver technique . . .

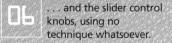

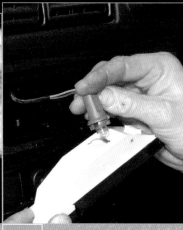

06 . . . and the slider control knobs, using no technique whatsoever.

07 Now, the whole heater control panel just prises out. Simple - and no nasty control cables to mess with, either . . .

08 . . . just this bulbholder to twist and pull out.

09 The only even-slightly-tricky bit. Use a small screwdriver to release the metal spring clips at the two top corners . . .

10 . . . before lifting out the centre panel.

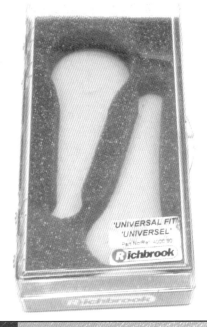
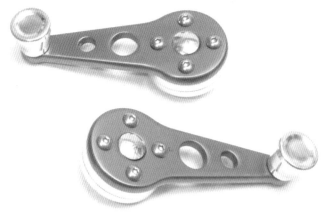

Window **winders**

01 Okay, so not everyone's got 'em, but if you do, you can't be happy with how they look! Removing the old ones can be a pain - use either of the methods described in "Door trim panel" earlier. Our new handles come in two parts - the base, which is secured to the regulator splines by a grub screw, and the handles themselves, which fit to the bases. So - slip the base onto the splines . . .

. . . and tighten the grub screw with the Allen key supplied. Worth getting it tight, or you'll suffer the embarrassment of it coming off in your hands (oo-er). With the window closed, look where the four holes for the handle will be - will this give you the desired "angle" for your handle? If not, re-position the base on its splines.

02

Offer on the handle, which colour-codes very nicely with this blue Fiesta we've borrowed for the occasion . . .

03

. . . and tighten the four screws. Now that's much better.

04

Other options

You might feel that all this anodised ally stuff's a bit tacky - after all, it has been done to death. That's how we felt, too, so we chose to remove a selection of bits from the door trim panel, and paint them instead. For more details on how to do this, see "Get the cans out" later on.

Door sill trims

01 You can get these in any colour you like, as long as it's chrome. One piece of advice, if you're planning major interior mods - fit the sill trims last. That way, there's less chance of scratching and scuffing 'em up during fitting the rest of the interior. Fitting isn't hard, but you will need a steady hand. First, peel up the ends of the rubber door seal (try and ignore the signs of rust).

02 Clean the sills with washing-up liquid (or, if they're really filthy, with wicked-strength solvent). Dry them off thoroughly before going any further.

03 Do a trial fitting before peeling off the backing paper, so you know what to line the trim up with on the car. Mark the end positions with a soft pencil, or masking tape, as a guide. Also note how far onto the sills the trims will come.

04 Peel off the backing from the sticky pads, and hold your breath.

05 The sticky on the sticky pads is very, very sticky indeed. Make sure you've lined up the sill trim accurately before finally smacking it in place, because it won't be coming off again without a fight! Hold the trim flat, angled towards you, line up the corners, then "roll" the trim down onto the sill.

06 Wipe over the tops of the trims, pressing down firmly to secure. If you find that the rubber door seal now covers the logo too much, fit the other sill trim slightly further out. Notice we did the passenger door first? Always a good idea - you can then make a better job of the one you and everyone else will see most of . . .

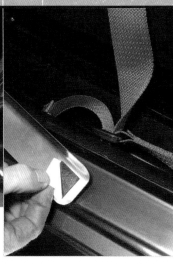

Anything but black?

The interior trim on the Fiesta at least hides its age well, and doesn't rattle much. And that's about it. Fortunately, there's plenty you can do to personalise it, and there are three main routes to take:

1) *Adhesive or shrink-fit film - available in various wild colours, carbon, ally, and, er... walnut (would you?). Probably best used on flatter surfaces, or at least those without complex curves, or you'll have to cut and join - spray is arguably better here. Some companies will sell you sheets of genuine carbon-fibre, with peel-off backing - looks and feels the part (nice if you have touchy-feely passengers).*

2) *Spray paint - available in any colour you like, as long as it's... not black. This Folia Tec stuff actually dyes softer plastics and leather, and comes in a multi-stage treatment, to suit all plastic types. Don't try to save money just buying the top coat, because it won't work! Special harder-wearing spray is required for use on steering wheels. Ordinary spray paint for bodywork might damage some plastics, and won't be elastic - good primer is essential. Make sure you also buy lots of masking tape.*

3) *Replacement panels - the easiest option, as the panels are supplied pre-cut, ready to fit. Of course, you're limited then to styling just the panels supplied.*

If you fancy something more posh, how about trimming your interior bits in leather? Very saucy. Available in various colours, and hardly any dearer than film, you also get that slight "ruffled" effect on tighter curves.

Filming your Fiesta

If you fancy creating a look that's a bit more special than plain paint colours, film is the answer - but be warned - it's not the easiest stuff in the world to use, and so isn't everyone's favourite. If you must have the brushed-aluminium look, or fancy giving your Fiesta the carbon-fibre treatment, there really is no alternative (apart from the lazy-man option of new panels, of course).

For our Fiesta, we chose to cover the dash top tray next to the instruments, and the passenger airbag.

01 Step 1 is cleaning and degreasing - see the advice in Step 1 for "Painting trim". On a heavily-grained finish, remember that the grain will show through thin film - this does slightly ruin the effect, and a deep grain means the film won't stick all over the surface. Not a good idea to go mad with the wet-and-dry (or Scotchbrite), to get rid of the grain - you'll destroy the surface totally.

If you're using thinner film, or covering a trickier object, a different approach is needed. Cut the film roughly to size, remembering to leave plenty of excess for trimming - it's also a good idea to have plenty to fold around the edges, because thin film has a nasty habit of peeling off, otherwise.

02 Our "real" carbon fibre sheet wasn't huge, so we took time getting the shape right before chopping it up. On the dash top, we used a piece of paper as a template, marking the shape of the tray recess with a pen . . .

Applying film

03 . . . while on the airbag, we made a template from wide strips of masking tape - mask over the whole front, then carefully trim out the shape of the airbag, and peel off.

Peel off the backing, being careful that the film stays as flat as possible. Also take care, when you pick the film up, that it doesn't stick to itself (our stuff seemed very keen to do this!).

07

08 Next, we gently warmed up both the panel, and the film itself. Just following the instructions provided, and who are we to argue?

09

04 Lightly tape the template onto the carbon sheet, and trim it out.

05 Peel off the backing, and stick it on straight (carbon fibre and brushed ally both look stupid if you get it stuck on un-straight, so take your time).

06 You now have one sexy-looking dash mat. Nice touch.

Bum notes

There are limitations to using film, and the quality of the film itself has a lot to do with that. We had major problems doing any kind of job with one particular make of brushed-aluminium-look film - it was a nightmare to work with, and the edges had peeled the next day. Buying quality film will give you a long-lasting result to be proud of, with much less skill requirement and lots less swearing. But it still pays not to be too ambitious with it.

10 Stick the film on straight - very important with any patterned finish. Start at one edge or corner, and work across, to keep the air bubbles and creases to a minimum. If you get a really bad crease, it's best to unpeel a bit and try again - the adhesive's very tacky, and there's no slide-age available.

11 Work out the worst of the air bubbles with a soft cloth - get the stuff to stick as best you can before trimming, or it'll all go horribly wrong. To be sure it's stuck (especially important on a grained surface), go over it firmly with the edge of your least-important piece of "plastic" - ie not a credit card.

12 Once the film's basically laid on, it's time for trimming - which as you've possibly guessed is the tricky bit. We found it was much easier to trim up the tricky bits once the film had been warmed up using a hairdryer or heat gun, but don't overdo it! Make sure you've also got a very sharp knife - a blunt one will ripple the film, and may tear it (one good thing about film is that blood wipes off it easily).

13 To get the film to wrap neatly round a curved edge, make several slits almost up to the edge, then wrap each sliver of film around, and stick on firmly. If the film's heated as you do this, it wraps round and keeps its shape - meaning it shouldn't try and spring back, ruining all your hard work.

Get the cans out

For the Fiesta interior, we found that the spray approach was the most successful - but that's just us, and for our chosen look. We tried (real) stick-on carbon-fibre for some things, otherwise our purple-and-silver look would've been a bit too much.

One thing to realise straight away with any painting process is that it's a multi-stage application. With the Folia Tec system, many of you apparently think you can get away just buying the top coat, which then looks like a cheap option compared to film - wrong! Even the proper interior spray top coat won't stay on for long without the matching primer, and the finish won't be wear-resistant without the finishing sealer spray. You don't need the special foaming cleaner - you could get by with a general-purpose degreaser, such as meths. Just watch the cloth doesn't suddenly turn black - if it does, you're damaging the finish! This might not be too important to you, as it's being sprayed over anyway, but if you take out the black too far on a part that's not being sprayed all over, you'll have to live with a cacky-looking white-black finish to any non-painted surface...

Providing you're a dab hand with the masking tape, paint gives you the flexibility to be more creative. With our interior, we decided to try colour-matching the exterior of the car - our Fiesta special edition came in purple metallic, which ain't bad for standard. Could we get ordinary car body paint to work on interior plastics? Only one way to find out...

Choice of paint's one thing, but what to paint? Well, not everything - for instance, you might want to avoid high-wear areas like door handles. Just makes for an easier life. The glovebox lid and heater panel are obvious first choices, as is the curvy instrument surround. The centre console's not lighting anyone's fire in standard Ford grey, so hit it with some spray too. The two console trays just pop out, giving you an easy opportunity to go for a contrasting colour (lots less masking needed) - just make sure whatever you're dismantling was meant to come apart, or it'll be out with the superglue instead of the cans.

Don't be afraid to experiment with a combination of styles - as long as you're confident you can blend it all together, anything goes! The top of the dash next to the instruments looked dull, as did our passenger airbag, but painting these would've been tricky, or just "too much". Out came the carbon-fibre sheet instead - neutral colours like this, or chrome, can be used to give a lift to dash bits that might look silly sprayed.

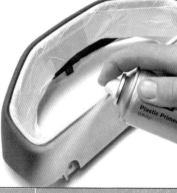

01 Clean up the surface to be sprayed, using a suitable degreaser - we used meths in the end, having tried some thinners initially (this started taking off the black). You must use something fairly evil, to get off any silicone-based products you or the previous owner may have used, as these are death to paint adhesion. If you're not going to paint the whole thing, don't degrease the whole thing, or you might ruin the finish on the black bits.

Painting trim

02 To be even more certain your chosen paint won't peel when the masking comes off, you need to get a bit brutal (no going back if you change your mind). You need some Scotchbrite, which is a bodyshop-spec scouring pad, available in several grades. Try a bodyshop or motor factors - it's not dear, and it's great for roughing-up any surface before spraying, giving the paint a "key". Cheaper alternatives may be available in Tesco's!

03 Mask up the bits you don't want sprayed, as necessary. Make sure you protect all surfaces from overspray - you can never do too much masking. After masking-up, give it a final wipe over with solvent, then apply a mist coat of primer - this is essential to help the paint "stick" to the plastic. Allow plenty of time for the primer to dry. If you're using ordinary spray as a topcoat (like we did), you'll need a special primer for plastics, which is available from places like Halfords.

04 Now for the colour coat - keep shaking the tin between passes, and don't bottle-out halfway across, or the can's nozzle will spit paint on, leaving nasty blobs in the finish. Also, don't try to cover the job in one coat, nor spray too close. You'll be a natural in the end - practice on some scrap card until you've mastered the technique (it's all in the wrist, y'know). Allow time for each coat to dry (a few minutes) before banging some more on.

05 Once you're happy that there's even coverage, let the last top coat dry, then slap on the sealer coat (or lacquer, in our case). This final coat is intended to improve wear-resistance (not much good if your carefully-applied paint rubs off in a few weeks, is it?). You should only need a light coat to finish the job.

06 Let the paint go tacky (rather than fully dry) before peeling off the masking, and take care when you do - if the paint's too dry, you'll peel some of the paint off with the mask! If you're in any doubt, take your steadiest hand and sharpest knife to the edges of the masking tape before peeling.

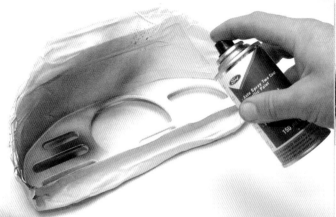

Ready-made panels

A far easier route to the brushed-ally or carbon look, pre-finished ("here's some we did earlier") panels are available from suppliers. As well as being far less aggro, with these, if the finish comes off, you can blame someone else! Bit of a limited range from some places - you'll probably still have to do some work to achieve your idea of a full-on interior, and will it all match? If you're determined that several panels are going to get "the treatment", don't be in too much of a hurry to take the easy option - mixing new panels with film is okay, but film with paint can look totally weak.

| 01 | Our Dash Dynamics kit came with its own wicked-strength degreaser/cleaner, so it seemed only fair to use it. Takes off paint inside, too, so it's pretty strong stuff. |

| 02 | A trial fitting isn't a bad idea, before peeling off the backing - it's sometimes not too obvious where the various kit bits are supposed to go! Next step is to heat up the area of dash you're about to transform. Doesn't hurt to warm the new trim pieces slightly, either - but we mean slightly (melted trim isn't a recognised style - yet). |

| 03 | Make sure your chosen trim piece is lined up nice and square, and keep it square as you press it on - the adhesive's usefully-sticky, meaning it will stay stuck whether you get it right or wrong. |

| 04 | And there we have it. Easier by far than trying to mask up and spray the edges of the vents (or the clock), which is what we'd probably have done otherwise. |

Gear knob

After the hassle we had getting the gaiter to fit neatly, we were hoping for an easier time with the new knob - and we got it. First, choose a rubber sleeve which is a nice tight fit (the way we like it) over the threaded end of the gear lever . . .

01

02 . . . then fit on the threaded collar which will screw up onto the new knob.

03 Loosen the grub screw on the new knob . . .

04 . . . then slide that on too.

05 Tighten the knob's grub screw . .

06 . . . then do up the collar below.

07 The final act is to tighten up the "laces" on your new gaiter, before basking in the reflective glory of all that lovely cool chrome.

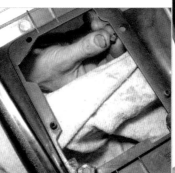

Interiors Gear gaiter

01 If you're changing the gaiter as well as the knob (and who wouldn't?), remove the centre console as described earlier (see "Centre console"). We're fitting a chrome surround as well as our new gaiter, so the four little plastic pegs around the gaiter hole will have to go - they just push out.

02 Our Richbrook gaiter looks the part, but wasn't really designed to work with our Fiesta console - some skill and judgement would be needed for a successful fitting, but we were up to the challenge. We decided first the elastic at the base of the gaiter would have to be cut through, before we'd get anywhere fitting it.

∧

At the back of the console hole are two sturdy plastic pegs. We thought we'd stretch the new gaiter over the two pegs, and **03** cut a hole in the leather at each corner to locate it.

With the gaiter now fitted at the back edge, the gaiter was stretched to see whether it **04** would reach the front corners. Yes - just.

The plan was to drill through the surround and console at the two front corners, using a drill bit slightly too big for our chosen screw, so the screw **05** wouldn't bite into the console - you'll see why in a minute.

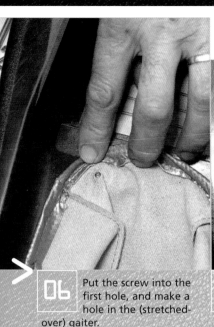

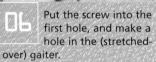

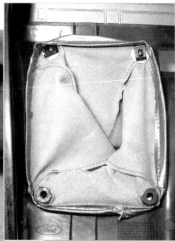

06 Put the screw into the first hole, and make a hole in the (stretched-over) gaiter.

07 Now, using a speed clip (and a large washer - optional), you can secure the chrome surround and the gaiter with one screw.

08 Repeat the process at the other front corner, and the gaiter's in place.

09 Before you drill and screw down the rest of the chrome surround, lift it up at the back edge, and drop in your two console retaining screws - otherwise, by the time the surround's in place, you won't be able to refit your console! Do we think of everything for you, or what?

Now you can drill and screw down the rest of the surround - remember to change the drill bit you used earlier for a slightly smaller one, as we want our screws to go into the plastic console, this **10** time.

When they're nearly all in, except the rear two corners, refit the console. You can tighten the console retaining screws through the rear corners of the chrome **11** surround, like this.

Of course, our two surround rear corner screws had nothing much to screw into, so we cheated, and glued the screws into the **12** holes.

And what a result! Who'd have thought fitting a gaiter could take so much **13** planning?

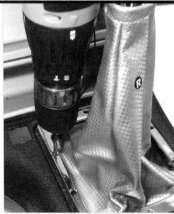

01 Your sexy new gear knob and gaiter's making the sad black stick behind look even worse, so get it sorted. The handbrake knob on the Fiesta just pulls straight off.

02 The gaiter's spectacularly easy to fit - just slip it over the lever . . .

03 . . . then part the flaps in the carpet, and tuck the base of the gaiter into it. If you find that the handbrake warning light won't go out easily after you've fitted your new gaiter, it's because there's too much gaiter been stuffed into the carpet, and you'll need to trim some away.

04 Now try your new handbrake knob for size. Ours was way too baggy a fit, so guess what? We had to wrap loads of gaffer tape round the lever, to take up the slack. If you resort to this method, the tape has to be put on evenly, which is easier than it sounds.

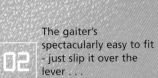

Handbrake
knobs & gaiters

05 Slide the new knob into place every so often, until it's a reasonably firm fit. If your tape doesn't go on evenly, the hole at the top of the new knob won't line up with the release button, and the button either won't work, or will jam up.

06 Another potential problem you might encounter - if the new knob doesn't go on far enough, you won't be able to press in the release button at the top. Which means the handbrake will be stuck on, and you won't be going very far. Using a pair of slip-joint pliers, crimp up the pressed-steel edges under the lever, to let the new knob slip further on.

07 When all is finally satisfactory, tighten up the grub screw below the knob . . .

08 . . . and tighten up the gaiter laces to complete.

Under neon light...

There's not a great deal to this, really - decide where you want 'em, where you're going to get a live and an earth (and a switch, if necessary), then fit 'em. We wanted our neons up under the dash, to light up the chequered footwells. The first thing we did was modify the neon mounting brackets by drilling some holes of our own . . .

So how much of a poser are you? How'd you like to show off all this funky chequer floor and sexy pedals to full effect, in the midnight hour? You need some neons, baby! Yeah!

02 . . . followed by some more holes under the dash.

Neon tubes don't exactly weigh lots, so threading a cable-tie **03** through our holes at each end was enough to hold them in place.

We didn't like the look of the switch which came with our neons, so we figured we'd be posh, and rigged our lights up to a Fiesta front foglight switch (from our local dealer).This meant the centre dash panel came out, and we fed our neon **04** wiring up behind it, trimming it to length.

 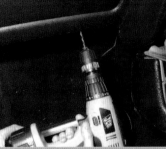 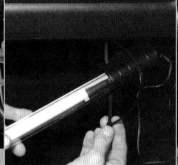 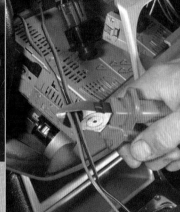

Our pair of neons would be fed by the same switch, so the two reds (live) and two blacks (earth) got joined **05** together, using two spade connectors . . .

. . . with the lives going to one "side" of our new switch (after testing with our meter, the two switch terminals we wanted were the copper-looking ones, rather than the brass ones, if you're interested). You can have a switch in either the **06** live or earth side of a circuit - it's up to you.

In our case, there's a handy live feed and earth available close by, in the wiring to the heater control panel illumination. The grey/yellow wire's the live, with brown earth. The live feed was cut into and connected **07** to the other side of our switch . . .

. . . and the earth joined to our two blacks from the neons. The heater illumination's only live when the sidelights are on, which seems appropriate - **08** neons show up best at night anyway.

 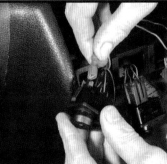 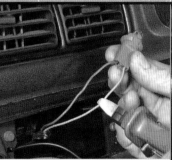 

Bum notes
: It appears that interior neons have recently been declared illegal, and this means, in the first place, you're unlikely to find anywhere that even sells them any more. Exterior neons have been illegal from day one. If you fit interior neons, make sure they're at least easily switched off, should you get pulled. Remember that driving at night with a brightly-lit interior makes it even harder to see out. Neons are best used for show purposes.

The personal touch – re-trimming

Okay, so you're definitely not happy with how the inside of your Fiesta looks, but you're not sold on any of the off-the-shelf options for tricking it up, either. You know how you want it to look, though, so get creative!

There are any number of upholstery companies in Yellow Pages, who will be able to create any look you want (we got one in our own back yard, almost - Pipers of Queen Camel, Somerset, who were extremely helpful in their contribution to this section). If your idea of Fiesta heaven is an interior swathed in black and purple leather, these guys can help. Don't assume that you'll have to go to Carisma, to get a car interior re-trimmed - they might well be the daddies at this, but any upholsterer worth the name should be able to help, even if they normally only do sofas!

Of course, if you're even slightly handy with things like glue and scissors, you might be able to use this one example we've got here as inspiration to get brave and DIY. An upholsterers will still be a useful source for your materials.

Seats

This is really one for a pro upholstery outfit - it involves pulling your seats to bits. For what it's worth, if you're determined to try trimming your seats on your own, our advice is to practise on a seat from the scrapyard first, 'til you've got the hang of it! Good luck, and we salute you!

For info on removing the standard seats, see "Are you sitting stylishly", further on.

Door trim panels

What applies to seats can also be applied to your door cards. If you're gonna DIY, practise on something old first. If you've had your seats trimmed, you'll obviously choose the same stuff for your doors - but here's a tip. Say you've gone for some nice bucket seats, in maybe a red-and-black pattern cloth. Would be nice to match your seats to the door panels here, too, wouldn't it? So how about doing what we did for another of our project cars, and contacting the seat manufacturer for a few square metres of the actual cloth they use to make the seats with? Should match then, shouldn't it? Hand material and cash to your upholstery experts, and wait. Or do it yourself.

01 We wanted a lush look for our sad Fiesta door trim panels, so we engaged the services of our local upholstery experts, Pipers. Following their advice, we went for a combination of alcantara and leather - nice. Here, the leather and its foam backing (to give a padded effect) are being trimmed to size.

02 Who'd have thought it? Spray glue in da house. Obviously, the leather's going to be stitched on eventually, but that's just for effect - this is what really locates everything, and who's to know?

03 With the foam backing in place, the leather gets the spray glue treatment too. On the alcantara, our man folded the material over a carefully-cut section of card, to give a nice edge where it meets the leather - the whole lot is then glued and stitched into place later.

04 A little warmth helps it all to go off that bit sooner, and removes any annoying creases.

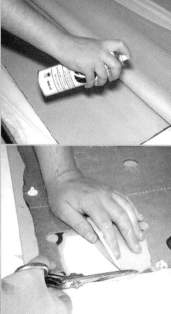

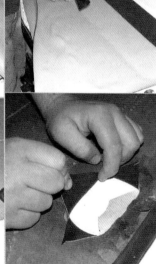

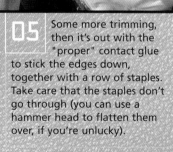

05 Some more trimming, then it's out with the "proper" contact glue to stick the edges down, together with a row of staples. Take care that the staples don't go through (you can use a hammer head to flatten them over, if you're unlucky).

06 No upholsterers would be complete without the sewing machine. Well really - did you think stitching was just stuck on, or something? Don't overlook the creative possibilities with the stitching process - there's various stitch styles and thread thicknesses, as well as complementary or contrasting colours, to consider.

07 Don't forget that your stylish new door trim still needs to be practical. Holes for things like speakers . . .

08 . . . and door lock handles will be a bonus. Carefully slice some neat holes for re-mounting the door pull, window winder (and in our case, tweeters) at the same time. So go on - have a go, and see what you can create. The worst that could happen is you have to go back to the boring grey original. Practise on any door trim panel from a scrapyard first, if it helps.

Are your dials all white?

White dial kits are not impossible to fit, but you will need some skill and patience not to damage the delicate bits inside your instrument panel - the risk is definitely worth it, to liven up that dark and depressing Fiesta dash, anyway. Just make sure you get the right kit for your car, and don't start stripping anything until you're sure it's the right one - look carefully. Most dial kit makers, for instance, want to know exactly what markings you have on your speedo and rev counter. If they don't ask, be worried - the kit they send could well be wrong for your car, and might not even fit. We were surprised to find that the standard Fiesta speedo goes to 140 mph - yeah, dream on!

If you haven't yet removed the steering wheel - don't! You don't really need to for this. Of course, if you're fitting a new wheel AND a dial kit, it's a good plan to do both at once - but are you that organised? First, remove two

01 cross-head screws (one either side) below the instrument cowl . . .

02 . . . and lift the cowl out, past the wheel.

03 Now there's four screws holding the clocks in - two above, and two below.

04 Unfortunately, that's not all there it to it - the speedo cable's gotta come off next. Pull the clocks out to give you some room . . .

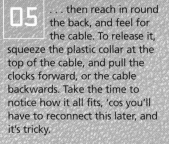

05 . . . then reach in round the back, and feel for the cable. To release it, squeeze the plastic collar at the top of the cable, and pull the clocks forward, or the cable backwards. Take the time to notice how it all fits, 'cos you'll have to reconnect this later, and it's tricky.

06 With the speedo cable off, all that remains is the main wiring plug - pull this out, and the clocks are at your mercy (cue evil laugh).

07 Take out the two bulbs at the top - these just twist and pull, like all the instrument panel bulbs . . .

08 . . . and unhook the printed circuit. Carefully.

09 Now use a small screwdriver to release the two plastic catches . . .

10 . . . and separate the lens cover from the clocks themselves.

11 This next bit's optional, and only for the brave - or mad. We wanted to colour-code the instrument surrounds, which sounds easy, but to get to it for spraying, the clear lens has to come off - and Ford didn't help by gluing it on. With some heat applied, careful use of the small screwdriver (and even a sharp knife, from inside) . . .

12 . . . the glue let go, and the lens eventually came away. Mostly undamaged. It's glued at the bottom corners (about four spots per side) and along the top edge. Just make sure the cracking noises you'll hear is the glue detaching, not the lens cracking.

>>

Let's tackle the big dials first. Hold the speedo needle up, and pull out the needle's stop peg with a pair of pliers. **13**

When you're ready, peel off the backing strips . . . **14**

. . . then hook the dial under the tip of the needle, and slide it up. That's the easy bit. **15**

The tricky bit is getting the centre hole to clip down over the needle hub - for that, you need at least one screwdriver to press down firmly on the dial. Keep the dial curved between your fingers, to help it clip down, and to stop the stickies from sticking. This is the point where you're in greatest danger of bending the needle, so keep your cool. **16**

17 Still keeping the dial curved to stop it from sticking, line it up with the dial underneath - on the speedo here, use the mileometer to check the new dial's straight.

18 Another confirmation that you've got the new dial on straight is that the stop peg hole should line up. Pop the peg back in, and feel smug - you've nearly white-ed your first dial.

19 Wipe over the front of the dial with a cloth, pressing firmly to stick it in place.

20 The fuel and temperature gauges are trickier, because you've got to do them both together, but don't panic. First, set the fuel gauge needle to about half-full, and peel off the backing bits.

21 Feed the temp gauge centre hole over the temp needle first . . .

22 . . . then slip the fuel gauge into position, keeping the pair of new dials curved between your fingers to stop them sticking prematurely. This is quite a problem with this part of the white-dialling - keep a small screwdriver handy, to lift the new dials off until they're on straight.

23 When it's all lined up, use the cloth again to stick the dials down firmly.

24 Now spot the deliberate mistake. Your new dials are white, and so are the needles. D'oh! Slip some paper behind the needles, mask up the needle edges for neatness, and get out the touch-up stick. We went for the Ford purple to match the car, and our newly-sprayed instrument surrounds. Red's a good bet too.

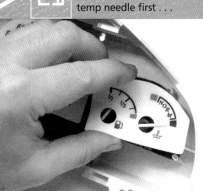

25 Those of you who were paying attention earlier will remember we un-glued our instrument lens, to colour the surround. So now we're gluing it back on. You could use superglue, but we chose black silicone, which doesn't go-off white and show through the clear plastic. Just a thought.

26 Press the lens back on, and wait. Black silicone isn't very sticky, and we left ours taped-down overnight.

27 And here's the result - now tell us all the effort wasn't worth it. With the instrument cowl colour-coded too, it's looking pretty saucy. Of course, purple might not be your thing, but you get the idea...

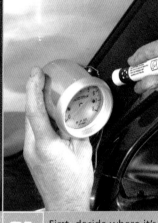

Rev counter

Those of you with the sports Fiesta models, who already have a rev counter (or tacho), ignore this bit. Or perhaps not - you might want a tidy little tacho mounted somewhere other than in the instrument podule. If so, we're here to help. Of course, you don't need a sports Fester to know how fast your engine's turning (and no, we're not trying to slag off the loud 'n' rattly old HCS engine) - even LX models came with a rev counter, but having a separate gauge mounted on the A-pillar, centre of the dash or centre console adds hugely to the racing look.

01 First, decide where it's going to go. Tucked into the centre console is cool, as is mounted on the centre of the dash, but we wanted the challenge of fitting to the A-pillar. Hold it up, and mark where the hole needs to be.

You could drill with the A-pillar trim fitted, but you run the risk of drilling through the wiring which sits behind. Better to remove the trim panel (which is described in the section on alarm fitting) and drill **02** the hole through, off the car.

The rev counter's mounted in place using a self-tapper and a speed clip - we were surprised just how sturdy a fixing we got, on the apparently-flimsy trim panel. Don't forget to set the toggle switch on the back of the gauge according to the number of cylinders (4, 6 or 8) **03** your Fiesta has. Anyone done a V8 conversion? Didn't think so.

∧

Now out comes our JCB again, **04** for another hole - this time for the rev counter wiring . . .

05 . . . which then gets fed through the panel - to go - where?

06 Our rev counter had three wires - live (red), earth (black) and signal (green). The signal wire comes from the ignition coil pack (no distributor on Mk 3 Fiestas), and can be traced to a large plug on the back of the instruments. You could trace the wire (also green) from the coil pack under the bonnet, but it means running your own wire through into the car. Either way, the rev counter wiring was too short, so we soldered on some extra . . .

07 . . . before feeding it down the A-pillar, through behind the driver's vent (these prise out) and in behind the instruments (removed as described in "Are your dials all white?"). Only the red and green wires were put through . . .

08 . . . we already had an idea where we'd get a good earth from - the same place as we used for the alarm.

Now repeat the same process with an ignition live wire - according to our Haynes wiring diagram, another of the instrument cluster wires (a black/yellow) will be suitable. Makes sense to take the wiring from the same general area. Start 'er up, and let rip. Funkier gauges come with an adjustable change-up light - where will you set yours?

As we said earlier, we were looking for a green wire on the instrument cluster wiring plug. Looks like we found it. Even though our car didn't have a tacho as standard, the wire's still there. Cut it through . . .

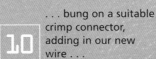

. . . bung on a suitable crimp connector, adding in our new wire . . .

09

10

11 . . . and join it back up.

12

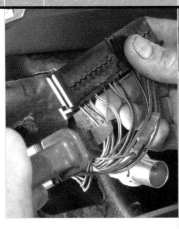
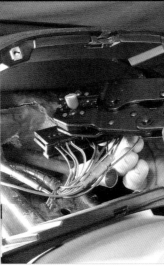

Racing starts

Like to have a racing-style starter button on your Fiesta? Read on! A very cool piece of kit, and not too bad a job to wire up - the most difficult bit's deciding where to mount the button (somewhere easy to get at, but still in full view so's you can impress your passengers!).

The idea of the racing starter button is that the ignition key is made redundant, beyond switching on the ignition lights (it'd be a pretty negative security feature, if you could start the engine without the key at all).

This is one job where you'll be messing with big wires, carrying serious current - more than any other electrical job, don't try and rush it, and don't skimp on the insulating tape. Do it properly, as we're about to show you, and there's no worries. Otherwise, at best, you'll be stranded - at worst, it could be a fire.

01 Our starter button was supplied by Richbrook, but the instructions here should be good for most makes. First, DISCONNECT THE BATTERY. You may have ignored this advice before. You may not. Don't do so now.

02 Before we got to the "tricky" wiring, we did the easy bit - mounting the button itself. We put ours in the right-hand switch blank below the heater controls, which meant the dash centre panel had to come out, as we covered in "Centre control/heater panel" earlier on. Prise out the blanking plate, and drill a hole big enough for the switch to fit.

03 The switch is secured from behind with a large nut. Once the switch is roughly in place, its wiring can be fed across the car towards the ignition switch.

04 Remove the column shrouds as described in "Wheely cool", later on in this section. Unfortunately, that's not the end of the dismantling - the instruments have to come out too, as described in "Are your dials all white?" earlier. What we're after behind the clocks is the main wiring plug, or more specifically, the blue wire on the main plug (which works the ignition/alternator warning light). Cut into this wire . . .

05 . . . and use a bullet connector to tap in the brown wire from the starter button.

06 Now working below the steering column, trace the wires from the ignition switch back to the large connector plug. Unclip the plug from under the column, and separate the two halves.

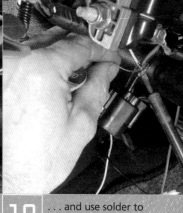

07 Cut the black/blue wire as shown, and join it to the blue wire from the new relay. Notice we say "cut" rather than "cut into" - once the black/blue wire has been cut, leave it cut. This is the starter solenoid wire, and leaving it cut means that the ignition key will no longer start the engine, which is the whole point of a starter button.

08 Now we need an ignition live feed, to join to the white wire which goes to one side of the fuseholder. Slice off a little insulation from the black wire on the back of the ignition switch plug . . .

09 . . . then strip the end from the white wire, wrap the wire around the stripped section of black . . .

10 . . . and use solder to make the joint permanent. Wrap the finished joint with insulating tape.

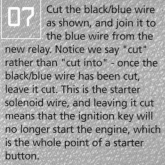

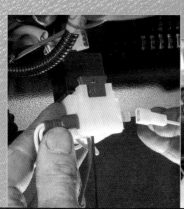

11 Take the white wire from the starter button, and the white wire from the relay, and join them together using a female spade connector. Plug this onto one side of the fuseholder, then join on the white wire which you just soldered onto the ignition live, using another spade connector.

12 The green wire from the starter button goes to a convenient earth point - we extended our green wire, and ran the earth to this bolt, on the right-hand side of the steering column.

13 The relay and fuseholder must be mounted somewhere reasonably easy to get at - our experience has been that the fuses can have a nasty habit of blowing. We tucked ours just under the dash, below the column, but we needed a screw hole first . . .

14 . . . before tucking the new assembly up and out of sight (but not out of reach). Apply one finger, and the racing Fiesta bursts into life. Fantastic stuff.

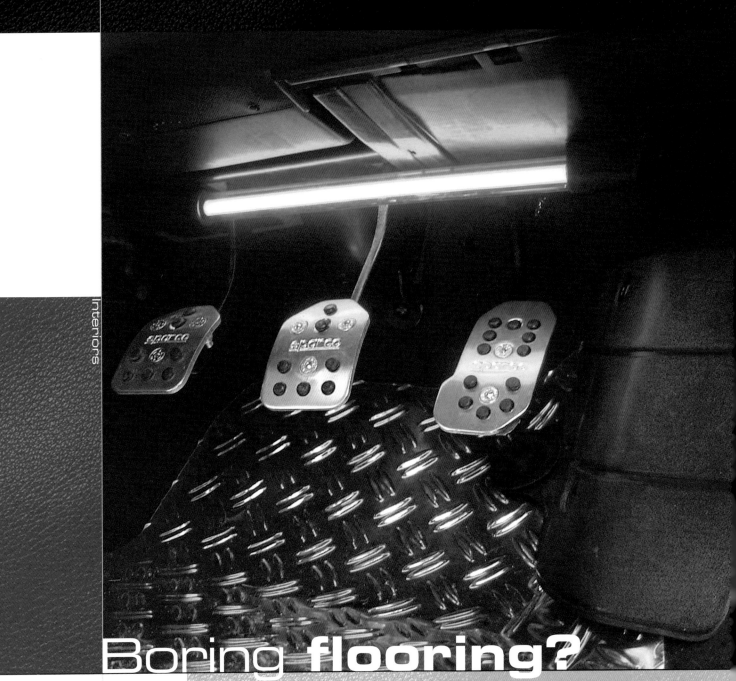

Boring flooring?

Alright, so carpets have always been a dull colour because they have to not show the dirt - when was the last time you heard of a car with white carpets? What goes on the floor needn't be entirely dull, though, and can still be easy to clean, if you're worried.

Ripping out the old carpets is actually quite a major undertaking - first, the seats have to come out (you might be fitting new ones anyway), but the carpets and underfelt fit right up under the dashboard, and under all the sill trims and centre console, etc. Carpet acts as sound-deadening, and is a useful thing to hide wiring under, too, so don't be in too great a hurry to ditch it completely.

A popular halfway measure to a fully decked-out chequerplate interior, tailored footwell 'plates are available from some suppliers - these are a big improvement on even the coolest carpet mats, and because they're a tailored fit, they should stay put, not slide up under your pedals.

Chequerplate is the current fashion in cool flooring, and it's easy to see why it'll probably have an enduring appeal - it's tough but flexible, fairly easy to cut and shape to fit, has a cool mirror finish, and it matches perfectly with the racing theme so often seen in the modified world, and with the ally trim that's widely used too.

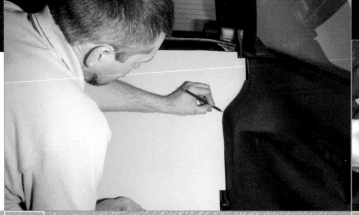

01 Aren't we lucky? We seem to have excessive amounts of chequerplate left over, and no rear seats. Perfect conditions for creating a back seat masterpiece. We unscrewed our backrest cushions, re-installed the metal backing, then made up a cardboard template of its shape inside the car.

02 Using our template, we marked up some hardboard (you could use thin MDF), then jigged out our backrest shape.

03 The MDF floor was going to sit up against the base of the backrest, but needed a "shelf" to rest on. We cut up three lengths of ally angle-plate we had lying about, then drilled and fitted them to the seat backrest.

Chequered
rear deck

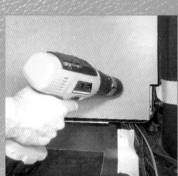

04 Then it's drill and fix the hardboard to the backrest . . .

05 . . . before offering in a sheet of chequer, and trimming it to shape.

06 The plate can be screwed-and-glued to the hardboard, but at the top, we used rivets for a tougher look. The top edge of the chequer just tucked inside the rolled top edge of the seat, once it had been trimmed to the right profile.

07 Our sheet of chequer wasn't quite wide enough to do the whole seat, but it was no trouble to trim up a small extra piece each side (matching the pattern's difficult, though) and stick it on with Evo.

Tips 'n' tricks
If you're completely replacing the carpet and felt with, say, chequerplate throughout, do this at a late stage, after the ICE install and any other electrical work's been done - that way, all the wiring can be neatly hidden underneath it.

Unless you buy real ally chequer, what you'll get is actually plastic, and must be supported by mounting it on hardboard. Take one of the lovely Ford mats which your car may have, and use it as a template to mark the shape onto the hardboard

01 (you could always make a template from some thin card).

With the shape marked out, it's time for the jigsaw - next to a cordless drill, this has to be one

02 of the most useful tools ever invented for the modder.

To make the hardboard fit better into the footwells, score it at the bend where it

03 goes up under the pedals . . .

The halfway-house to a fully-plated interior is to make up your own tailored mats (hell, you can buy ready-mades if you're not allowed to play with sharp knives).

Fully-tailored
chequer mats

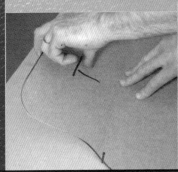   

04 . . . then carefully "fold" the hardboard back to the required shape - trust us, this will make your new chequer mats fit superbly.

05 Not unlike this in fact. Try your hardboard mat in place, and trim the corners and edges as necessary to get it fitting as flat as poss.

06 Now you can use your hardboard as a template, for cutting out the chequer. Try to make the chequer fractionally bigger overall than the hardboard, so you don't see the wood edge (you shouldn't anyway, if your board is a tidy fit). Stick the chequer to the board, using some decent glue - spray glue's convenient, but usually not quite up to the job. You can't beat good old brush-on Evo-Stik (and no, we're not being paid to say that).

08 Do it right, and you too can have a floor like this - looks sweet, and the mats don't slip. Sorted.

One rather unfortunate feature in a lesser Fiesta's interior décor is that you get a grandstand view of the ugly black heater box, every time you get in. There it is, staring back at you from the footwell. Help is at hand, however, in the form of some chrome footwell trim plates. These won't fit in with everyone's chosen interior theme, but they sure did with our silver pedals and chequer floor.

01 When we offered our plates into place, it soon became obvious that the heater box would need modifying. We chopped off this little right-angled flange in the plastic, which is actually used to send the air supply to the driver's feet, to let our plate sit in better.

02 Mark where the holes need to be, ensuring that we get maximum coverage of the ugly heater . . .

Footwell trim plates

03 . . . then get the drill out. This drilling operation's not remotely scary - you're in no danger of hitting the heater matrix, drilling through the centre console . . .

04 Our plates came with some very bizarre-looking screw fixings, which are fitted in two parts - the outer part fits to the large hole at the two corners of the plate, and the whole lot's secured using a very small screw in the centre.

05 Repeat the drilling process at the top corner, now holding your breath in case any sudden leaks develop. We're very close to the heater matrix here. Only drill a shallow hole - don't press too hard, and be ready to stop.

06 Turn on the neons, and you could charge for admission. Haven't got neons yet? Get some.

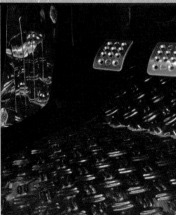

Wheely cool

A new steering wheel is an essential purchase as a first step to personalising your Fiesta. It's one of the main points of contact between you and the car, it's sat right in front of you, and the standard ones are dull as a very dull thing. Sort it out now!

Don't be tempted to fit too small a wheel if you've not got power steering. Fiesta steering isn't exactly heavy, but a tiny-rimmed steering wheel will make manoeuvring very difficult, especially with fat tyres.

One bit of good news is that, once you've shelled out for your wheel, it may be possible to fit it to your next car, too. When you buy a new wheel, you usually have to buy a boss (or mount) to go with it - the mounts are less pricey, so one wheel could be fitted to another completely different car, for minimum cost.

A trick feature worth investigating is the detachable wheel/boss. This feature comes in handy when you park up and would rather the car was still there when you come back (something most people find a bonus). It's all very well having a steering wheel immobiliser or steering lock, but I doubt many thieves will be driving off in your car if the steering wheel's completely missing! Also, removing the wheel may remove the temptation to break in and pinch . . . your wheel!

A word about **airbags**

Many Fiestas will have a driver's airbag fitted to the original wheel. So far, the market for replacement wheels with airbags doesn't seem to have materialised, so fitting your tasty new wheel means losing what some people think is a valuable safety feature.

But the problem with airbags doesn't end with simply disconnecting the damn thing, because all that'll happen then is your AIRBAG warning light will be on permanently. Not only is this extremely irritating, it'll also be one of the reasons your newly-modded motor will fail the MOT (having the airbag itself isn't compulsory, but if the warning light's on, it's a fail - at least at the time this was written). Two ways round this - either take out the clocks (see the section "Are your dials all white?") and remove the offending warning light bulb, or bridge the airbag connector plug pins with two lengths of wire attached to either side of a 5A fuse. Bridging the pins this way "fools" the test circuit (which fires up every time you switch on the ignition) into thinking the airbag's still there, and the warning light will go out as it should.

Disabling the airbag is yet another issue which will interest your insurance company, so don't do it without consulting them first. We're just telling you, that's all.

Airbags are expensive to replace (several £100s), and are classed as an explosive!!! Funny, that - for a safety item, there's any number of ways they can cause injuries or damage if you're not careful - check this lot out:

a Before removing the airbag, the battery MUST be disconnected (don't whinge about it wiping out your stereo pre-sets). When the battery's off, don't start taking out the airbag for another 10 minutes or so. The airbag system stores an electrical charge - if you whip it out too quick, you might set it off, even with the battery disconnected. True.

b When the airbag's out, it must be stored the correct way up.

c The airbag is sensitive to impact - dropping it from sufficient height might set it off. Even if dropping it doesn't actually set it off, it probably won't work again, anyway. By the way, once an airbag's gone off, it's scrap. You can't stuff it back inside.

d If you intend to keep the airbag with a view to refitting it at some stage (like when you sell the car), store it in a cool place - but bear in mind that the storage area must be suitable, so that if the airbag went off by accident, it would not cause damage to anything or anyone. Sticking it under your bed might not be such a good idea.

e If you're not keeping the airbag, it must be disposed of correctly (don't just put it out for the bin men!). Contact your local authority for advice.

f Airbags must not be subjected to temperatures in excess of 90°C (194°F) - just remember that bit about airbags being an explosive - you don't store dynamite in a furnace, now do you? Realistically in this country, the only time you'll get that hot is in a paint-drying oven.

Fitting a
Momo wheel

Fiestas without airbags have it easy - just prise out the Ford badge, and skip to the bit where we undo the steering wheel nut. If you've got an airbag, the column shrouds must come off. The lower shroud's not too bad a job - it's held by four screws (two cross-heads, and two different-size Torx).

01

Attention!
If you remove an airbag, you are disabling a safety-related system. Make sure you tell your insurance company.

They didn't want these shrouds to fall off, did they? The upper half is held by two Torx screws from the top . . .

02

∧

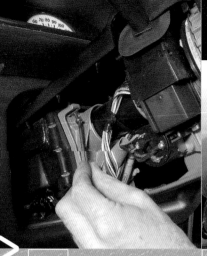

03 . . . and by a further two Torx screws inside (one each side).

04 Now the instrument cowl has to come off, to make room for the upper shroud to come out. Fortunately, the cowl's only held by two (cross-head) screws underneath.

05 With some careful wiggling, the upper shroud can now be persuaded out of position.

Before you go messing with that airbag, disconnect the battery, and wait at least ten minutes before you carry on. If you don't there's an excellent chance you'll set off **06** the airbag, which could ruin your day big-time.

The two airbag Torx screws are fitted into the steering wheel from the rear. Insert a long T30 Torx key (or socket) into the holes behind the wheel, and remove the screws - **07** they may be very tight!

Now that airbag "pad" can be lifted out of the wheel, and the yellow connector pulled off. Remove the airbag to a safe place. A "safe place" is not on the pavement, by your car. Get it indoors, in a cupboard, or maybe in the loft. Our workshop (like any decent garage) actually has a wall safe for storing airbags, to **08** meet Health & Safety regs. That's how scary airbags are.

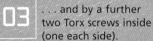

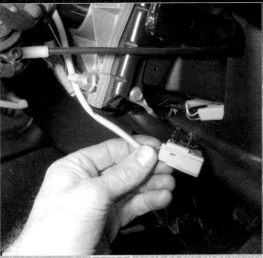

09 Before the wheel can safely come off, the rest of the airbag wiring has to be unplugged and unclipped. Disconnect this plug on the right-hand side of the column . . .

10 . . . then trace the yellow wire back to the airbag, unclipping it and cutting through any cable-ties holding it in place.

11 The steering wheel nut's not done up mega-tight (or it wasn't on ours, anyway). Hold onto the wheel to stop it turning while you undo the nut - don't just let the steering lock take the strain, as you might bust it. Before you go much further, make sure that the steering wheel's straight - as confirmation, look to see that the front wheels are pointing straight-ahead.

The wheel should now be reasonably easy to pull off its splines. Just in case it isn't, pop the wheel nut back on loosely, to stop the wheel flying off.

12

Let's deal with the issue of the very annoying light which you'll find won't go out. We're talking airbag warning light here. If you've only got a driver's airbag, you can bridge the pins in the yellow connector plug using a 5-amp fuse (solder two short lengths of wire to a blade fuse). Now the light will come on, and more importantly go out, just as it did before.

13

Our Fiesta had a passenger bag too, which we'd removed previously. We could've bridged its wiring connector too, but decided that the safest option was simply to remove the flippin' bulb from the instrument panel. Getting the clocks out isn't too big a chore (see the section "Are your dials all white?"). Just make sure you unscrew the right bulb!

14

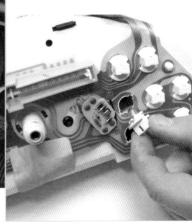

15 Check that the front wheels are still straight, then fit the new wheel boss, with the "TOP" mark - duh-uh - at the top!

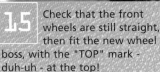

16 Fit the wheel mounting bolt, and tighten it to the proper torque (50 Nm) if you've got a wrench. If you haven't, do it up like your life depended on it. Which of course, it does. Hold the boss with your other hand - don't rely on the steering lock, or you'll bust it.

17 Even though we weren't connecting up the horn buttons on our wheel (why should we, when there's a perfectly good horn button on the end of the stalk?), the wiring on the back of the wheel was still an issue. We could've just chopped it, but Momo provide this spacer plate to stop the wires getting crushed, so we played along.

18 Feed the wires down into the boss you just fitted, and offer the wheel on.

Bum notes

Our new wheel went on very well, but when we'd finished, we found that the indicators didn't self-cancel any more. This was because we'd removed the airbag "clockspring", or contact unit, which serves the dual role of switching off the indicators. Momo's instructions go into great detail about how to refit the clockspring during fitting the new wheel, but don't say why our clockspring refused to mate up with the new boss when we tried following those instructions. Guess we'll just have to get used to DIY cancelling from now on - worked for Citroëns, for years…

. . . and tighten them securely with the Allen key provided. Depending on how nervous you are about your new wheel coming off in your hands one day, a drop of thread-locking fluid on the six screws will be a good idea - or not.

Now we see what those two little buttons are for - double-shot of nitrous, anyone?

19 Fit the six Allen screws . . .

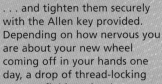

20

21

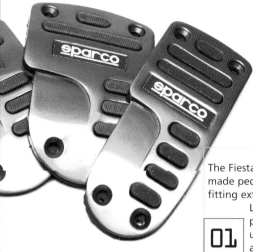

Pedalling your Fiesta

The Fiesta's got such cheaply-made pedals in the first place, fitting extensions is easy. Ea-sy. Let's start with the loud pedal - hold the plate up in the right place, and mark it.

01

02 Drill straight through that quality plastic . . .

03 . . . fit a bolt, and tighten up the nut from behind. Fit at least two nuts and bolts per extension.

A very nice race-equipment touch to your modded machine, pedal extensions really look the part when combined with full chequerplate mats - available in several styles and (anodised) colours. Not sure how well the anodising will wear, though...

04 The clutch and brake pedals have rubber covers - for safety, your new extensions should also make some concession to non-slip, or the MOT crew will have something to say. Try sourcing some little rubber grommets from a motor factors (or just don't buy any extensions that don't come with them in the first place).

05 Before we get to drilling any more holes, let's see how the rest of the pedal set fits. Hmmm - badly, it seems. Here we see our mechanic finding another use for an axle stand - as a bending platform and hammer, for plates that are just too flat. Worked very well, actually.

06 Blu-tac or tape comes in handy for trying the plates on. Before any more drilling gets done, check the spacing of the plates, and especially the gaps between (not just for style and appearance - there's a safety benefit in not hitting two pedals at once).

07 Drilling through the plates into the pedals means there's less chance of mucking it up. Placing an old piece of wood behind the pedal means there's less chance of drilling the carpet. Now it's nuts, bolts, tighten, etc. Just remember to check every so often that the nuts haven't come loose.

Achtung!
Check your insurance company's position regarding pedal extensions. A while ago there was a big fuss after a couple of cars fitted with pedal extensions crashed, which resulted in pedal extensions being withdrawn from sale at a lot of places.

Are you sitting stylishly?

The perfect complement to your lovingly-sorted suspension, because you need something better than the standard seats to hold you in, now that you can corner so much faster... and they look brutal, by way of a bonus. Besides the seat itself, remember to price up the subframe to adapt it to the mounting points in your car. Most people also choose the three- or four-point harnesses to go with it (looks a bit daft to fit a racing seat without it), but make sure the harness you buy is EC-approved, or an eagle-eyed MOT tester might make you take 'em out.

Reclining seats are pricier than non-recliners, but are worth the extra. With non-adjustable seats, how are your mates meant to get in the back? Through the tailgate? Or maybe there is no back seat... You can get subframes which tilt, so that non-reclining seats can move forward. Non-reclining racing seats should be tried for fit before you buy.

An alternative to expensive racing seats would be to have your existing seats re-upholstered in your chosen colours/fabrics, to match your interior theme. You might be surprised what's possible, and the result could be something truly unique. If you've got a basic model, try sourcing XR2i or (yes!!) RS1800 seats from a breakers. A secondhand interior bought here will be a lot cheaper than buying new goodies, and you know it'll fit easily (all Fiestas are the same underneath) - but - it won't have that unique style. Specialist breakers may be able to supply something more rad, such as a wicked leather interior from a top-spec Mondeo or Granada - might take some persuading to get it in, though!

01 Whipping out the old front chairs is easy. First, depending on which model you've got, you may find this plastic trim on the outside of your seat, which just prises off.

02 And, er, undo the bolts. You might need to slide the seat fully back for access. These will be re-used for your new seats, so it's worth noting which ones went where (if you're that organised).

03 Our front bolts were hidden under a flap of carpet - but this didn't have us fooled for long.

04 Slide the seat forwards to get at the rear bolts, and soon those unimpressive grey velour nasties will be just a bad memory.

Removing
seats

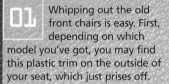

Not everyone will want to be as vicious with their back seats (which are quite useful for carrying mates around), but we wanted to strip our Fiesta, for maximum power-to-weight. Or something like that. The rear seat back is held in by hinges at either side, which have large Torx screws.

05

Our Fester has a single-piece backrest, which comes out in, er, one piece. For models with split rear seats, you just have to work a bit harder - there's more hinges.

06

The cushion has three screws along the front edge, then it's a case of unhooking the catches at the back, by pushing down. Now you've (almost) turned your Fiesta into a van!

07

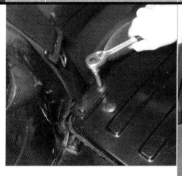

01 The first job (apart from working out which base is for left and right) is to fit the bases to the new seats. As we're talking about a fairly important safety item, which we wouldn't want to come loose, we felt that a drop of thread-lock on the frame-to-seat bolts was a good move . . .

02 . . . especially since it's also not easy to tighten a cheese-head screw really tight, as you should - ideally, use a screwdriver which has a hex fitting below the main handle, and tighten it with a spanner.

03 The new chairs are now ready to fit - hopefully, the bolt holes in the new bases will line up with the holes in the floor.

Fitting new Corbeaus

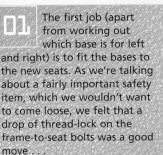

Tricks 'n' tips
During fitting, the seats will have to slide forwards or back, to gain access to the mounting bolts. Make sure the bases are bolted in firmly before you slide the seat, or there's a risk of twisting the seat relative to the base, and it will jam up solid. Trust us - we've been there.

The seat mounting bolts are, of course, the old ones you took out. Which are probably rusty as hell, so treat them to some copper grease, instead of just bunging them straight back in.

04

The bolts should really be tightened using a torque wrench (30 Nm), but if you haven't got one handy, just do them up good 'n' tight. Make sure the bolt heads don't pull through the bases, by using big washers where necessary.

05

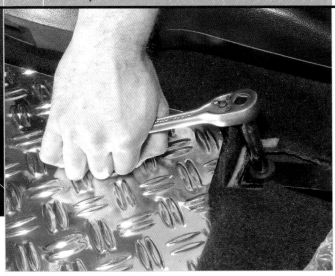

How strapped are you?

It's true that not everyone likes racing harnesses, but the majority of those who don't are "plump". And boring. You don't fit sexy race seats and then not fit race belts, do you?

The only problem with harnesses is caused by where you have to mount them. Even with a three-point harness, you end up using one of the rear seat belt mounts, and it seriously reduces your ability to carry bodies in the back seats (webbing everywhere). The MOT crew say that, if you've got rear seats, you must have rear seat belts fitted, so you either "double-up" on your rear belt mounts (use the same mounts for your harnesses and rear belts), or you take the back seats out altogether. Removing the rear seats leaves the rear deck free for chequerplate, speakers, roll cages - whatever you like. It's just important to understand how fundamental harnesses can end up being to the whole look of your car - there's almost no half-measures with race belts, so you've got to really want 'em.

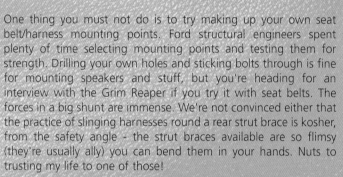

One thing you must not do is to try making up your own seat belt/harness mounting points. Ford structural engineers spent plenty of time selecting mounting points and testing them for strength. Drilling your own holes and sticking bolts through is fine for mounting speakers and stuff, but you're heading for an interview with the Grim Reaper if you try it with seat belts. The forces in a big shunt are immense. We're not convinced either that the practice of slinging harnesses round a rear strut brace is kosher, from the safety angle - the strut braces available are so flimsy (they're usually ally) you can bend them in your hands. Nuts to trusting my life to one of those!

01 Before you can fit your new harnesses, the old belts have to at least be disturbed, if not ripped out completely. As we said earlier, you must use the existing seat belt mounts, for safety. The front belt is mounted to the floor, on a sliding rail. The rail front bolt is hiding behind a plastic cover. Undo the bolt, then unhook the rail at the rear, and slide the seat belt off it.

02 The seat belt upper mounting (Torx) bolt is hidden behind another plastic trim, which just clips off.

Racing harnesses

03 That was the easy bit. To get to the inertia reel, the side trim panel's got to come off. The rear seat cushion's best removed first, as described in "Removing seats", then prise up this push-in clip at the base of the panel.

04 Remove the screw at the back of the panel, and unclip the panel edges . . .

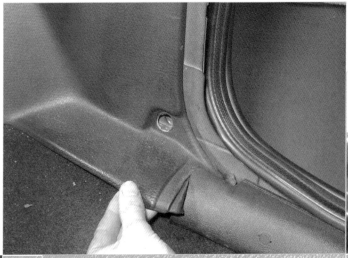

05 . . . then pull off the rubber door seal at the front, and unclip the side trim from the sill trim.

06 Partially unclip the B-pillar trim panel, to release the side trim from under it. The side trim panel can now come out (try not to break/lose too many of the clips behind).

07 The belt reel can now be unbolted and removed - it's held in by a major Torx bolt underneath, and by a small screw at the side.

11 Fitting the new harnesses is a walk in the park, compared to taking out the naff old belts. The harnesses clip onto "eyes", which you screw in, in place of the old seat belt bolts. The only trick is tightening the eyes sufficiently to be safe - they must go in all the way down to the shoulder - use a big screwdriver to help with final tightening, as shown.

12 Hooking-on the new harness is made very easy by the spring-loaded tag which you pull back.

13 Up at the front, use the bolt hole where the old sliding rail was fitted, for the outer half of the harness. The inner half of the harness mounts directly onto the seat base, using one of the holes they will have provided. What you probably won't have is a suitable nut, to fit onto your "eye" - get a Nyloc (self-locking) type, with a plastic thread insert.

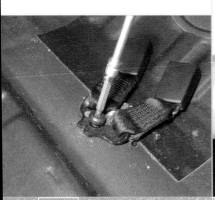

08 The rear belt buckles unbolt from the floor (seen again with the rear seat removed) . . .

09 . . . while the rear upper mountings are very similar to the front belts.

10 The rear belt reels are tucked under the parcel shelf side supports, and present no challenge to anyone with the right-size Torx bit.

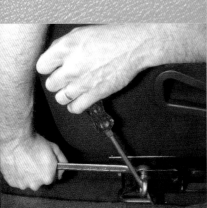

14 Tighten the nut and eye with the big screwdriver and spanner arrangement, like this . . .

15 . . . then you can feed your harness through the holes in your seats . . .

16 . . . and clip on your harness to the seat mounting, safe in the knowledge that you're, er, safe.

ICE
Headset

Ford's head units could also be described as well-matched to the speakers - ie cheap and nasty. Fine if all you want to do is aimlessly listen to the radio with your arm out the window, but not - definitely not - if you want to impress your mates with the depth and volume of your bass. Or, of course, if you want to listen to CDs. It's got to go - and there's plenty of decent headsets out there which will give you a night-and-day difference in sound quality and features. The headset is the heart of your new install - always go for the best you can afford. Ask the experts if you're not sure what features to look out for, if you're building a full system.

01 First, the old set's got to be shifted. Resist the urge to just crowbar the thing out of the dash - you'll be needing two of the standard radio removal tools to do the job with less damage. These tools can be bought over the counter, by anyone - and they call this security? You will, however, need the code if you're planning on selling the old set at a car boot. Better to keep it, to put back in when you sell the car?

02 Slide the set out of its cage, and pull out the wiring plugs. You might not want the speaker plug again, but the permanent live (red) ignition live (yellow) and earth (phat brown) wires may come in handy, as will the aerial lead. Prise up the retaining lugs, and take out the old cage - put it with the old headset.

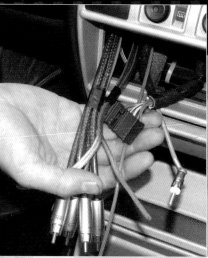

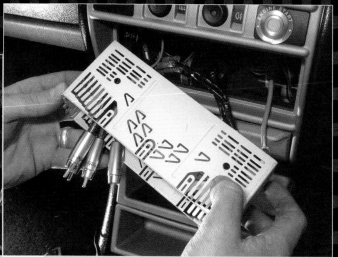

03 First job with the new unit is to feed round all your new speaker wiring and RCAs (if you're running amps). If you're at the lower end of the spending scale, it's time to consult your Haynes wiring diagram, and tap into the existing speaker wiring. This is just some of the wiring going to our new Alpine head unit - here we have two sets of RCAs, rear shelf speaker wiring, a battery live feed, and the good old aerial.

04 Many high-power sets now require a direct power connection from the battery (fused, of course) - here, we're connecting ours to the headset wiring plug. This is just one of many wires to be connected to the headset loom provided - read your instruction book to see what's supposed to go where. Use bullet connectors rather than blocks, and please not Scotchloks. Use insulating tape round any bullet connection, as it also helps stop them from coming apart.

05 When the headset loom's ready, slip the new cage over all your wiring, and lock it into place. Alpine units have cage retaining lugs which click into place on their own. Other, lesser, sets need a hand from a small screwdriver. Just bend a few of the lugs over, enough to hold the cage in place - do too good a job, and you won't get the cage out easily when you sell the car.

Plug in the aerial and the headset loom wiring plug, and you're there. Your CD multi-changer gets plugged in as well, if you've got one. It's not a bad idea to test that everything's working at this point, before pushing the unit home into its cage - just make sure it's not hanging by the wiring.

If all's well, push the headset home until the cage clips click in. Sounds easy, but you'll almost certainly have to reach in behind the set, and straighten out the wiring before the set will go in. Do not force it in, or you could end up having a very bad day. Success! Now get out the instruction manual again, and set the levels properly. Enjoy.

Connect up those RCAs, checking that you've got the colour-coding right. We've only got one amp in this install, so why two sets of leads? It's usually one set of RCAs per amp, but this head unit has a **06** subwoofer pre-out, giving direct sub control via the headset (this is good, better still is an LPL controller, but that's another story).

07

08

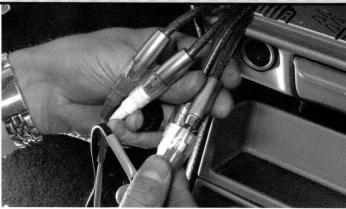

Front speakers

The standard items in the Fiesta speak volumes (hur-hur) about Ford's general feelings on car building - spend as little as poss. What does it cost Ford for the speakers in a Fiesta? If it's more than a fiver a set, they're being robbed. Low on power, and with nasty paper cones which disintegrate after a few years, fitting ANY aftermarket speakers is going to be an upgrade. But we don't want to give you that - how about showing you how to fit some tasty JL components? Properly, that is, with the help of our friends at Liquid ICE, in Yeovil.

Once you've got the door trim panel off, and have removed (and burnt) the old speaker, it's time to think about upgrading the wiring. You CAN cheat and use the existing Ford wiring for low-power speakers, but you don't want low-power speakers up front. Let's do it right. Fiesta door wiring sits in a screw-on rubber boot, and the first job is getting the boot off the door. Use a medium screwdriver to prise the boot out, and a smaller one to release the plastic lugs holding the end fitting in the door.

01

Unscrew the other end of the boot, and unclip the inner part of the plug from the door pillar. Choosing your spot carefully, drill through the door pillar just below where the plug was - this hole will be where you feed your new speaker wiring through.

02

So that you don't suddenly end up with no sound (or a blown channel on your headset/amp), put a grommet into the hole you just drilled. Or use lots of insulating tape when you "loom" the speaker wires. You know it makes sense.

03

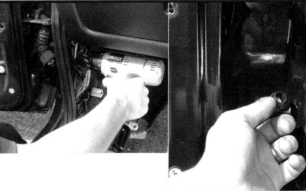

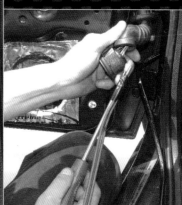

> **04** Peel back the rubber boot from the screw fitting . . .

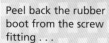

05 . . . and cut a small slit at the bottom. This will be where you feed in your speaker wire, after it's come through your newly-drilled hole. It then goes through the rubber boot, and into the door - now d'you see how neat an idea this is?

06 Now you know the theory, let's see it in action. Take your new speaker wire, and feed it through your new hole. Okay so far? Of course, if you're fitting mids and tweets, you'll be needing TWO wires at this point.

07 Before you try feeding into that curvy rubber boot - think. Will the curviness and rubberiness make pushing a wire through a tad tricky? Correct. So tape your wire to a screwdriver handle, and push it through. Easy when you know how. Your wire should now be in the door, ready to take crimps for connecting to the speaker. Refit the rubber boot fully, screwing it back onto the plug in the door pillar, and the worst is over.

If you don't want all that kicking power to set your door panel tizzing, you need to invest in some Dynamat. Expensive? Yes. For perfectionists? Yes. Worth it, all the same? Hell, yes.

08 Clean up the door panel with some decent solvent . . .

. . . then cut it, and get it on. Real pro's will sound-deaden the outer door panel, too - for the best results, you'll need to budget for at least a sheet of 'mat per door, if not more.

09

10 If nothing else, do the section of door around where the speaker will sit. When the Dynamat's on, slice it across the speaker hole . . .

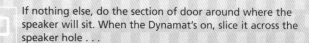

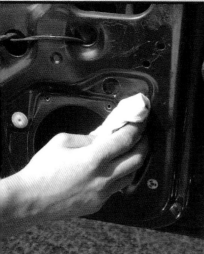

11 . . . and tuck in the excess behind. Two things about Dynamat - use it warm (warm it up with a heat gun, on a cold day), and watch your fingers (the metal foil edges are sharp!).

12 A fully-Dynamatted door looks almost too good to cover up with the door trim!

13 With the door glass wound fully down, try the speaker in its hole. If it's too deep, you might need to make up a spacer, from some MDF. We used the (un-burnt) old speaker to mark round, so we got the shape on the door right . . .

14 . . . then marked the speaker holes onto that, using the new mounting ring.

> **Achtung!**
> MDF dust is nasty stuff to breathe in. Wear a mask when you're cutting, drilling or sanding it.

15 With an electric planer, we then chamfered the piece of MDF we were using. Why go to this trouble? Well, it pulls the speaker down slightly, so the door trim panel doesn't cover it, and also pulls the speaker out from the window glass. The angle helps to "aim" the sound up, towards your lugs. If you have to make a spacer, make it work for you!

16 Stop all this mucking about with spacers and matting - let's get the wiring on the speakers, and the speakers in the doors. Decide which "half" of your speaker wire is going to be "pos" (+) first - most wire has one part with writing on, and the other without, for identification. Stick to the same rule with all the wiring you're putting in the car. Crimp on the right-size connectors, and plug onto your speaker terminals.

17 It's worth cable-tying the speaker wire back to the speaker frame, to stop it flapping about and possibly getting hooked on the bottom of the door glass.

18 Think about which way up the speaker terminals will be, when the speaker's fitted. Facing upwards is often best. Drill through and screw, and the speaker's in. Even a rotten old Ford head unit will sound better with decent speakers - but you don't wanna do that...

19 As we said, these are JL components, so where are the tweeters? Before we mount those, let's deal with the crossovers. Proper components will come with matched crossovers, with the best frequencies already dialled-in. All you have to do is connect up the wires.

20 Here's one we connected earlier. The crossover input comes from one channel on the amp (the lower two terminals), and gets split into mid-range and treble (top two pairs of connections) - all clearly marked, and backed up with decent instructions. The crossovers have a self-adhesive backing, so poking them up under the dash is a whole lot easier.

21 Our low-rent Fiesta actually has electric windows, leaving this blanking plug where the window winder would be, in the door trim panel. Almost tweeter-size, and in a nice spot too. Hmmm…

22 But, because we didn't want to wimp out, we cut our own hole, which also lined up better with a hole on the door frame itself. Cut the vinyl and the fluff underneath with a blade - don't drill through, or the fluff just wraps round the drill bit. We know, because we went there.

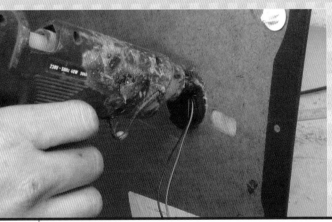

23 One hole saw later for the hardboard backing, and we got us a hole.

24 Slip the tweeter into its new orifice . . .

25 . . . secure from behind with a hot-glue gun. Connect up the wiring, refit the door trim, and caress your ears with crystal-clear sound.

Rear shelf & speakers

Okay, we know that the Fiesta has rear speaker grilles in the parcel shelf side supports - depending on which model you've got, there might even be speakers in them - but you're not getting any 6x9s in there! No speaker's going to work any sense mounted in flimsy plastic, so shelf-mounting is the only option. If you don't want to butcher your standard shelf, either make a new one from MDF (using your stock shelf as a template), or buy a ready-made acoustic shelf. A ready-made shelf comes trimmed in shelf cloth, and looks the business for not much money - it's hardly worth making your own.

01 First job with our new shelf is to mark the speaker positions. Not tricky.

02 With a speaker outline marked, drill a nice big hole somewhere inside it . .

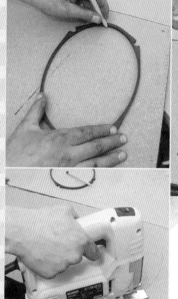

03 . . . and get busy

04 with the jigsaw. Use the speaker mounts as a template to drill the mounting holes . . .

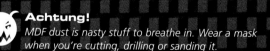

Achtung!
MDF dust is nasty stuff to breathe in. Wear a mask when you're cutting, drilling or sanding it.

> **05** ... then screw on the speakers themselves. We're running these Phoenix Gold 6x9s off the headset, to provide a little "rear fill" to the sound.

06 If you plan on being able to take the shelf out easily, you'll be needing a Neutrik plug and socket, which allows quick and easy wiring disconnection. Using the instructions provided with the connector, connect up your pos and neg speaker wires, and assemble the plug.

07 Find a suitable spot to mount the Neutrik socket, and drill yourself a hole.

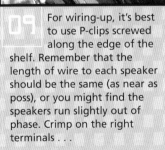

08 Wire up the socket using the same pos-and-neg, left-and-right locations as for the plug, and slip it into its new hole. The socket can be held by a screw if necessary - our hole was so tight it didn't need one.

09 For wiring-up, it's best to use P-clips screwed along the edge of the shelf. Remember that the length of wire to each speaker should be the same (as near as poss), or you might find the speakers run slightly out of phase. Crimp on the right terminals . . .

10 . . . and connect up your speakers.

11 Now we got us a speaker-equipped shelf. If you're putting a sub box in the boot as well, it's not a bad idea to plonk the box and shelf in, to check your speaker magnets will clear above the box. Just a thought... We marked the speaker position on the underside of the shelf carefully to get both speakers in the same place.

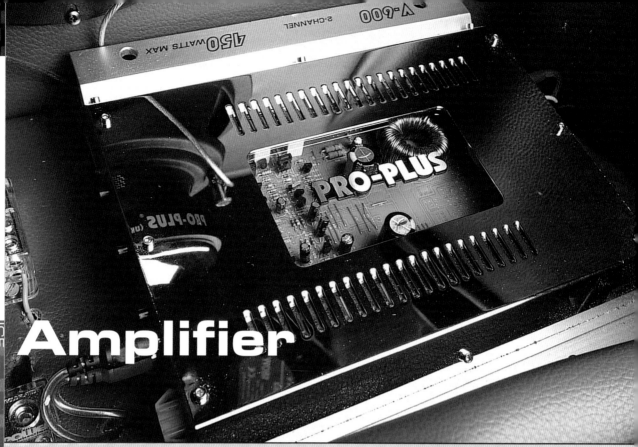

Amplifier

So, how many amps do we want in our car? One school of thought says each pair of speakers, and each sub, should have an individual amp - by setting the output from each amp separately, you can control each aspect of the sound, before you even need to think about adding a graphic equaliser. You can also better match your speakers to the level of power they need, to work best. Trouble is, running several amps means doubling-up on wiring, and you could end up drawing an awful lot of power from that battery.

Our new system seriously kicks, with just one four-channel amp - choose the right one carefully (and the components to go with it), and just one will do. Our chosen amp is one of the new Phoenix Gold "Tantrum" series, and has all the toys, including being LPL (low-pass level, or sub) control-ready.

Decide where you'll mount the amp carefully. One factor to consider is that it must be adequately cooled - don't cover it up, and don't hang it upside-down from your shelf. Our lads at Liquid ICE are doing us a fancy false floor, so only the top part of the amp will be on **01** display - with the amp in position, drill and screw it down.

Look at this flippin' lot! Feed all the power, RCA, speaker, LPL control and P-cont (remote switch-on) wires through from inside the car, and decide how they'll be arranged around the amp. If possible, trim the wires to length now - keep the **02** speaker and RCA wiring away from the power and earth cables.

Achtung! *MDF dust is nasty stuff to breathe in. Wear a mask when you're cutting, drilling or sanding it.*

Oh yes - the earth cable! We nearly forgot that. Make an earth cable from the same-thickness wire as you've used for your live feed. In our case, it was four-gauge, so we found a nice dark piece for our earth. Now to find an earth point - you can use almost any handy bolt in

03 the boot area, but seat and seat belt mounting bolts must be re-done up tight, of course. You can always make your own hole (just don't go through the fuel tank) . . .

. . . and pin your wire, suitably ring-terminalled, to the floor with a large self-tapper (or better still, drill through to the outside world, and fit a nut and bolt through your hole). Notice too how we scratched away the boot

04 floor paint, to make a better earth connection - nothing left to chance.

Now we're into the serious wiring-up. Read the amp's instruction book carefully when connecting any wires, or you might regret it. Make sure you're happy about your speaker pos and neg/left and right wires, and get

05 them screwed on. It's not essential to use ring terminals on speaker wiring . . .

06 . . . but, on a hefty and important wire like the live feed, a ring terminal is a must, and wrap the end with tape, to prevent it shorting across the other connections.

07 And there it is - a complete set of speaker, sub, power, remote and earth connections.

08 Seen nestling inside its false floor, the amp is just one part of a very neat install. One any competent DIY-er can aspire to - and it sounds LUSH.

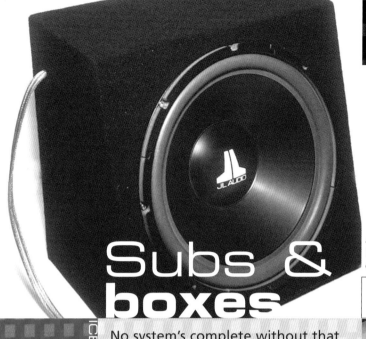

Subs & boxes

No system's complete without that essential deep bass boom and rumble. Don't muck about with bass tubes - get the real thing to avoid disappointment. So you lose some of your boot space - so what? Is getting the shopping in an issue? We think not.

Most people opt for the easy life when it comes to boxes, at least until they're ready for a full-on mental install. The Fiesta at least has a roomy boot, so most standard boxes will fit easily. Making up your own box isn't hard though, especially if you were any good at maths and geometry. Oh, and woodwork. Most subs come with instructions telling you what volume of box they work best in - the standard boxes are just fine, and aren't dear. The only real reason to build your own is if you've got an odd-shaped boot (or just like a challenge).

Another plus with a ready-made box is that the speaker connection plate is usually pre-fitted, meaning all you have to do is connect speaker wire to it . . .

01

02 . . . and to the speaker connections on the sub itself.

03 Lining, and then filling, your new box with Dacron, is thought to be a good way to smooth out the bass sound. Makes a bit of a nonsense of all your precise volume calculations, if you built your own box, but we won't argue with the experts.

04 All that's left is to drill and screw your sub into place. Make sure you fit the gasket (or sections of gasket) between the speaker and box, and do the screws up tight - vibration might just be a bit of a problem here...

ICE

Wiring-up

For most people, this is the scariest part of an install - just the thought of masses of multi-coloured spaghetti sticking out of your dash might have you running to the experts (or a knowledgeable mate). But - if you do everything in a logical order, and observe a few simple rules, wiring-up isn't half as brain-numbing as it seems.

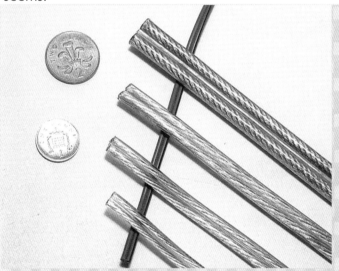

If you're running a modern head unit, or a brace of amplifiers, you'll be needing a new live feed, taken straight off the battery. Re-using any of the standard Ford stereo wiring is a bad move - the stock wire is probably only good for about 15 amps, tops, so don't go fitting a bigger fuse, or you'll have a meltdown (and maybe, a fire).

Get some decent "four-gauge" wire (which is about as thick as battery cable - serious stuff) and a matching fuseholder. If you're running more than one item off this feed wire, get a distribution block too, which splits the feed up, with a separate fuse for each item - who'd have thought electrical safety can look trick too?

Live feeds

First step in running a live feed is deciding where best to run the wire into the car - try and go for the most direct route. On our CFi-engined Fiesta, there's this plate at the back of the engine bay, which hides the injection "brain" - it's held on by rivets and a "security" Torx bolt, and is no match for a drill.

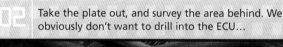

01

02 Take the plate out, and survey the area behind. We obviously don't want to drill into the ECU...

03 Our man at Liquid ICE knows where he's going with the drill, and heads off well to the side of the brain.

04 Fit a grommet to the hole you've just made. No, this is not optional - that's a live feed, going through a sharp-edged hole, which will provide an excellent earth path if the wire gets chopped. Feed in some of that nice four-gauge wire, and get a mate to pull a decent length through inside. On our install, we're using four-gauge for the amp supply, and a separate (thinner, but still heavy-duty) wire for the headset power - both wires can be pushed through the same hole.

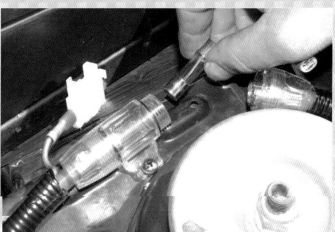

05 It's not a bad idea to silicone-up your new hole, or any water that gets in will run straight down your new wire, into the back of your stereo (or new distribution block), and it's adios muchachos.

06 Here's the battery-end of our new lead, receiving its new fuseholder. There's something really satisfying about assembling one of these - they're just Designed For The Job. Behind it, you can see the more conventional blade-type fuseholder we've rigged into our headset live feed.

07 The new fuseholder can be screwed to the inner wing, and here's the new fuse going in place (get a fuse the same rating as your amp, or the total load on your distribution block - ask a pro for advice). Make sure you use four-gauge wire from the fuseholder to the battery, and crimp on a ring terminal big enough to deal with such hefty wire. Don't get carried away and connect up your live feed until you're ready - remember, this feed is NOT ignition-switched!

Speaker and RCA wiring

As with virtually all wiring, the lesson here is to be neat and orderly - or - you'll be sorry! RCA leads and speaker wires are prone to picking up interference (from just about anywhere), so the first trick to learn when running ICE wiring is to keep it away from live feeds, and also if possible, away from the car's ECUs. Another favourite way to interference-hell is to loop up your wiring, when you find you've got too much (we've all been there). Finding a way to lose any excess lengths of wire without bunching can be an art - laying it out in a zig-zag, taping it to the floor as you go, is just one solution.

Another lesson in neatness is finding out what kinds of cable clips are available, and where to use them. There's various stick-on clips which can be used as an alternative to gaffer tape on floors, and then "P-clips", which look exactly as their name suggests, and can be screwed down (to speaker shelves, for instance). "Looming" your wiring is another lesson well-learned - this just means wrapping tape around, particularly on pairs of speaker wires or RCAs. As we've already said, don't loom speaker wire with power cables (or even with earths).

The last point is also about tidiness - mental tidiness. When you're dealing with speaker and RCA wiring, keep two ideas in mind - positive and negative. Each speaker has a pos (+) and neg (-) terminal. Mixing these up is not an option, so work out a system of your own, for keeping positive and negative in the right places on your headset and amp connections. Decent speaker cable is always two wires joined together - look closely, and you'll see that one wire has writing (or a stripe) on, and the other is plain. Use the wire with writing for pos connections throughout your system, and you'll never be confused again. While we're at it, RCA leads have red and white connector plugs - Red is for Right (usually).

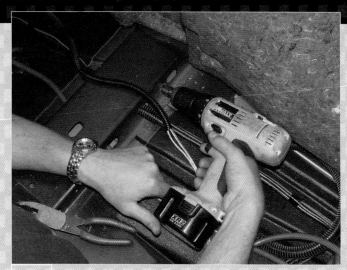

01 Here we see just one solution to a little wiring problem. We have two RCA leads, some speaker wiring, and a power feed, all going to our amp in the boot. We can't run all the wires together, so we must separate them. We've removed the passenger seat, to make life easier, but here's the first obstacle - a ridge in the floor. To avoid laying the wires on top, out comes the drill . . .

02 . . . and having made our holes, in goes a grommet. There are ready-made holes too, in a Fiesta - just not enough for three sets of wires.

03 If you prefer, or are using a odd-shaped hole for which no grommet has yet been made, you can sleeve your wiring with this plastic cable-trunking. Nice.

04 With strips of gaffer tape to keep it all neatly tied down, this is how a professional wiring install should look.

12 Engines

Faster, faster!

So now your car talks the talk, but does it walk the walk, as in walking away from everything at the next set of lights... Not everyone's into mega-performance, which is why the bolt-on goodies like induction kits and big-bore exhausts are such big business. Serious engine tuning costs, and not just in the initial expense - it goes without saying that your insurance company will throw a wobbly at a gas-flowed head, and might refuse to cover you altogether if you go for that 1.9 litre CVH conversion.

The induction kit and sports exhaust are undoubtedly good fun things to fit, and they're claimed to improve the airflow through the engine, helping it to "breathe" better - this they do, and very well-documented a fact it is too. This improved breathing helps when you go for the accelerator initially, so improving the response you feel, while the rear box sounds nice and fruity, so everyone's happy. Now, the harsh and painful truth. Unless you really spend a fortune, and seriously modify or even replace your standard engine, you will not gain much extra "real" power. Sorry, but it's a myth. Time and again, people fit induction kits and back boxes, expecting huge power gains, and those in the know have a quiet chuckle. All these things really do is make the car sound sportier, and improve the response - accept this, and you won't be disappointed.

If you don't believe us, point your lightly-modified engine in the direction of a rolling road, and we'll stand back and laugh when the result shows a 2 or 3 per cent gain, or less. If you're still not convinced, ask yourself why most insurance companies don't generally increase premiums for the likes of a performance rear box or induction kit. The answer is - because (on their own) they don't make enough difference!

All later Fiestas (with "cats") have fuel injection, and all the sports ones had it anyway, from day one. The fuelling arrangements for fuel injection are based largely on the volume of incoming air. If you start feeding the injection system an unusually large amount of air (by fitting an induction kit, for instance), the management system will compensate by throwing in more fuel. The net result could be that the car will drink petrol and your exhaust emissions will be screwed up, inviting an MOT failure. We're not saying "don't do it", just remember that power gains can be exaggerated, and that there can be pitfalls.

The bolt-on performance goodies have more effect as part of an engine "makeover" package, and setting-up the engine properly after fitting these parts can make a huge difference. If you're halfway serious about increasing the go of your Fiesta, talk to someone with access to a rolling road, so you can prove that what's been done has actually made a useful gain. If you've spent time and a ton of money on your car, of course you're going to think it feels faster, but is it?

Fitting all the performance goodies in the world will be pretty pointless if the engine's already well worn, but it might not be as bad as you think. One of the best ways to start on the performance road is simply to ensure that the car's serviced properly - new spark plugs, HT leads, and an oil and filter change, are a good basis to begin from. Correct any obvious faults, such as hoses or wiring plugs hanging off, and look for any obviously-damaged or leaking components, too.

Breathe with me...

One of the simplest items to fit, the replacement air filter element, has been around for years, and has only recently been overtaken in popularity by the induction kit (which is generally only available for fuel injection engines).

The idea of these items is to increase the flow of air into the engine, supposedly to help the engine to "breathe", but they can actually upset the air/fuel mixture and cause poor running. If you're serious about increasing performance, fitting an adjustable fuel pressure regulator (for fuel injection engines) is a must for any useful effect - and any setting-up really should be done by a professional, preferably with access to a rolling road. On fuel injection engines, feeding in extra air will "fool" the injection system into providing more fuel - ultimately, this will increase performance a bit, but will greatly increase fuel consumption and lead to an over-rich mixture, which could cause the car to fail the MOT.

Replacement element

This a replacement element which fits inside the standard air filter box, and it's therefore a very discreet way of tweaking your engine - no-one can tell it's fitted, looking under the bonnet. A replacement air filter is dead easy to fit - release the clips securing the air cleaner top cover, then lift the cover enough to lift out the old element. Before you fit the new element, if you can, clean out the inside of the filter housing. Some performance filters have to be oiled before fitting - follow the instructions provided; don't ignore this part, or the filter won't be effective.

Fit the new element the right way up - it may have a "TOP" or arrow marking, or may only fit one way. If the filter won't fit, check whether you actually have the right one - don't force it in, and don't cut it to fit, as either of these will result in gaps, which would allow unfiltered air to get in. Refit the air cleaner cover, and secure with the clips.

Achtung!
Don't simply take out the air filter completely - this is a really dumb idea. The fuel system's air intake sucks in air, and also dust, dirt and leaves from the front of the car - it's also designed to suck in oil fumes from the engine itself (through the "breather" connection). Without a filter, all this muck would end up in the sensitive parts of the fuel system, and will quickly make the car undriveable. Worse, if any of it makes it into the engine, this will lead to engine wear. Cheaper performance filters can be of very suspect quality - if your new filter disintegrates completely inside six months, it'll do wonders for the airflow, but it'll also be letting in all sorts of rubbish!

Induction kit

These are supposed to allow even more air into the system than a normal replacement filter, and are a very popular fitment. As mentioned previously, it's best if the fuel system is set up professionally after fitting, otherwise the results could be disappointing.

With an induction kit, the standard air filter housing and ducting are junked, and the new filter bolts directly to the airflow meter, using a special adapter supplied with the kit. Most kits also feature special air inlet ducting (hoses) to feed the new filter with the coldest possible air from the front of the car - cold air is denser, and improves engine power. Feeding the filter with cold air is in theory good for maximum performance with a hot engine or in hot weather, but in colder conditions with a cold engine, driveability and fuel economy might suffer.

As a final bonus, the induction kit, which operates without all the normal ducting provided as standard, gives the engine a real throaty roar when you go for the loud pedal - certainly true of our kit, made by Green Filters. Actually, our kit isn't a true, traditional "induction kit", but it does the same job - the only difference in fitting a more normal kit would be fitting the mounting bracket for the cone, and working out where to route the cold-air pipe (neither of which is difficult).

01 Remove the three screws securing the air cleaner to the throttle body . . .

02 . . . then release the spring-type hose clip, and pull the breather pipe off the oil filler cap.

03 Trace the breather pipe up to the base of the air cleaner, twist it to the right to free it, then pull the fitting down out of the air cleaner. That's the last you'll see of that grey plastic splat on top of your engine.

04 Pull the breather pipe off the plastic fitting that used to sit under the air cleaner . . .

Engines

05 . . . and fit the restrictor into the pipe end, followed by this rather cute breather filter . . .

06 . . . which you secure to the pipe using a cable-tie.

07 The breather filter for the oil filler cap gets a Jubilee clip to retain it . . .

08 . . . as does the main filter, which sits on the throttle body.

09 Make sure the clip is done up tight, or you'll have an air leak.

10 Our instructions claimed that the main filter could be bolted down, but this turned out to be a bit of a whopper. For sake of appearance, we had to do something with the two bolt holes we had left in the filter, so we glued in some suitable screws we found lying about.

11 And this is the finished result - green filters from Green Filters everywhere! And yes, the bonnet will shut - just.

Finally...

Once you've fitted your new filter or induction kit, even if you don't take the car to a rolling road for setting up, at least take it to a garage and have the emissions checked - any minor adjustments should mean that the engine will still tick over okay, and should ensure an MOT emissions pass.

No quicker? An RS Turbo should be quick enuff for anyone, surely?

No quicker
but it looks nice

Of course, if you're embarrassed about how your engine looks, you could always claim your bonnet pull's broken, and only open the bonnet while no-one else is around. But come on, even a boggo Fiesta's engine bay can be made to look well smart, with just a few simple mods.

N366 AYA

First up - try cleaning the engine! How do you expect to emulate the show-stopping cars if your gearbox is covered in grot? Get busy with the degreaser (Gunk's a good bet), then get the hosepipe out. You can take it down to the local jetwash if you like, but remember your mobile - if you get carried away with the high-power spray, you might find the car won't start afterwards!

When it's all dry (and running again), you can start in. Get the polish to all the painted surfaces you reasonably can, and don't be afraid to unbolt a few of the simpler items to gain better access. We're assuming you've already fitted your induction kit, but if not, these nicely do away with a load of ugly plastic airbox/air cleaner and trunking, in favour of nice-looking product. Take off the rocker cover (or engine cover), and paint it to match your chosen scheme (heat-resistant paint is a must, really, such as brake caliper paint), set off with a funky oil filler cap. A strut brace is a nice underbonnet feature, especially when chromed. Braided hose covers (or coloured hose sets), ally battery covers and bottles, mirror panels - all give the underbonnet a touch of glamour.

Coloured HT leads

01 Brighten up the underbonnet, and maybe (if you believe what it says on the tin) make your car go better too? Gotta be worth a punt, to find out. Work on one lead at a time here - pull this end off the spark plug . . .

02 . . . unclip it from the rocker cover . . .

03 . . . then reach round the back of the engine, squeeze the two clips together, and pull it off the coil pack (your Fiesta doesn't actually have a distributor, so sound like a smarty and call it by its proper name).

04 Lay the new leads out, and choose the lead closest in length to the one you've just pulled off. All our new leads were, in fact, way too long.

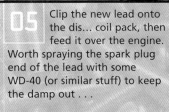

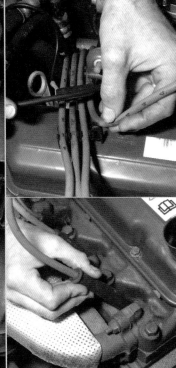

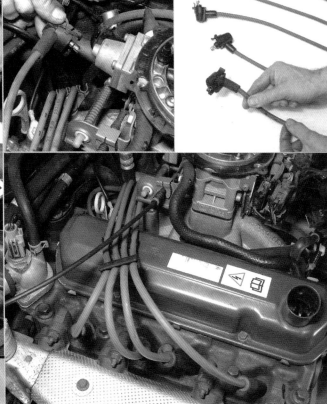

05 Clip the new lead onto the dis... coil pack, then feed it over the engine. Worth spraying the spark plug end of the lead with some WD-40 (or similar stuff) to keep the damp out . . .

06 . . . then push the new lead home.

07 And here's one we did earlier. Don't like blue? Well, they also come in red, yellow...

Achtung!
Switch off the ignition and remove the key before starting this job. You don't want to be on the wrong end of 40,000 volts.

Adjustable fuel
pressure regulator
(power boost valve)

Generally only available for Fiestas with multi-point injection (Si, XR and RS models), these valves allow the fuel system pressure to be increased over the standard regulator valve. Contrary to what you might think, they don't actually provide much more fuel (this is regulated separately by the injection ECU). The effect of increasing the injection pressure is to improve the injector spray pattern, which helps the fuel to burn more efficiently, and has the effect of increasing engine power while actually reducing emission levels.

To see the true effect of these valves, they must be set up using emission test gear and ideally a rolling road - merely turning the pressure up to the maximum level might not produce the desired effect. Fitting one of these valves involves breaking into the high-pressure fuel line, which is potentially dangerous for the inexperienced - also, if the valve is poorly fitted (or the fuel lines are in poor condition), you could end up with fuel spraying out under pressure onto a hot engine. Make sure you know what you're doing - take great care when dealing with petrol, and watch carefully for any sign of fuel leakage after fitting, even if this is done by a professional.

Braided hoses

Turning your engine bay into something resembling that of a racing machine should only be done when the engine's completely cold to start with - like first thing in the morning, NOT when you've just got back from Ripspeed. With the state of the NHS these days, visiting the burns unit should be avoided wherever possible. Depending on which hoses you decide to treat, you could be removing ones containing hot coolant or fuel, and you don't play games with either, so be careful.

First step is to remove your chosen hose. If supplies of braiding are limited, go for the hoses at the top of the engine first, then the ones underneath you can't see won't matter so much. Ford tend to use spring-type clips, best released using pliers . . .

01

... but you'll find Jubilee clips too.

02

If the hose is stuck, be careful how you free it, or you could snap the pipe stub underneath (some are only plastic). This sort of thing can really ruin your day.

03

Unroll your braiding, then expand it to the right size using a suitable blunt object. Like a screwdriver handle, we mean.

04

05 Once the braiding's roughly the right size, you can slip your pipe in (lovely). Smooth out the braiding round the bends, as it tends to gather up and look naff otherwise . . .

06 . . . then trim off the excess from the ends.

07 Slide a new Jubilee clip over the braiding at one end, then slip one of the end fittings over the clip. Repeat this process at the other end of your chosen hose, and it'll be ready to fit back on.

08 When you're sure the hose is fully onto its fitting, tighten the hose clip securely to avoid embarrassing leakage. If any of the end fittings rattle annoyingly, you can put a stop to it by packing the fittings with silicone (preferably black).

Engine painting

01 Our minter of a Fiesta was rather shiny under the bonnet to start with, but only shiny grey and black. Time to change all that, with some Folia Tec engine paint (two-pack, heat-resistant - basically the same as brake caliper paint). An obvious first candidate was our HCS rocker cover, which does not require much genius to remove.

02 Once off, the first task is to remove any rusty bits, and stickers.

03 The kit we had included a degreaser spray. We'd already done a lot more than just degrease at this point, but we thought we'd show this step anyway.

04 And on goes the paint. Once mixed, this paint will go off (solid in the tin) inside two hours, so it pays to prepare everything you want to paint before getting the brush out. This stuff also needs plenty of coats, to cover properly.

05 The end result's not everyone's cuppa, but it's certainly not dull. As you can see, we didn't stop at the rocker cover - but then we're Haynes, and not shy about pulling things to bits...

Chrome battery cover

You'd really think there wouldn't be much to this, wouldn't you? Get a chrome battery cover, stick it on your battery, job done. Well, yes, except that you'd quite likely have a fire if you did just stick it on. Any cover worth having's made of metal, which will do a great job of shorting-out your battery terminals if you let it. We chose

01 the safe option of fitting a piece of hardboard inside (you can use anything non-conductive - like cardboard, if you want). Measure up . . .

02 . . . then get out the jigsaw (or scissors), and try the finished article in place for size.

03 We thought it might be nice if our hardboard terminal protector didn't fall off, so out came the sticky double-sided tape . . .

 04 . . . before the hardboard was finally stuck in position.

05 And now, safe in the knowledge that our battery won't suffer meltdown, we can fit our shiny new cover. Phew.

ECU "chipping"

Fiestas with "cats" have fuel injection, as do all the sports models bar the 1.6 S. The injection system is controlled by an engine management system with a "computer" at its heart, known as the ECU, or Electronic Control Unit.

The ECU contains several computer chips, at least one of which has programmed onto it the preferred fuel/air mixture and ignition advance setting for any given engine speed or load - this information is known as a computer "map", and the system refers to it constantly while the car's being driven. Obviously, with the current trend towards fuel economy and reducing harmful exhaust emissions, the values in this "map" are set, well, conservatively, let's say (read "boring"). With a little tweaking - like richening-up the mixture, say - the engine can be made to produce more power, or response will be improved, or both. At the expense of the environment. Oh well.

Companies like Superchips offer replacement computer chips which feature a computer map where driveability and performance are given priority over outright economy (although the company claims that, under certain conditions, even fuel economy can be better, with their products). While a chip like this does offer proven power gains on its own, it's obviously best to combine a chip with other enhancements, and to have the whole lot set up at the same time. By the time you've fitted an induction kit, four-branch manifold, big-bore pipe, and maybe even a fast-road cam, adding a chip is the icing on the cake - chipping an already-modified motor will liberate even more horses, or at least combine it with majorly-improved response. Ford tuning specialists are best placed to advise you on the most effective tuning mods.

Another feature programmed into the ECU is a rev limiter, which cuts the ignition (or fuel) progressively when the pre-set rev limit is reached. Most replacement chips have the rev limiter reset higher, or removed altogether. Not totally sure this is a good thing - if the engine's not maintained properly (low oil level, cambelt changes neglected), removing the rev limiter and running beyond the red line would be a quick way to kill it.

Now the bad news

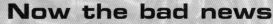

Chipping is often thought of as an easy, "no-tell" route to increased performance and driveability - after all, the ECU is well-buried inside the car, not on show under the bonnet, so who's gonna know? Needless to say, the insurance companies have been wise to this trick for a long time. A sure way to tell whether a "performance" product does what it says on the tin is to see what it'll do to your premium - telling them you're fitting a sports ROM chip will cost. Big-time. But, in the event of a claim, if they suspect your car's been "chipped", rest assured, they will make efforts to find out, because if you haven't told them about it, it means they save on paying out. What's an insurance assessor's salary for one day, compared to the thousands you could be claiming in case of an accident or theft? Do it by all means, but at least be honest.

Gaining access to the ECU

On all Fiestas, the ECU (brain) is tucked inside the car, above the passenger footwell. To be safe (the ECU is a bit fragile, and a bit expensive too), this needs two people to remove - one under the bonnet, one in the car. Speaking of safety, disconnect the battery before doing this job (or at least make sure the ignition's off, by taking out the key). First job under the bonnet is to remove the ECU

01 cover, which is held on by two rivets at the top . . .

. . . and by a "security" Torx screw at the bottom. If you haven't got a suitable Torx bit, pliers work well, as does the

02 drill (of course, we shouldn't really be telling you this).

Now undo the two nuts which hold the ECU rubber cover on (one either

03 side) . . .

04 . . . and lift the cover away.

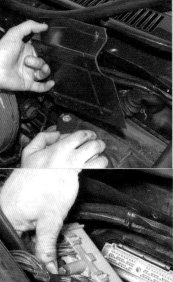

05 The ECU multi-plug is held in place by a single bolt (no loose connections here, then). Make a final check that the battery's off, or that the ignition key's out, then undo the bolt . . .

06 . . . and disconnect the multi-plug.

07 The ECU and its mounting bracket are held up by two spring-loaded clips, which are released from the engine compartment side. If you just release them, however, the brain will simply plummet into the inside of the car, landing heavily and damaging itself in the process. You don't want a brain-damaged Fiesta on your drive, so get someone (preferably with all their mental faculties) inside the footwell, ready to catch it.

08 And there we are - one brain successfully removed inside the car by our resident surgeon. Didn't hurt a bit. Just treat it carefully once it's been removed (not dropping it on the floor or playing with it in the bath are good places to start).

Engine tuning

So you've done the airbox/induction kit, exhaust and chip - what's next, short of going for a complete engine swap? We'll assume you've got a capacity-challenged Fiesta first. Well, you'll have an easier time extracting more oomph from a CVH engine than from the humble HCS pushrod unit, but that doesn't mean there's no point in trying with a 1.1 (or especially, a 1.3 litre). These little beauties respond really well to a camshaft change, with as much as 30 bhp more available from a Kent cam conversion. Only problem is - unlike the overhead-cam CVH engine, swapping a cam on an HCS motor is not the work of a morning. Try taking the engine out, instead - the cam won't really come out any other way, unless you fancy pulling the offside front wing off . . . And you're really gonna put that engine back in, once it's come out?

The CVH engines respond well to cam swaps as well, but more can be gained from having the head gas-flowed, ported, skimmed (to increase compression) and bigger valves fitted. If you've got the early 1.6 S, dump the original carb and get a Weber 34 DMTR (or the Weber 32 DFT fitted to the Mk 2 XR2 up to 1985, and a popular mod for the 1986-on ones). Most carburettor specialists have now "moved on" to fuel injection and engine management, but the knowledge is still out there. Get busy with the Yellow Pages.

The most tune-able engine of all is, of course, the RS Turbo lump. Superchips are a good first step, but a Unichip offers more scope for monster power, being upgradeable. Exhausts apparently make little difference to outright power, but a replacement hybrid turbo will soon have power approaching the 200 mark. Serious RST owners go for partial or total Zetec engine swaps - few people realise that the Zetec was intended as a direct replacement for the CVH motor, and is so similar in terms of dimensions that various swaps are possible. Specialist stuff, then, and companies such as Vulcan, Power Engineering and Specialised Engines are the boys to talk to.

The Zetecs are limited by their engine management systems, so specialist help will soon be needed for more than a mild tweak. However, if you've got a 105 bhp XR2i, you could get 130 bhp RS1800 power by swapping the injection system throttle body from 47 mm diameter to 52 mm, together with the matching ECU. Zetecs were also fitted to Mondeos, remember - could be a rich source of engine bits from scrapyards, and the Mondy went up to 2.0 litre as well. Hmmm…

Replacement engine

If the engine really is past it, or you'd like a simpler route to better performance, why not consider an engine change? The trick is, of course, to make absolutely sure the "new" engine's better than the old one - some so-called "reconditioned" engines may actually be worse!

Especially if you're good with engines, or know someone who is, an engine change can easily be done in a day (with the right equipment). If your car's done a huge mileage, dropping in a newer lower-mileage motor will make a big difference. As long as the new engine's the same size as the old one, it won't affect the insurance - all you do is tell the DVLA about the change, and they'll update the car's registration document with the new engine number.

One advantage of owning a Fiesta is that there's the whole Ford engine family to choose from - one of the more popular "advanced" mods for a basic model is to pull out a 1.6 litre CVH engine (perhaps from a cheap old Escort) and slot it in under the bonnet. It's not quite that easy of course, or everyone would be doing it. Then there's the very tune-able Fiesta/Escort RS Turbo motor, with 133 bhp (stock), the Zetecs, and 1.9 litre CVH conversions. Of course, there's always the ultimate Ford motor - how would 200-plus brake from a Cossie feel in a Fiesta? Wick-ed! Trouble is, the Cosworth motor's the wrong way round for an easy conversion - but don't let minor details like that put you off turning that Fiesta into a beast.

Fitting a larger engine should be an easy enough upgrade for an experienced DIY-er, but this time, the insurance must be told, and it's likely they'll insist on a full engineer's report (these aren't especially expensive - look one up in the Yellow Pages, under "Garage Services" or "Vehicle Inspection").

Exhausts

It's gotta be done, hasn't it? Your rusty old exhaust lacks the girth to impress the girls, and doesn't so much growl as miaow. Don't be a wimp and fit an exhaust trim - they'll fool nobody who really knows, and they certainly won't add to your aural pleasure (oo-er). Sort yourself out a decent back box upgrade, and even a timid 1.0 litre Fiesta can begin to cut it at the cruise.

What a back box won't do on its own is increase engine power - although it'll certainly sound like it has, provided you choose the right one, and fit it properly. Check when you're buying that it can be fitted to a standard system - you'll probably need something called a reducing sleeve for a decent fit, which is a section of pipe designed to bridge the difference between your small-diameter pipe and the larger-diameter silencer. Try and measure your standard pipe as accurately as possible, or you'll have major problems trying to get a decent seal between the old and new bits - don't assume that exhaust paste will sort everything out, because it won't.

Fashion has even entered the aftermarket exhaust scene, with different rear pipe designs going in and out of style. Everyone's done the upswept twin-pipe "DTM" style pipes, while currently the trend in single pipes is "the bigger the better", or fat oval (or twin-oval) designs. Particularly with the upswept pipes, your rear bodywork may need protecting from the heat of the exhaust gases, and a trendy add-on is the heat-reflective ally panel - needless to say, this is also available in several designs, with the riveted look (similar to the ally filler cap) gaining most approval. Some people, though, reckon these panels are just tacky, and serve no useful purpose whatsoever! If you

Know your enemy - this is what your cat looks like inside. Is it any wonder they restrict gas flow?

must have the phattest Fiesta on the block, you can't beat a twin-exit system, even though it'll mean losing your spare wheel in the fitting process. Well, when was the last time you had a puncture? And what are mobiles and breakdown cover for, anyway?

If you've got a capacity-challenged Fiesta, you might need to lightly modify even your standard rear bodywork to accommodate a bigger rear pipe; if you're going for a bodykit later, your back box will have to come off again, so it can be poked through your rear valance/mesh.

You'll see some useful power gains if you go for the complete performance exhaust system, rather than just the back box. Like the factory-fit system, the sports silencer again will only work at its best if combined with the front pipe and manifold it was designed for! Performance four-branch manifolds alone can give very useful power gains for some Fiestas. Watch what you buy, though - cheap exhaust manifolds which crack for a pastime are not unknown, and many aftermarket systems need careful fitting and fettling before you'll stop it resonating or banging away underneath. A sports rear box alone shouldn't attract an increased insurance premium, but a full system probably will.

Later Fiestas are fitted with a catalytic converter (or "cat"), and you're no doubt aware that the cat acts like a restrictor in the exhaust, inhibiting the gas flow and sapping some engine power (maybe 5 to 10%). Several companies and exhaust specialists market replacement sections which do away with the cat (a "de-cat

pipe"), and these will have a useful effect, to be sure. You could easily have one made up, if you know someone handy with the welder - all you need is the two flanges and some half-decent pipe (from a scrapyard or motor factors). You could even get the non-cat replacement section for earlier Fiestas, direct from your local exhaust-u-like centre - but is it the same length? Unfortunately, by taking off or disabling the cat, your car won't be able to pass the emissions test at MOT time, so you'll have to "re-convert" the car every 12 months. This fact, arguably, means that the car is illegal on the road with a de-cat pipe fitted - you'd have no defence for this, if questions were asked at the roadside, and potentially no insurance if the unthinkable happens. Sorry, but we have to say it…

One other point to consider, if your Fiesta's been slammed to the floor - will your big new sports system be leaving behind a trail of sparks as it scrapes along the deck? Shouldn't do, if it's been properly fitted, but will the local multi-storey be out-of-bounds for your Fiesta, from now on? And - pub trivia moment - you can actually be done for causing damage to the highway, if your exhaust's dragging. Well, blummin' marvellous.

You probably couldn't give a stuff if your loud system's a very loud major public nuisance, but will that loud pipe start interfering with your sound system? If you rack up many motorway miles, you might find the constant drone of a loud pipe gets to be a real pain on a long trip, too…

Fitting a **back box**

First we've got to lose some rusty bits. It helps to remove the offside rear wheel for this, but it's not absolutely essential. Jack up the back end of the car - have a look in "Wheels 'n' tyres" for more info on jacking up. The back box splits just behind the rear axle. First, loosen off the clamp nuts **01** (hopefully, not too rusty - WD-40 works wonders).

Our box was suspended just at the rear, on a single rubber. The only trick required to make life easier here was to bend up the **02** tag on the metal peg, where it pokes through the rubber . . .

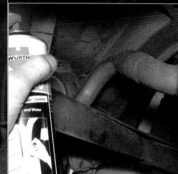

03 . . . before sliding the rubber off the peg. These can be very hard to get free, sometimes - use your largest screwdriver as a lever (some of that WD-40 might help, too).

04 Now all you've got to do is separate the pipes - ie split the box from the rest of the system. We won't try and pretend it's easy - large hammers, chisels and plenty of swearing are usually compulsory for this. Soak the joint in some more of that wonderful aerosol spray, and give it a few taps with a hammer (denting the pipes won't help them separate, but might relieve the frustration). Usually, twisting the pipes relative to each other is the most successful way to separate them. Good luck!

05 Before you go offering up your new silencer, clean up the joint area on the front pipe, then smear on some exhaust assembly paste. Put some inside the end of the new silencer too, if you like, but don't use too much, or lumps of it will break off and partly block your new free-flowing system - not good!

Our Peco system came with its own hanger, designed specially for use with a Fiesta - not often you see that, and it saves a lot of mucking about. Once the box is in, there's a clamp bolt to do up, at the side.

06

07 This is what we've been waiting for! Look at the pipe on that! Slide it into your new hanger, then slip a new exhaust clamp on at the front . . .

08 . . . connect up the front of the box, and tighten the new clamp nuts. So come on, what's it sound like?

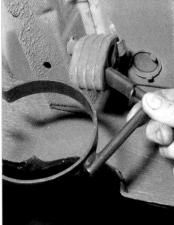

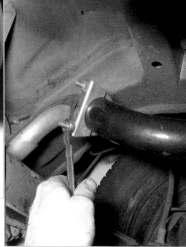

Four-exit system

Phat single pipes like our Peco are a good first-time choice for an exhaust upgrade, but if you're determined your Fiesta's going to turn heads and impress at the cruise, you'll need more than one pipe at the back end. Our Ashley four-pipe system is a "universal" fit (which means more work fitting than usual, but at least they supply plenty of bits in the kit!), and access to a welder is advisable. Fitting a multi-exit rear system should, of course, only be attempted during (or after) fitting that bodykit or rear bumper - we left the final fitting of our system to "our bodywork man" Ed, at SAD Motorsport.

01 Time to wave goodbye to that simply lovely spare wheel. For those of you who've never had to use it before, this is how it comes out. Wind down the spare wheel carrier at the back, using the large bolt at the back of the boot floor (note the cut-out which Liquid ICE cleverly made in our false floor).

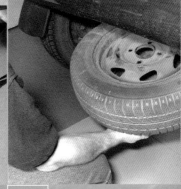

02 Eventually, the spare wheel can be taken out . . .

03 . . . which leaves behind the carrier itself. This can be unhooked from under the car, once you remove the clamp washers from the ends of the hooks.

04 All that's left is unscrewing the hook which the carrier used to hang on. You'll probably need to do what we did, and clamp the hook with a pair of pliers, while unscrewing it from the top. It's not meant to unscrew as far as we're going to, so put some effort into it!

05 Finally, the offending object is removed, leaving a clear playing field under the back end for all your new pipework. Lovely.

06 Fitting a four-exit system will obviously involve modifying your rear bodywork, and more than just slightly. Our new 12-bore rear bumper is about to get the fright of its life - first we mark up the bits we don't want (all three holes here will be meshed later) . . .

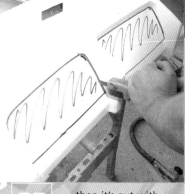

07 . . . then it's out with the sharp objects to make us some exhaust-friendly holes. Notice we didn't cut the whole section out - leaving some glassfibre at the bottom will make meshing a lot easier.

08 Now hang the rear bumper back on, to see what else is in the way, behind our new holes. Oh dear - looks like the old rear valance is about to get chopped as well.

09 Ed's air hacksaw takes no prisoners, and the offending metalwork soon surrenders.

10 Remove the sharp edge with a touch of the grinder, and add some paint, to help fend off the tin worm.

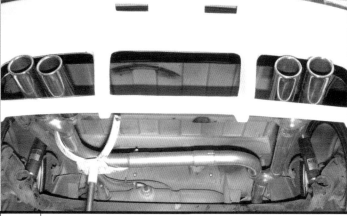

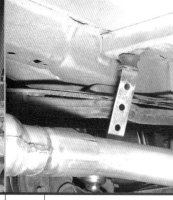

11 Our universal rear box came with all sorts of pipes, bends and joints - now we have to assemble them as best we can, to see what fits, and what needs chopping. This all looks pretty pukka. When the fit's satisfactory, make alignment marks across the pipe joints, so they can be welded in the right places.

12 One disadvantage with anything "universal" is that it always needs more effort and expertise to fit. If you're not too hot at welding, find someone who is. The bends have to be welded at the right angle, or none of it will fit. This is why marking the sections relative to each other is so important, to preserve the alignment, and reduce the need for much bending later.

13 Some home-made brackets will almost certainly be needed, and existing ones may need "adjustment". Hang the new pipework up so that it's supported but not under strain - any pipe or bracket that's being stressed will crack sooner or later. Decent welding on any made-up bracket is a must, and use rubber mounts between metal brackets and metal car.

Safety and tools

Safety

We all know that working on your car can be dangerous - and we're not talking about the danger of losing your street cred by fitting naff alloys or furry dice! Okay, so you'd be hard-pushed to injure yourself fitting some cool floor mats or a tax disc holder, but tackle more-serious mods, and you could be treading dangerous ground. Let's be honest - we have to put this safety section in to cover ourselves, but now it's in, it would be nice if you read it…

Burning/scalding

The only way you'll really burn yourself is if your car's just been running - avoid this, and you won't get burned. Easy, eh? Otherwise, you risk burns from any hot parts of the engine (and especially the exhaust - if you've got one, the cat runs very hot), or from spilling hot coolant if you undo the radiator hoses or filler cap, as you might when you're braiding hoses.

Fire

Sadly, there's several ways your car could catch fire, when you think about it. You've got a big tank full of fuel (and other flammable liquids about, like brake fluid), together with electrics - some of which run to very high voltages. If you smoke too, this could be even worse for your health than you thought.

a Liquid fuel is flammable. Fuel vapour can explode - don't smoke, or create any kind of spark, if there's fuel vapour (fuel smell) about.

b Letting fuel spill onto a hot engine is dangerous, but brake fluid spills go up even more readily. Respect is due with brake fluid, which also attacks paintwork and plastics - wash off with water.

c Fires can also be started by careless modding involving the electrical system. It's possible to overload (and overheat) existing wiring by tapping off too many times for new live feeds. Not insulating bare wires or connections can lead to short-circuits, and the sparks or overheated wiring which results can start a fire. Always investigate any newly-wired-in kit which stops working, or which keeps blowing fuses - those wires could already be smouldering…

Crushing

Having your car land on top of you is no laughing matter, and it's a nasty accident waiting to happen if you risk using dodgy old jacks, bricks, and other means of lifting/supporting your car. Please don't.

Your standard vehicle jack is for emergency roadside use only - a proper trolley jack and a set of axle stands won't break the overdraft, and might save broken bones. Don't buy a cheap trolley jack, and don't expect a well-used secondhand one to be perfect, either - when the hydraulic seals start to fail, a trolley jack will drop very fast; this is why you should always have decent stands in place under the car as well.

Steering, suspension & brakes

Screwing up any one of these on your car, through badly-fitted mods, could land you and others in hospital or worse. Nuff said? It's always worth getting a mate, or a friendly garage, to check over what you've just fitted (or even what you've just had fitted, in some cases - not all "pro" fitters are perfect!). Pay attention to tightening vital nuts and bolts properly - buy or borrow a torque wrench.

To be absolutely sure, take your newly-modded machine to a friendly MOT tester (if there is such a thing) - this man's your ultimate authority on safety, after all. Even if he's normally a pain once a year, he could save your life. Think it over.

Even properly-fitted mods can radically alter the car's handling - and not always for the better. Take a few days getting used to how the car feels before showing off.

Wheels

Don't take liberties fitting wheels. Make sure the wheels have the right stud/bolt hole pattern for your car, and that the wheel nuts/bolts are doing their job. Bolts which are too long might catch on your brakes (especially rear drums) - too short, and, well, the wheels are just waiting to fall off. Not nice. Also pay attention to the bolt heads or wheel nuts - some are supposed to have large tapered washers fitted, to locate properly in the wheel. If the nuts/bolts "pull through" the wheel when tightened, the wheel's gonna fall off, isn't it?

Asbestos

Only likely to be a major worry when working on, or near, your brakes. That black dust that gets all over your alloys comes from your brake pads, and it may contain asbestos. Breathing in asbestos dust can lead to a disease called asbestosis (inflammation of the lungs - very nasty indeed), so try not to inhale brake dust when you're changing your pads or discs.

Airbags

Unless you run into something at high speed, the only time an airbag will enter your life is when you change your steering wheel for something more sexy, and have to disable the airbag in the process. Pay attention to all the precautionary advice given in our text, and you'll have no problems.

One more thing - don't tap into the airbag wiring to run any extra electrical kit. Any mods to the airbag circuit could set it off unexpectedly.

Exhaust gases

Even on cars with cats, exhaust fumes are still potentially lethal. Don't work in an unventilated garage with the engine running. When fitting new exhaust bits, be sure that there's no gas leakage from the joints. When modifying in the tailgate area, note that exhaust gas can get sucked into the car through badly-fitting tailgate seals/joints (or even through your rear arches, if they've been trimmed so much there's holes into the car).

Tools

In writing this book, we've assumed you already have a selection of basic tools - screwdrivers, socket set, spanners, hammer, sharp knife, power drill. Any unusual extra tools you might need are mentioned in the relevant text. Torx and Allen screws are often found on trim panels, so a set of keys of each type is a wise purchase.

From a safety angle, always buy the best tools you can afford - or if you must use cheap ones, remember that they can break under stress or unusual usage (and we've all got the busted screwdrivers to prove it!).

DO Wear goggles when using power tools.

DO Keep loose clothing/long hair away from moving engine parts.

DO Take off watches and jewellery when working on electrics.

DO Keep the work area tidy - stops accidents and losing parts.

DON'T Rush a job, or take stupid short-cuts.

DON'T Use the wrong tools for the job, or ones which don't fit.

DON'T Let kids or pets play around your car when you're working.

DON'T Work entirely alone under a car that's been jacked up.

Legal modding?
No such thing!!

The harsh & painful truth

The minute you start down the road to a modified motor, you stand a good chance of being in trouble with the Man. It seems like there's almost nothing worthwhile you can do to your car, without breaking some sort of law. So the answer's not to do it at all, then? Well, no, but let's keep it real.

There's this bunch of vehicle-related regulations called Construction & Use. It's a huge set of books, used by the car manufacturers and the Department of Transport among others, and it sets out in black and white all the legal issues that could land you in trouble. It's the ultimate authority for modifying, in theory. But few people (and even fewer policemen) know all of it inside-out, and it's forever being updated and revised, so it's not often enforced to the letter at the roadside - just in court. Despite the existence of C & U, in trying to put together any guide to the law and modifying, it quickly becomes clear that almost everything's a "grey area", with no-one prepared to go on record and say what is okay to modify and what's not. Well, brilliant. So if there's no fixed rules (in the real world), how are you meant to live by them? In the circumstances, all we can promise to do is help to make sense of nonsense...

Avoiding roadside interviews

Why do some people get pulled all the time, and others hardly ever? It's often all about attitude. We'd all like to be free to drive around "in yer face", windows down, system full up, loud exhaust bellowing, sparks striking, tyres squealing - but - nothing is a bigger "come-on" to the boys in blue than "irresponsible" driving like this. Rest assured,

if your motor's anywhere near fully sorted, the coppers will find something they can nick you for, when they pull you over - it's a dead cert. Trying not to wind them up too much before this happens (and certainly not once you're stopped) will make for an easier life. There's showing off, and then there's taking the pee. Save it for the next cruise.

The worst thing from your point of view is that, once you've been stopped, it's down to that particular copper's judgement as to whether your car's illegal. If he/she's having a bad day anyway, smart-mouthing-off isn't gonna help your case at all. If you can persuade him/her that you're at least taking on board what's being said, you might be let off with a warning. If it goes further, you'll be reported for an offence - while this doesn't mean you'll end up being prosecuted for it, it ain't good. Some defects (like worn tyres) will result in a so-called "seven-day wonder", which usually means you have to fix whatever's deemed wrong, maybe get the car inspected, and present yourself with the proof at a police station, inside seven days, or face prosecution.

If you can manage to drive reasonably sensibly when the law's about, and can ideally show that you've tried to keep your car legal when you get questioned, you stand a much better chance of enjoying your relationship with your modded beast. This guide is intended to help you steer clear of the more obvious things you could get pulled for. By reading it, you might even be able to have an informed, well-mannered discussion about things legal with the next officer of the law you meet at the side of the road. As in: "Oh really, officer? I was not aware of that. Thank you for pointing it out." Just don't argue with them, that's all...

Documents

The first thing you'll be asked to produce. If you're driving around without tax, MOT or insurance, we might as well stop now, as you won't be doing much more driving of anything after just one pull.

Okay, so you don't normally carry all your car-related documents with you - for safety, you've got them stashed carefully at home, haven't you? But carrying photocopies of your licence, MOT and insurance certificate is a good idea. While they're not legally-binding absolute proof, producing these in a roadside check might mean you don't have to produce the real things at a copshop later in the week. Shows a certain responsibility, and confidence in your own legality on the road, too. In some parts of the country, it's even said to be a good idea to carry copies of any receipts for your stereo gear - if there's any suspicion about it being stolen (surely not), some coppers have been known to confiscate it (or the car it's in) on the spot!

Number plates

One of the simplest mods, and one of the easiest to spot (and prove) if you're a copper. Nowadays, any changes made to the standard approved character font (such as italics or fancy type), spacing, or size of the plate constitutes an offence. Remember too that if you've moved the rear plate from its original spot (like from the tailgate recess, during smoothing) it still has to be properly lit at night. You're unlikely to even buy an illegal plate now, as the companies making them are also liable for prosecution if you get stopped. It's all just something else to blame on speed cameras - plates have to be easy for them to shoot, and modding yours suggests you're trying to escape a speeding conviction (well, who isn't?).

Getting pulled for an illegal plate is for suckers - you're making it too easy for them. While this offence only entails a small fine and confiscation of the plates, you're drawing unwelcome police attention to the rest of your car. Not smart. At all.

Sunstrips and tints

The sunstrip is now an essential item for any modded motor, but telling Mr Plod you had to fit one is no defence if you've gone a bit too far. The sunstrip should not be so low down the screen that it interferes with your ability to see out. Is this obvious? Apparently not. As a guide, if the strip's so low your wiper(s) touch it, it's too low. Don't try fitting short wiper blades to get round this - the police aren't as stupid as that, and you could get done for wipers that don't clear a sufficient area of the screen. Push it so far, and no further!

Window tinting is a trickier area. It seems you can have up to a 25% tint on a windscreen, and up to 30% on all other glass - but how do you measure this? Er. And what do you do if your glass is tinted to start with? Er, probably nothing. Of course you can buy window film in various "darknesses", from not-very-dark to "ambulance-black", but being able to buy it does not make it legal for road use (most companies cover themselves by saying "for show use only"). Go for just a light smoke on the side and rear glass, and you'd have to be unlucky to get done for it. If you must fit really dark tints, you're safest doing the rear side windows only.

Some forces now have a light meter to test light transmission through glass at the roadside - fail this, and it's a big on-the-spot fine.

Single wiper conversion

Not usually a problem, and certainly not worth a pull on its own, but combine a big sunstrip with a short wiper blade, and you're just asking for trouble. Insufficient view of the road ahead. There's also the question of whether it's legal to have the arm parking vertically, in the centre of the screen, as it obscures your vision. Probably not legal, then - even if it looks cool. Unfortunately, the Man doesn't do cool.

Lights

Lights of all kinds have to be one of the single biggest problem areas in modifying, and the police are depressingly well-informed. Most people make light mods a priority, whether it's Morette conversions for headlights or Lexus-style rear clusters. If they fit alright, and work, what's the problem?

First off, don't bother with any lights which aren't fully UK-legal - it's just too much hassle. Being "E-marked" only makes them legal in Europe, and most of our Euro-chums drive on the right. One of our project cars ended up with left-hand-drive rear clusters, and as a result, had no rear reflectors and a rear foglight on the wrong side (should be on the right). Getting stopped for not having rear reflectors would be a bit harsh, but why risk it, even to save a few quid?

Once you've had any headlight mods done (other than light brows) always have the beam alignment checked - it's part of the MOT, after all. The same applies to any front fogs or spots you've fitted (the various points of law involved here are too many to mention - light colour, height, spacing, operation with main/dipped headlights - ask at an MOT centre before fitting, and have them checked out after fitting).

If Plod's really having a bad day, he might even question the legality of your new blue headlight bulbs - are they too powerful? Keeping the bulb packaging in the glovebox might be a neat solution here (60/55W max).

Many modders favour spraying rear light clusters to make them look trick, as opposed to replacing them - but there's trouble in store here, too. One of the greyest of grey areas is - how much light tinting is too much? The much-talked-about but not-often-seen "common sense" comes into play here. Making your lights so dim that they're reduced to a feeble red/orange glow is pretty dim itself. If you're spraying, only use proper light-tinting spray, and not too many coats of that. Colour-coding lights with ordinary spray paint is best left to a pro sprayer or bodyshop (it can be done by mixing lots of lacquer with not much paint, for instance). Tinted lights are actually more of a problem in daylight than at night, so check yours while the sun's out.

Lastly, two words about neons. Oh, dear. It seems that neons of all kinds have now been deemed illegal for road use (and that's

interior ones as well as exteriors, which have pretty much always been a no-no). If you fit neons inside, make sure you rig in a switch so you can easily turn them off when the law arrives - or don't drive around with them on (save it for when you're parked up). Distracts other road users, apparently.

ICE

Jungle massive, or massive public nuisance? The two sides of the ICE argument in a nutshell. If you've been around the modding scene for any length of time, you'll already know stories of people who've been done for playing car stereos too loud. Seems some local authorities now have by-laws concerning "music audible from outside a vehicle", and hefty fines if you're caught. Even where this isn't the case, and assuming a dB meter isn't on hand to prove the offence of "excessive noise", the police can still prosecute for "disturbing the peace" - on the basis of one officer's judgement of the noise level. If a case is proved, you could lose your gear. Whoops. Seems we're back to "do it - but don't over-do it" again. If you really want to demo your system, pick somewhere a bit less public (like a quiet trading estate, after dark) or go for safety in numbers (at a cruise).

Big alloys/tyres

One of the first things to go on any lad's car, sexy alloys are right at the heart of car modifying. So what'll interest the law?

Well, the first thing every copper's going to wonder is - are the wheels nicked? He'd need a good reason to accuse you, but this is another instance where having copies of receipts might prove useful.

Otherwise, the wheels mustn't rub on, or stick out from, the arches - either of these will prove to be a problem if you get stopped. And you don't need to drive a modded motor to get done for having bald tyres…

Lowered suspension

Of course you have to lower your car, to have any hope of street cred. But did you know it's actually an offence to cause damage to the road surface, if your car's so low (or your mates so lardy) that it grounds out? Apparently so! Never mind what damage it might be doing to your exhaust, or the brake/fuel lines under the car - you can actually get done for risking damage to the road. Well, great. What's the answer? Once you've lowered the car, load it up with your biggest mates, and test it over roads you normally use - or else find a route into town that avoids all speed bumps. If you've got coilovers, you'll have an easier time tuning out the scraping noises.

Remember that your new big-bore exhaust or backbox must be hung up well enough that it doesn't hit the deck, even if you

haven't absolutely slammed your car on the floor. At night, leaving a trail of sparks behind is a bit of a giveaway…

Exhausts

One of the easiest-to-fit performance upgrades, and another essential item if you want to be taken seriously on the street. Unless your chosen pipe/system is just too damn loud, you'd be very unlucky to get stopped for it, but if you will draw attention this way, you could be kicking yourself later.

For instance - have you in fact fitted a home-made straight-through pipe, to a car which used to have a "cat"? By drawing Plod's attention with that extra-loud system, he could then ask you to get the car's emissions tested - worse, you could get pulled for a "random" roadside emissions check. Fail this (and you surely will), and you could be right in the brown stuff. Even if you re-convert the car back to stock for the MOT, you'll be illegal on the road (and therefore without insurance) whenever your loud pipe's on. Still sound like fun, or would you be happier with just a back box?

It's also worth mentioning that your tailpipe mustn't stick out beyond the very back of the car, or in any other way which might be dangerous to pedestrians. Come on - you were a ped once!

Bodykits

The popular bodykits for the UK market have all passed the relevant tests, and are fully-approved for use on the specific vehicles they're intended for. As long as you haven't messed up fitting a standard kit, you should be fine, legally-speaking. The trouble starts when you do your own little mods and tweaks, such as bodging on that huge whale-tail spoiler or front air dam/splitter - it can be argued in some cases that these aren't appropriate on safety grounds, and you can get prosecuted. If any bodywork is fitted so it obscured your lights, or so badly attached that a strong breeze might blow it off, you can see their point. At least there's no such thing as Style Police. Not yet, anyway.

Seats and harnesses

Have to meet the UK safety standards, and must be securely bolted in. That's about it. It should be possible to fasten and release any seat belt or harness with one hand. Given that seat belts are pretty important safety features, it's understandable then that the police don't like to see flimsy alloy rear strut braces used as seat harness mounting points. Any other signs of bodging will also spell trouble. It's unlikely they'd bother with a full safety inspection at the roadside, but they could insist on a full MOT test/engineer's report inside 7 days. It's your life.

While we're on the subject of crash safety, the police also don't like to see sub boxes and amps just lying on the carpet, where the back seat used to be - if it's not anchored down, where are these items gonna end up, in a big shunt? Embedded in you, possibly?

Other mods

We'll never cover everything else here, and the law's always changing anyway, so we're fighting a losing battle in a book like this, but here goes with some other legalistic points we've noted on the way:

a It's illegal to remove side repeaters from front wings, even to create the ultimate smoothed/flushed motor. Sorry.

b All except the most prehistoric cars must have at least one rear foglight. If there's only one, it must be fitted on the right. We've never heard of anyone getting stopped for it, but you must also have a pair of rear reflectors. If your rear clusters ain't got 'em, can you get trendy ones? Er, no.

c Fuel filler caps have to be fitted so there's no danger of fuel spillage, or of excess fumes leaking from the top of the filler neck. This means using an appropriate petrol-resistant sealer (should be supplied in the kit). Oh, and not bodging the job in general seems a good idea. Unlikely to attract a pull, though.

d Front doors have to retain a manual means of opening from outside, even if they've been de-locked for remote locking. This means you can't take off the front door handles, usually. It seems that rear door handles can be removed if you like.

e Tailgates have to have some means of opening, even if it's only from inside, once the lock/handle's been removed. We think it's another safety thing - means of escape in a crash, and all that.

f You have to have at least one exterior mirror, and it must be capable of being adjusted somehow.

g If you fit new fog and spotlights, they actually have to work. No-one fits new lights just for show (or do they?), but if they stop working later when a fuse blows, relay packs up, or the wiring connectors rust up, you'd better fix 'em or remove 'em.

h Pedal extensions must have rubbers fitted on the brake and clutch pedals, and must be spaced sufficiently so there's no chance of hitting two pedals at once. This last bit sounds obvious, but lots of extension sets out there are so hard to fit that achieving this can be rather difficult. Don't get caught out.

i On cars with airbags, if you fit a sports wheel and disconnect the airbag in the process, the airbag warning light will be on permanently. Apart from being annoying, this is also illegal.

j Pace-car strobe lights (or any other flashing lights, apart from indicators) are illegal for road use. Of course.

k Anything else we didn't think of - is probably illegal too. Sorry.

Any questions? Try the MOT Helpline (0845 6005977). Yes, really.

Thanks to Andrew Dare of the Vehicle Inspectorate, Exeter, for his help in steering us through this minefield!

This Safety Devices rear roll cage (with diagonal) was fitted to our Fiesta just too late for a procedure to be featured in the book. Sorry!

Thanks to:

We gratefully acknowledge all the help and advice offered from the following suppliers, without whom, etc, etc. Many of those credited below went way beyond the call of duty to help us produce this book - you know who you are. Cheers, guys! Roll the credits…

A & I Peco
0151 647 6041

Ashley Competition Exhausts
01922 720767

Auto Imparts
01525 382713

Auto Tint Design
0113 289 1500

Autoleads
01420 476767

Britania Cars
01442 490700

BBG
0208 863 9117

Brown & Geeson Distribution Ltd (Momo)
01268 764411

Cambridgeshire Chemicals Limited (Rage paint)
01480 880100

Champion
0151 522 3000

Corbeau Seats Ltd
01424 854499

Dash Dynamics
01942 222531

Demon Tweeks
01978 663000

Dimma UK
01606 854377

ESP
01621 869 866

Eurostyling (Folia Tec)
01908 324950

Fibre Sports
01268 282723

GP Automotive
01562 67610

Green Filters
(Auto Imparts)
01525 382713

H & R Springs
01375 489500

Halfords
08457 626 625

LA & RW Piper
(car trimming)
01935 851676

Liquid ICE
01935 433500

Lockwood International
0113 272 3200

Mono Style
0870 742 5181

R & A Design
01472 811711

Red Dot Racing
020 8888 2354

RGM
01525 853888

Richbrook
0208 543 7111

Ripspeed at Halfords
0845 609 1259

S.A.D Motorsport (Ed)
(body styling)
01935 432352

Safety Devices
01353 724201

Toyo Tyres
01933 411144

Trillogy
01280 822865

Ultra World
0800 652 2155

Wolfrace Wheels
01621 843770

Yokohama Ltd
01908 625625

A special thank you to:
Brodie Baxter
Jon Hill (cover shots)
Bryn Musselwhite

Project Manager	Matthew Minter
Designer	Simon Larkin
Page Build	James Robertson
Workshop	Paul Buckland Pete Trott
Editor	Ian Barnes
Project Co-ordinator	Carole Turk
Production Control	Kevin Heals

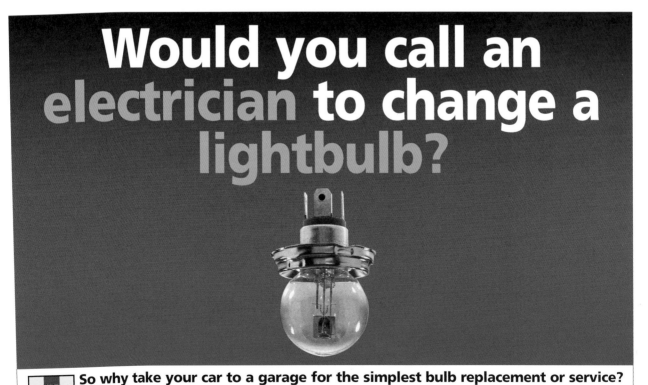

Haynes Car Manuals

Haynes Manuals

Alfa Romeo Alfasud/Sprint (74 - 88) 0292
Alfa Romeo Alfetta (73 - 87) 0531
Audi 80 (72 - Feb 79) 0207
Audi 80, 90 (79 - Oct 86) & Coupe (81 - Nov 88) 0605
Audi 80, 90 (Oct 86 - 90) & Coupe (Nov 88 - 90) 1491
Audi 100 (Oct 82 - 90) & 200 (Feb 84 - Oct 89) 0907
Audi 100 & A6 Petrol & Diesel (May 91 - May 97) 3504
Audi A4 (95 - Feb 00) 3575
Austin A35 & A40 (56 - 67) 0118
Austin Allegro 1100, 1300, 1.0, 1.1 & 1.3 (73 - 82) 0164
Austin Healey 100/6 & 3000 (56 - 68) 0049
Austin/MG/Rover Maestro 1.3 & 1.6 (83 - 95) 0922
Austin/MG Metro (80 - May 90) 0718
Austin/Rover Montego 1.3 & 1.6 (84 - 94) 1066
Austin/MG/Rover Montego 2.0 (84 - 95) 1067
Austin/Rover 2.0 litre Diesel Engine (86 - 93) 1857
Bedford CF (69 - 87) 0163
Bedford/Vauxhall Rascal & Suzuki Supercarry (86 - Oct 94) 3015
BMW 1500, 1502, 1600, 1602, 2000 & 2002 (59 - 77) 0240
BMW 316, 320 & 320i (4-cyl) (75 - Feb 83) 0276
BMW 320, 320i, 323i & 325i (6-cyl) (Oct 77 - Sept 87) 0815
BMW 3-Series (Apr 91 - 96) 3210
BMW 3- & 5-Series (sohc)(81 - 91) 1948
BMW 520i & 525e (Oct 81 - June 88) 1560
BMW 525, 528 & 528i (73 - Sept 81) 0632
Citroën 2CV, Ami & Dyane (67 - 90) 0196
Citroën AX Petrol & Diesel (87 - 97) 3014
Citroën BX (83 - 94) 0908
Citroën C15 Van Petrol & Diesel (89 - Oct 98) 3509
Citroën CX (75 - 88) 0528
Citroën Saxo Petrol & Diesel (96 - 01) 3506
Citroën Visa (79 - 88) 0620
Citroën Xantia Petrol & Diesel (93 - 98) 3082
Citroën XM Petrol & Diesel (89 - 98) 3451
Citroën Xsara Petrol & Diesel (97 - Sept 00) 3751
Citroën ZX Diesel (91 - 98) 1922
Citroën ZX Petrol (91 - 98) 1881
Citroën 1.7 & 1.9 litre Diesel Engine (84 - 96) 1379
Fiat 126 (73 - 87) 0305
Fiat 500 (57 - 73) 0090
Fiat Bravo & Brava (95 - 00) 3572
Fiat Cinquecento (93 - 98) 3501
Fiat Panda (81 - 95) 0793
Fiat Punto Petrol & Diesel (94 - Oct 99) 3251
Fiat Regata (84 - 88) 1167
Fiat Tipo (88 - 91) 1625
Fiat Uno (83 - 95) 0923
Fiat X1/9 (74 - 89) 0273
Ford Anglia (59 - 68) 0001
Ford Capri II (& III) 1.6 & 2.0 (74 - 87) 0283
Ford Capri II (& III) 2.8 & 3.0 (74 - 87) 1309
Ford Cortina Mk III 1300 & 1600 (70 - 76) 0070
Ford Cortina Mk IV (& V) 1.6 & 2.0 (76 - 83) 0343
Ford Cortina Mk IV (& V) 2.3 V6 (77 - 83) 0426
Ford Escort Mk I 1100 & 1300 (68 - 74) 0171
Ford Escort Mk I Mexico, RS 1600 & RS 2000 (70 - 74) 0139
Ford Escort Mk II Mexico, RS 1800 & RS 2000 (75 - 80) 0735
Ford Escort (75 - Aug 80) 0280
Ford Escort (Sept 80 - Sept 90) 0686
Ford Escort & Orion (Sept 90 - 00) 1737
Ford Fiesta (76 - Aug 83) 0334
Ford Fiesta (Aug 83 - Feb 89) 1030
Ford Fiesta (Feb 89 - Oct 95) 1595
Ford Fiesta (Oct 95 - 01) 3397
Ford Focus (98 - 01) 3759
Ford Granada (Sept 77 - Feb 85) 0481
Ford Granada & Scorpio (Mar 85 - 94) 1245
Ford Ka (96 - 99) 3570
Ford Mondeo Petrol (93 - 99) 1923
Ford Mondeo Diesel (93 - 96) 3465
Ford Orion (83 - Sept 90) 1009
Ford Sierra 4 cyl. (82 - 93) 0903
Ford Sierra V6 (82 - 91) 0904
Ford Transit Petrol (Mk 2) (78 - Jan 86) 0719
Ford Transit Petrol (Mk 3) (Feb 86 - 89) 1468
Ford Transit Diesel (Feb 86 - 99) 3019
Ford 1.6 & 1.8 litre Diesel Engine (84 - 96) 1172
Ford 2.1, 2.3 & 2.5 litre Diesel Engine (77 - 90) 1606
Freight Rover Sherpa (74 - 87) 0463
Hillman Avenger (70 - 82) 0037
Hillman Imp (63 - 76) 0022
Honda Accord (76 - Feb 84) 0351
Honda Civic (Feb 84 - Oct 87) 1226
Honda Civic (Nov 91 - 96) 3199
Hyundai Pony (85 - 94) 3398
Jaguar E Type (61 - 72) 0140
Jaguar Mk I & II, 240 & 340 (55 - 69) 0098

Jaguar XJ6, XJ & Sovereign; Daimler Sovereign (68 - Oct 86) 0242
Jaguar XJ6 & Sovereign (Oct 86 - Sept 94) 3261
Jaguar XJ12, XJS & Sovereign; Daimler Double Six (72 - 88) 0478
Jeep Cherokee Petrol (93 - 96) 1943
Lada 1200, 1300, 1500 & 1600 (74 - 91) 0413
Lada Samara (87 - 91) 1610
Land Rover 90, 110 & Defender Diesel (83 - 95) 3017
Land Rover Discovery Petrol & Diesel (89 - 98) 3016
Land Rover Series IIA & III Diesel (58 - 85) 0529
Land Rover Series II, IIA & III Petrol (58 - 85) 0314
Mazda 323 (Mar 81 - Oct 89) 1608
Mazda 323 (Oct 89 - 98) 3455
Mazda 626 (May 83 - Sept 87) 0929
Mazda B-1600, B-1800 & B-2000 Pick-up (72 - 88) 0267
Mazda RX-7 (79 - 85) 0460
Mercedes-Benz 190, 190E & 190D Petrol & Diesel (83 - 93) 3450
Mercedes-Benz 200, 240, 300 Diesel (Oct 76 - 85) 1114
Mercedes-Benz 250 & 280 (68 - 72) 0346
Mercedes-Benz 250 & 280 (123 Series) (Oct 76 - 84) 0677
Mercedes-Benz 124 Series (85 - Aug 93) 3253
Mercedes-Benz C-Class Petrol & Diesel (93 - Aug 00) 3511
MGA (55 - 62) 0475
MGB (62 - 80) 0111
MG Midget & AH Sprite (58 - 80) 0265
Mini (59 - 69) 0527
Mini (69 - Oct 96) 0646
Mitsubishi Shogun & L200 Pick-Ups (83 - 94) 1944
Morris Ital 1.3 (80 - 84) 0705
Morris Minor 1000 (56 - 71) 0024
Nissan Bluebird (May 84 - Mar 86) 1223
Nissan Bluebird (Mar 86 - 90) 1473
Nissan Cherry (Sept 82 - 86) 1031
Nissan Micra (83 - Jan 93) 0931
Nissan Micra (93 - 99) 3254
Nissan Primera (90 - Aug 99) 1851
Nissan Stanza (82 - 86) 0824
Nissan Sunny (May 82 - Oct 86) 0895
Nissan Sunny (Oct 86 - Mar 91) 1378
Nissan Sunny (Apr 91 - 95) 3219
Opel Ascona & Manta (B Series) (Sept 75 - 88) 0316
Opel Kadett (Nov 79 - Oct 84) 0634
Opel Rekord (Feb 78 - Oct 86) 0543
Peugeot 106 Petrol & Diesel (91 - 01) 1882
Peugeot 205 Petrol (83 - 97) 0932
Peugeot 206 Petrol and Diesel (98 - 01) 3757
Peugeot 305 (78 - 89) 0538
Peugeot 306 Petrol & Diesel (93 - 99) 3073
Peugeot 309 (86 - 93) 1266
Peugeot 405 Petrol (88 - 97) 1559
Peugeot 405 Diesel (88 - 97) 3198
Peugeot 406 Petrol & Diesel (96 - 97) 3394
Peugeot 505 (79 - 89) 0762
Peugeot 1.7/1.8 & 1.9 litre Diesel Engine (82 - 96) 0950
Peugeot 2.0, 2.1, 2.3 & 2.5 litre Diesel Engines (74 - 90) 1607
Porsche 911 (65 - 85) 0264
Porsche 924 & 924 Turbo (76 - 85) 0397
Proton (89 - 97) 3255
Range Rover V8 (70 - Oct 92) 0606
Reliant Robin & Kitten (73 - 83) 0436
Renault 4 (61 - 86) 0072
Renault 5 (Feb 85 - 96) 1219
Renault 9 & 11 (82 - 89) 0822
Renault 18 (79 - 86) 0598
Renault 19 Petrol (89 - 94) 1646
Renault 19 Diesel (89 - 95) 1946
Renault 21 (86 - 94) 1397
Renault 25 (84 - 92) 1228
Renault Clio Petrol (91 - May 98) 1853
Renault Clio Diesel (91 - June 96) 3031
Renault Clio Petrol & Diesel (May 98 - May 01) 3906
Renault Espace Petrol & Diesel (85 - 96) 3197
Renault Fuego (80 - 86) 0764
Renault Laguna Petrol & Diesel (94 - 00) 3252
Renault Mégane & Scénic Petrol & Diesel (96 - 98) 3395
Rover 213 & 216 (84 - 89) 1116
Rover 214 & 414 (89 - 96) 1689
Rover 216 & 416 (89 - 96) 1830
Rover 211, 214, 216, 218 & 220 Petrol & Diesel (Dec 95 - 98) 3399
Rover 414, 416 & 420 Petrol & Diesel (May 95 - 98) 3453
Rover 618, 620 & 623 (93 - 97) 3257
Rover 820, 825 & 827 (86 - 95) 1380
Rover 3500 (76 - 87) 0365
Rover Metro, 111 & 114 (May 90 - 98) 1711
Saab 90, 99 & 900 (79 - Oct 93) 0765
Saab 95 & 96 (66 - 76) 0198
Saab 99 (69 - 79) 0247

Saab 900 (Oct 93 - 98) 3512
Saab 9000 (4-cyl) (85 - 98) 1686
Seat Ibiza & Cordoba Petrol & Diesel (Oct 93 - Oct 99) 3571
Seat Ibiza & Malaga (85 - 92) 1609
Skoda Estelle (77 - 89) 0604
Skoda Favorit (89 - 96) 1801
Skoda Felicia Petrol & Diesel (95 - 99) 3505
Subaru 1600 & 1800 (Nov 79 - 90) 0995
Sunbeam Alpine, Rapier & H120 (67 - 76) 0051
Suzuki Supercarry (86 - Oct 94)
Suzuki SJ Series, Samurai & Vitara (4-cyl) (82 - 97) 1942
Talbot Alpine, Solara, Minx & Rapier (75 - 86) 0337
Talbot Horizon (78 - 86) 0473
Talbot Samba (82 - 86) 0823
Toyota Carina E (May 92 - 97) 3256
Toyota Corolla (Sept 83 - Sept 87) 1024
Toyota Corolla (80 - 85) 0683
Toyota Corolla (Sept 87 - Aug 92) 1683
Toyota Corolla (Aug 92 - 97) 3259
Toyota Hi-Ace & Hi-Lux (69 - Oct 83) 0304
Triumph Acclaim (81 - 84) 0792
Triumph GT6 & Vitesse (62 - 74) 0112
Triumph Herald (59 - 71) 0010
Triumph Spitfire (62 - 81) 0113
Triumph Stag (70 - 78) 0441
Triumph TR2, 3, 3A, 4 & 4A (52 - 67) 0028
Triumph TR5 & 6 (67 - 75) 0031
Triumph TR7 (75 - 82) 0322
Vauxhall Astra (80 - Oct 84) 0635
Vauxhall Astra & Belmont (Oct 84 - Oct 91) 1136
Vauxhall Astra (Oct 91 - Feb 98) 1832
Vauxhall/Opel Astra & Zafira Diesel (Feb 98 - Sept 00) 3797
Vauxhall/Opel Astra & Zafira Petrol (Feb 98 - Sept 00) 3758
Vauxhall/Opel Calibra (90 - 98) 3502
Vauxhall Carlton (Oct 78 - Oct 86) 0480
Vauxhall Carlton & Senator (Nov 86 - 94) 1469
Vauxhall Cavalier 1300 (77 - July 81) 0461
Vauxhall Cavalier 1600, 1900 & 2000 (75 - July 81) 0315
Vauxhall Cavalier (81 - Oct 88) 0812
Vauxhall Cavalier (Oct 88 - 95) 1570
Vauxhall Chevette (75 - 84) 0285
Vauxhall Corsa (Mar 93 - 97) 1985
Vauxhall/Opel Frontera Petrol & Diesel (91 - Sept 98) 3454
Vauxhall Nova (83 - 93) 0909
Vauxhall/Opel Omega (94 - 99) 3510
Vauxhall Vectra Petrol & Diesel (95 - 98) 3396
Vauxhall/Opel 1.5, 1.6 & 1.7 litre Diesel Engine (82 - 96) 1222
Volkswagen 411 & 412 (68 - 75) 0091
Volkswagen Beetle 1200 (54 - 77) 0036
Volkswagen Beetle 1300 & 1500 (65 - 75) 0039
Volkswagen Beetle 1302 & 1302S (70 - 72) 0110
Volkswagen Beetle 1303, 1303S & GT (72 - 75) 0159
Volkswagen Beetle (Apr 99 - 01) 3798
Volkswagen Golf & Jetta Mk 1 1.1 & 1.3 (74 - 84) 0716
Volkswagen Golf, Jetta & Scirocco Mk 1 1.5, 1.6 & 1.8 (74 - 84) 0726
Volkswagen Golf & Jetta Mk 1 Diesel (78 - 84) 0451
Volkswagen Golf & Jetta Mk 2 (Mar 84 - Feb 92) 1081
Volkswagen Golf & Vento Petrol & Diesel (Feb 92 - 96) 3097
Volkswagen Golf & Bora Petrol & Diesel (April 98 - 00) 3727
Volkswagen LT vans & light trucks (76 - 87) 0637
Volkswagen Passat & Santana (Sept 81 - May 88) 0814
Volkswagen Passat Petrol & Diesel (May 88 - 96) 3498
Volkswagen Polo & Derby (76 - Jan 82) 0335
Volkswagen Polo (82 - Oct 90) 0813
Volkswagen Polo (Nov 90 - Aug 94) 3245
Volkswagen Polo Hatchback Petrol & Diesel (94 - 99) 3500
Volkswagen Scirocco (82 - 90) 1224
Volkswagen Transporter 1600 (68 - 79) 0082
Volkswagen Transporter 1700, 1800 & 2000 (72 - 79) 0226
Volkswagen Transporter (air-cooled) (79 - 82) 0638
Volkswagen Transporter (water-cooled) (82 - 90) 3452
Volkswagen Type 3 (63 - 73) 0084
Volvo 120 & 130 Series (& P1800)(61 - 73) 0203
Volvo 142, 144 & 145 (66 - 74) 0129
Volvo 240 Series (74 - 93) 0270
Volvo 262, 264 & 260/265 (75 - 85) 0400
Volvo 340, 343, 345 & 360 (76 - 91) 0715
Volvo 440, 460 & 480 (87 - 97) 1691
Volvo 740 & 760 (82 - 91) 1258
Volvo 850 (92 - 96) 3260
Volvo 940 (90 - 96) 3249
Volvo S40 & V40 (96 - 99) 3569
Volvo S70, V70 & C70 (96 - 99) 3573

Haynes Car Service and Repair Manuals are available from car accessory retailers.

For further information or to find your nearest stockist, call

01963 442030 or visit

www.haynes.co.uk